What Is God Like?

Philosophers and "Hereticks" on the Triune God: The Sundry Paths of Orthodoxy from Plato, Augustine, Samuel Johnson, Nietzsche, Camus, and Flannery O'Connor, Even to Charlie Brown and the Wodehouse Clergy

James V. Schall, S.J.

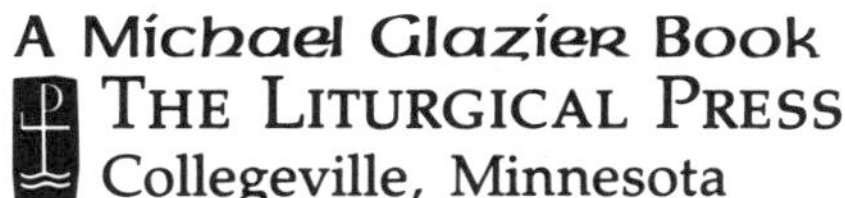
A Michael Glazier Book
THE LITURGICAL PRESS
Collegeville, Minnesota

A Michael Glazier Book published by The Liturgical Press

Cover design by David Manahan, O.S.B.
Cover photograph by Annette Brophy, O.S.B.

Acknowledgement is given to *World & I,* which originally published chapter V, under the title, *Albert Camus: Deprived of Grace,* vol. 4, June 1989, 543–63.

1 2 3 4 5 6 7 8 9

Library of Congress Cataloging-in-Publication Data

Schall, James V.
What is God like? / James V. Schall.
p. cm.
"A Michael Glazier Book."
Includes bibliographical references.
ISBN 0-8146-5020-1
1. God. 2. Christian life—Catholic authors. I. Title.
BT102.S297 1992
231—dc20 92-24774
CIP

I should recommend Dr. (Samuel) Clarke's Sermons *were they orthodox. However, it is very well known* where *he was not orthodox, which was upon the Doctrine of the Trinity, so as to which he is a condemned heretick.*

Dr. Samuel Johnson, April 7, 1778.

One of the most convenient Hieroglyphicks of God, is a Circle; and a Circle is endlesse; whom God loves, hee loves to the end: and not onely to their own end, to their death, but to his end, and his end is, that he might love them still.

John Donne, Christmas Day, 1624.

The bishop (of Stortford) came to himself with a start. He had been thinking of an article which he had just completed for a leading review on the subject of Miracles, and was regretting that the tone he had taken, though in keeping with the trend of Modern Thought, had been tinged with something approaching scepticism.

"The Bishop's Move,"
The World of the Wodehouse Clergy, 1984.

Contents

Preface

The Audience Who Think God Is Dead

The first question we ask ourselves is simply, "Is God?" "The fool in his heart says there is no God," Scripture tells us (Psalm 14:1), while St. Paul maintained to the Romans (1:18-19) that we are culpable if we do not see the evidence for the divine existence. The second question follows on this initial query: not "does God exist?" but "what is God like?" Both of these questions were asked and answered in a most positive and precise manner by St. Thomas Aquinas (*ST* I, q. 2–43). But each of us must ask them again in a world in which many deny God's existence or knowability. This situation is not new. It was mentioned in book ten of Plato's *Laws*.

I want to talk about what God is like. Our understanding of God's existence will be much clearer, I think, if we reflect on what God might be like. The question of "what God might be like" is related to what it is we want, to what is our destiny, if we could have it. I do not argue from desire to reality. Yet a remarkable coincidence exists in the universe between what we want in the depths of our being and what sort of a reality God is. At the most perplexing points of freedom, sin, evil, and death, what God "is like" coheres most delicately with what it is we are. My premise is, briefly, that it is all right for human beings *to exist*, even in the fallen manner in which we find them, even in the likes of ourselves.

In the "Prologue" to Nietzsche's *Thus Spoke Zarathustra* is found the famous passage: "Could it be possible? This old saint in the forest has not heard anything of this, that God is *dead?*"[1] These words, which remain an underlying theme in much of modern thought, were written about a century ago. Nietzsche had the honesty to add that God was "killed." God did not simply die. Indeed, God may not even be dead. We have the power within ourselves so to exclude God that the world goes on as if God were killed. To act as if God did not exist, we must find, or better, select an explanation for the everything *that is* that formerly was explained by God's existence. The comparison of the new world of human making with the old world of God's making remains the central intellectual exercise we undertake for ourselves. The argument for God in the modern world begins with the arguments about what we have wrought by ourselves without God.

Eric Voegelin, in a famous essay, "The Murder of God," took up this disturbing Nietzschean theme of God's death at human hands. Voegelin's discussion was no longer the familiar one of who killed Socrates or who killed Christ, in which there could be some assignment of responsibility to historical, individual persons, in known trials. "The murder of God is committed speculatively by explaining divine being as the work of men," Voegelin wrote.[2] With God eliminated, we can replace the Divine Reality with our own norms and constructs. Ironically, this death of God has not been, as Nietzsche imagined, followed by some superman, made to our own image. Instead, "historically, the murder of God is . . . followed . . . by the murder of man. . . ."[3] In getting what we wanted we lost what we are from nature.

This murder of God is essentially the construct of a philosophical system, the effort of modern philosophy.[4] However, if this philosophic elaboration is not closed except by our *choice*, by implication we remain open to an influence, to a presence that is not included within our self-made system. If God is eliminated by "dialectics," as Voegelin argued to be

[1]Friedrich Nietzsche, *Thus Spoke Zarathustra*, I, 3, *The Portable Nietzsche*, ed. Walter Kaufmann (Harmondsworth: Penguin, 1968) 124.

[2]Eric Voegelin, "The Murder of God," *Science, Politics, and Gnosticism* (Chicago: Regnery-Gateway, 1968) 54.

[3]Ibid., 64.

[4]Ibid., 69-70.

the purpose of modern thought, perhaps God remains alive if we see the incompleteness of our thought systems. The key word, again, is "choose." For the death of God, as even Nietzsche understood, is something we do to God by our choices. It is not possible for God to be suicidal. We are never more than a choice away from God. Such is the structure of our being, made in God's image, in the image of someone who commands and it is done. We can act, and it is accomplished. But this human activity is so because God sustains our reality and brings all things to God's end, even ourselves, though only if we choose. *Fiat. Fiat Lux. Fiat Voluntas Tua. Fiat Secundum Verbum Tuum.*

In Charles Schultz' *And the Beagles and the Bunnies Shall Lie Down Together*, a park scene shows Violet confusedly looking at Charlie Brown. Charlie happily tells her, "And right after church next Sunday, we're all going on a picnic." The second scene is a close-up in which Violet remarks to a blank-faced Charlie, "I didn't know your family belonged to a church." As they walk rapidly away, both with eyes forward, Charlie responds, "Sure, doesn't yours?" Sitting forlornly on a bench, Violet explains, with sadness, "They used to, now they belong to a Coffee House."[5]

Where is the audience for wondering *what God is like*? In the churches? In the coffee houses? In the academies wherein God seems mostly dead? All of the above? None of the above? Flannery O'Connor, in a letter of August 2, 1955, observed, "I believe too that there is only one Reality and that is the end of it." Yet, for such a writer this belief caused her audience not to understand her world, what she was talking about when she talked about the problems of people insofar as they seek the end of what they are. "One of the awful things about writing when you are a Christian," she continued, "is that for you the ultimate reality is the Incarnation, the present reality is the Incarnation, and nobody believes in the Incarnation; that is, nobody in your audience. *My audience are the people who think God is dead.* At least these are the people I am con-

[5]Charles M. Schultz, *And the Beagles and the Bunnies Shall Lie Down Together: The Theology in 'Peanuts'* (New York: Holt, 1984).

scious of writing for.''[6] Flannery O'Connor, devised a way of speaking about ultimate reality, while at the same time she aroused the interest and attention of the actual audience. The world in which ''God is dead'' is a given proposition for many for whom like Violet's parents coffee houses have replaced churches. Indeed too often the churches have conceived themselves to be coffee houses.

This counterbalancing of coffee houses and churches, however, is not to suggest that there is no place for coffee houses. Coffee houses, pubs, cafes, not to mention parks and gardens, are natural places in which to wonder what God is like, sometimes by ourselves, sometimes in conversation with others. No place, not even the Gulags, as Solzhenitsyn told us, is incapable of teaching us what God is like. Our places of happiness and our places of sadness, our places of beauty and our places of ugliness all show forth something of what God is like. But we must know where to look, and we must actually look. We even learn much about what God is like by knowing what God definitely is *not* like. Our sins and evils form a record of what God is not like. At our worst we can indeed become like only ourselves, a classic definition not of God but of hell.

I do not write this book as a philosophical polemic. I think combative argument has its place. Indeed, ''combative'' is one of the things we are. We are ''altercators,'' quibblers, and debaters. I have, admittedly, a bit of such disputation in these pages. Yet St. Thomas, in the beginning of his *Summa Contra Gentiles*, a work he addressed to those who did not share his revelational background, calmly remarked, ''Not everything which is said about God, although it cannot be investigated by reason, must be immediately rejected as false'' (I, 3). Aquinas had a pretty good idea of what could and what could not be investigated by reason. Without being irrational or contradictory, a reasonable case could be made for what was in itself beyond *our* reason, as the fundamental things of God are.

[6]Flannery O'Connor, *The Habit of Being*, ed. Sally Fitzgerald (New York: Vintage, 1979) 92. Italics added.

I have written a good deal about the dangers of political or social thought becoming, in effect, a substitute for thought about God. The modern totalitarian state became a real alternative to God. All the worst things I could have imagined about politics substituting itself for divinity have come to pass, often within religious circles themselves. Politics is not transcendence, but a point comes, if only for our own peace of mind, when it is well to confront that transcendence itself. The word transcendence, to be sure, has become a kind of excuse for not speaking about God. Though of noble lineage, this word remains vague enough to permit continued ambiguity. An unclear notion of transcendence can serve to undermine any sense of right and wrong, truth and falsity.

We have, however, made God more arcane than the evidence warrants. We will always come to the higher things by the lower ones. We come to anything gradually as befits the finiteness that is the condition of our being. God is not vague. Everything about God is as particular as we can possibly imagine, including the divine relationship to us. God, as we recall from Genesis, is fond of naming things. We should name things too. Indeed, this naming was a responsibility Yahweh assigned to Adam. And it is a sign of our glory.

Talk about what God is like includes formal, philosophical discourse. Yet, to some degree it must reflect our own experience. Does the account of God seeking us correspond with our own seeking God? Erasmo Leiva-Merikakis wrote of Dante: "The originality of Dante's poem is that it everywhere presupposes the intimate unity that exists between his personal history and the history of God's self-revelation to mankind. Without such revelation . . . one's personal history has no mainstay, no shaping principle; and without the real details and time-bound milestones of a personal history, the divine revelation remains theoretical, a matter for speculation. . . ."[7] Attention both to autobiography and to doctrine is essential when it comes to the question of what God is like.[8] We learn

[7]Erasmo Leiva-Merikakis, "*Fides Quaerens Experientiam*: The Flesh of Dante's Belief," *Faith and Reason*, VI (Fall, 1980) 205.

[8]See James V. Schall, *Unexpected Meditations Late in the XXth Century* (Chicago: Franciscan Herald Press, 1985).

what God is like primarily by being attentive to how God deals with us. But we will not be able to understand how we are dealt with unless we know how God has dealt with specific people, particularly Christ.

This age is skeptical. Its presuppositions are that we can know little or nothing about the important things. Any claim that we do know things "for certain" challenges the world built upon the supposition that God is dead, the world that thought it had to murder God to claim its heritage. We are reminded by the skeptics themselves that evil in the world is caused by those who "claim" they know the truth. Yet, those who claim that there is no truth leave the world to the ideologues. These ideologues at least understand enough about the structure of our minds to know that we cannot and will not ever be satisfied with knowing nothing about ultimate things.

I am in much sympathy with Dorothy Sayers when she wrote, annoyed by this same mentality, "Official Christianity, of late years, has been having what is known as a bad press. We are constantly assured that the churches are empty because preachers insist too much upon doctrine—dull dogma as people call it. The fact is the precise opposite. It is the neglect of dogma that makes for dullness. The Christian faith is the most exciting drama that ever staggered the imagination of man—and the dogma is the drama."[9] To prevent our personal lives from being dull, let alone hopeless or meaningless, we must understand that they are only adequately explained by the dogmas of creation, fall, incarnation, resurrection, and eternal life. Nothing else will do.

On his visit to Ferney, near Geneva, James Boswell recounted how, on Christmas Eve, 1764, he took a coach to this "seat of the illustrious Monsieur de Voltaire": "I was in true spirits; the earth was covered with snow; I surveyed wild nature with a noble eye. I called up the grand ideas which I have ever entertained of Voltaire. The first object that struck me was his church with this inscription: '*Deo erexit Voltaire* MDCCLXI.' " No doubt, as Boswell sensed, something deliciously saucy, if not blasphemous, is found here, with Voltaire

[9]Dorothy Sayers, "The Greatest Drama Ever Staged," *The Whimsical Christian* (New York: Macmillan, 1978) 11.

in person erecting his own Church to God. The irony is not to be missed.[10]

We see that even when the audience for our acts is, as for Voltaire's famous church, ostensibly the very Godhead, we can make this God seem not to exist. St. Thomas found so much falsity often mixed up in human reasonings and conceptions, especially about God, that even when there is a demonstrated truth, "the force of the demonstration will be ignored, especially when normal people see that diverse things are argued and taught by differing thinkers who are deemed to be wise" (CG I, 4). Aquinas thought that this confusion was one of the main reasons why we needed to have revelation. He continued, "It is salubrious, then, for the divine clemency to provide that also those things which reason investigates are commanded to be held by faith in order that all might more easily participate in the divine knowledge and this without doubt or error." As Chesterton said of him on this very point, Aquinas was a great democrat who could not conceive that in their pursuit of him, God left the many to the mercy of the intelligentsia.[11]

To arrive at what God might be like, I have relied on much that I have known, read, or experienced. The place for us human beings to begin to think about God, it seems to me, is from our weakness, from our fragility and frailty, as I call it. We all are aware of how God looks to those about us. Ours is the culture which invented the idea that God might be dead, killed by ourselves. But it is not enough to understand the closed world of our ideologies and philosophic systems. What breaks into this world will not be only God himself but especially laughter and friendship, two experiences that strike me as inexplicable except in terms of what God is like.

Two writers in particular were of help to me because they wrote journals or books, "confessions," as they have come to be called. Raissa Maritain and St. Augustine have been guides to the highest things, which neither hesitates to name. I have

[10]James Boswell, *On the Grand Tour: Germany and Switzerland*, ed. Frederick A. Pottle (New York: McGraw-Hill, 1953) 279.

[11]G. K. Chesterton, *St. Thomas Aquinas*, in *Collected Works*, Vol. II (San Francisco: Ignatius Press, 1986).

paid attention to them because while they grasped our sinful condition, they realized that we are made to understand, to comprehend what we are and where we are in the world.

Next, I have taken a look at God as such, as it were, reconsidering the Trinity, that central doctrine about the inner life of God around which all else turns, even our own autobiographies.

Finally, since the triune God is a God to whom we pray, I have thought it important to consider this devotional aspect of what God is like. God is indeed an object of contemplation as the Greeks thought. But God's inner life reveals a diversity of Persons within this inner life. Our prayerful relation to God more than anything else reveals whether we know what God is like.

Even if we believe in the incarnation, we still talk to a world for which in many ways God is dead. Flannery O'Connor was right about which audience to address ourselves to. The audience that I propose for myself here is not that of abstract philosophy, nor that of ordinary piety, though I have tried to respect both, to talk to both. Rather I wish to address those who realize, now ever more vividly with the Marxist collapse, that the ideologies have failed us. We are each being called to judgment and resurrection, a call which does not in the least hold that our life in this world is either unimportant or the less poignant because we do not see the whole structure of what we are before the triune God. We are not passive beings. The world ought to be different because of what we understand about God and how we relate to him. Still God is not primarily about politics. God is concerned with our ultimate redemption.

Some attention must also be paid to intelligence, especially intelligence as it relates to holiness. In this effort, I think, no two writers in this century are more helpful and incisive than the Englishman G. K. Chesterton and the French Algerian Albert Camus. The value of existence stands before a modern thought that denies grace. We live in a world that has, in large part, denied grace. Not surprisingly, it is also a world that can no longer understand existence. The great political thinker Leo Strauss surmised that our age had rejected the tradition of revelation without really purging itself of the elevated vistas which grace had opened to mankind.[12] To know what God is like we need to sense the wonder of our very existence, as Chesterton did. We need to suspect what we have lost, as Camus did. Both of these experiences lead to the great Christian truth that intelligence and holiness are not opposed to each other except for those who choose to make their own intelligence to be the only intelligence in the universe.

Peter Berger, speaking of the contemporary politicization of religion, wrote: "Our congregations are full of individuals with a multitude of afflictions and sorrows, very few of which have anything to do with the allegedly great issues of history. These individuals come to receive the consolation and solace of the Gospel, instead of which they get a lot of politics."[13] This book is addressed to those who seek to know about God, not politics. In knowing something about politics, especially about its limits, we are constrained to know about something more than politics. We seek to know something of what God is like in a world in which this very search is either prohibited by law or custom, by our pride, by our business, by our escaping to something else that seems more immediate, or by our sins. We always find ourselves back with ourselves. Our true concern, and it is a noble one, is that we might see God. We need not be apologetic. This seeing is indeed that for which we are created. One of Nietzsche's maxims was "The mother of dissipation is not joy but joylessness."[14] We all know enough about "dissipation," I suppose, to know that Nietzsche was close to the mark. The aim of this book, however, is to inquire about the "mother of joy." In a column in the London *Illustrated News*, on June 9, 1906, G. K. Chesterton wrote: "It is the test of a responsible religion or theory whether it can take examples from pots and pans and boots and butter-tubs. It is the test of a good philosophy whether you can defend it grotesquely. It is the test of a good religion whether you can

[12]Leo Strauss, *Thoughts on Machiavelli* (Glencoe, Ill.: The Free Press, 1958).

[13]Peter Berger, "Different Gospels: The Social Sources of Apostasy," The Third Annual Erasmus Lecture (New York: Rockford Institute, 1987) 14.

[14]Nietzsche, *Thus Spoke Zarathustra*, no. 77, p. 64.

joke about it."[15] The theme of joy is really what this book on what God is like is ultimately about.

Thus, I take the jokes seriously, and I believe in the pots, pans, boots, and butter-tubs of the ordinary people who look for God in the midst of such pedestrian things. The dogma is the drama. The drama is the dogma. If each individual with a name, including my name, is to experience joy in any final sense, it is only because God is joy. This joy somehow means that God is triune, that the Word became flesh and dwelt amongst us, was crucified, died, and was buried. The rising again is the only doctrine that addresses itself in a final way to our joys as they are in our own being, especially our highest joys of love and friendship, not merely with our kind but also with the triune God. God is like this, like someone who addresses us in that wholeness in which we most are. We are struck by this, by the fact that what we most want is indeed a surprise. But we begin in our smallness, in our frailty. In humility we begin our wonderment about who God is, what he is like.

[15]G. K. Chesterton, *Collected Works,* Vol. XXVII (San Francisco: Ignatius Press, 1986) 206.

Chapter I

On Not Obscuring What Is Very Plain

Just after it had been published in 1755, James Boswell was discussing some of the few quaint errors that had subsequently been found in Samuel Johnson's famous *Dictionary*. "A lady once asked him (Johnson) how he came to define *Pastern* (actually part of the foot) as the *knee* of the horse: instead of making an elaborate defence, as she expected, he at once answered, 'Ignorance, Madam, pure ignorance.' His definition of *Network* (to wit, 'anything reticulated, or decussated at equal distances with interstices between the intersections') has been often quoted with sportive malignity, *as obscuring a thing in itself very plain*."[1] Such a passage indicates the spirit in which I would present these reflections on "what God is like." It is a spirit willing to confront ultimate issues, with a realization that we can make errors, that we can obscure what is already quite clear.

This book does not intend either to obscure what is very plain, or to mis-define the parts of horses or other creatures. My errors, like Johnson's, are best acknowledged by frankly admitting ignorance. Yet something is to be said for addressing myself to what will seem at first sight an impossible topic, to a topic wherein ignorance might modestly prevail as the better part of intellectual valor. "What is God like?" may well be a question tinged with "sportive malignity." I may succeed

[1]James Boswell, *Life of Johnson* I (London: Oxford, 1931) 198. Italics added.

in only making something very plain to be quite obscure. Yet, some questions we must formulate, at least for ourselves, if we are to be human beings. The present query is one of them: ''What, indeed, is God like?'' I make no ''elaborate defence'' of what I do here, but, like Johnson's *Dictionary,* I feel that it ought to be attempted even if a few errors might creep in. Aristotle encouraged us to spend our lives on the highest questions about our existence, including its causes. Even if we know but little of their full implications, their pursuit is, nevertheless, worth the dedication and passion of our lives (*Ethics* X, 7).

In the First Epistle of John, we read, ''Little children, let us love in deed and in truth and not merely talk about it'' (3:18). We are not to understand this passage as forbidding us from earnestly ''talking'' about what it means to love in truth, or better to love the truth. St. Ignatius of Loyola said that we are created ''to know, love, and praise God and by this means to save our souls.'' This is what we should be about. Yet, we talk about everything else today except what it means to save our own particular souls. We are accused of being selfish even to bring up the topic. We are to ''save'' everything but our own soul in an intellectual world wherein the word ''save'' has taken on a political, not transcendent meaning. This particular phrase, ''to save our souls,'' can suggest that the ''real'' person is only a ''soul.'' In its proper context the phrase identifies what is of highest moment in each human life, namely, its final status. The soul's ''salvation'' results from a person's decision to order his life to achieve it. Though we are more than souls, still we have a soul. Through this very soul each of us has his own proper activity at the highest levels of loving and knowing. We are to believe and to act, both.

We search not just for ''transcendence'' or the ''higher things,'' but for reality, for God. We do in truth want to know whether these ''higher things'' themselves have personal existence. We want to know if what transcends our world and our life is itself only inner-worldly. If what we call ''transcendent'' is itself merely finite, we cannot avoid the realization, if we are logical, that ultimately at the heart of being there is only despair. Joseph Ratzinger remarked that ours is a ''praying religion,'' which indicates the importance of the Christological and Trinitarian doctrines of God. There is *someone* to whom to pray. In contrast, Aristotle's God, who moved indeed by knowing and loving, was said to have no interest in what was not itself. Ratzinger wrote: "But the retreat to a rationally presentable monotheism is always merely the first step. Next comes the abandonment of the relational categories of creation and revelation. Thus this God himself fades into the concept of 'transcendence.' The possibility of prayer being 'heard' dwindles, and faith becomes 'self-transcendence.' "[2] Historically, the earlier purification of philosophy from mythology by the Greeks was itself a necessary preparation for further intellectual and revelational understanding of what God is like. But when we lose faith and reverse the process, taking personhood out of God, we move back not to God but through abstractions like justice and good back to ourselves.

The title of this book, *What Is God Like?*, will make us wonder about how anyone, including myself, can possibly know what God is like. The very phrase, as I use it, though provocative, is intended to be familiar in manner. St. Thomas Aquinas reminded us, on a more philosophic basis, that the primary question that we humans ask about God is not "what is God (*quid sit Deus?*)," but rather "whether God is or exists (*an Deus sit?*)." On the basis of this latter question, "Is God?", we might, with sufficient reflection, be able to say something about God's nature, provided we remember that everything we say, though rooted in God's existence, is negative, what God is not.[3] This negative intellectual approach is quite valid and necessary. Knowing what is not true is a necessary beginning. It is indeed a form of knowing. I will presuppose St. Thomas' position in everything that I say here. He remains, I think, though so pedestrian on first reading, the most exciting of the thinkers.

My question, however, is precisely "what is God *like*"? This question will mean what is he like "for me." But, as E. F. Schumacher argued, we must first know what goes on inside of us before we can begin to understand and communi-

[2]Joseph Ratzinger, *Feast of Faith* (San Francisco: Ignatius Press, 1986) 22.

[3]See Josef Pieper, *The Silence of St. Thomas*, trans. John Murray, S.J. and Daniel O'Connor (Chicago: Regnery-Logos, 1957) 87–91.

cate with what goes on inside someone else, including God.[4] Arguing for the importance, even for society, of knowing our inner-selves, Schumacher wrote:

> Since we have no direct access to the inner experiences of other beings, obtaining indirect access is one of man's most important tasks as a social being. This indirect access can be gained only through self-knowledge, which shows that it is a grave error to accuse a man who pursues self-knowledge of having "turned his back on society." The opposite would be more nearly true: that a man who fails to pursue self-knowledge is and remains a danger to society, for he will tend to misunderstand everything that other people say or do, and remain blissfully unaware of the significance of many of the things he does himself.[5]

We must begin with an accurate knowledge of ourselves. We ourselves in our particularity, in our individual lives, do reach even to God beyond any possible societal order. Society does not mediate everything between God and ourselves. Good people save their souls in badly ordered regimes, while people who do evil things are found in the best of societies. How are we to understand this paradox? In history we have examples of people of the highest sort but not of the best cities, Leo Strauss wrote; one transcends the city only by "pursuing true happiness."[6] At the limits of our encounters we meet what we do not make.

The last myth in *The Republic* of Plato, the myth of Er, taught us that we only have one life and that we ought to choose what is right while we live it. A cartoon in the *New Yorker* (November 30, 1987) showed two ex-human, angelic types, with seraphic wings, arms over the knees, sitting on a couple of clouds, earnestly conversing. One Platonic-oriented man-angel said to the other, "Well, this proves it. You only live once."

God is rather different, I think, for each of us. He treats each of us in quite diverse ways and differently at different

[4]E. F. Schumacher, *A Guide for the Perplexed* (New York: Harper Colophon, 1977) 62–79.

[5]Ibid., 119.

[6]Leo Strauss, *City and Man* (Chicago: University of Chicago Press, 1964) 49.

times in our lives. We only do live once. God is someone who understands that it is the greater drama to live once not twice. One life is far more dramatic than a multiplicity of sundry reincarnations. But God does deal directly and personally with each of us in the events and choices of our individual lives, in the people we are given, in the people we meet, in the only life we live. To some he gives suffering, to others exquisite happiness, to others power, to others tragedy, to a few all of these and more. We are often tempted to conclude from this that God is unjust (which is untrue) and "plays favorites" (which is true in the sense that everyone is treated uniquely). Or else we are lured into holding that both evil (how could God permit it?) and human accomplishments (why do we need anything but ourselves?) are arguments against God's very being or existence. Yet, neither evil nor finiteness militates against God. God will not be defeated by either. But God will not call evil good nor make us other sorts of creatures than we already are.

When James Boswell was on his Grand Tour in 1764, one of the high points was his visit with Jean-Jacques Rousseau in Neufchatel. Boswell at the time was a brash young man of twenty-four, who wanted to bare his soul to the great philosopher. After Boswell had recounted some of his less than edifying exploits to him, Rousseau remarked, "You have no right to do evil for the sake of good." Boswell replied, "True. None the less, I can imagine some very embarrassing situations. And pray tell me how I can expiate the evil I have done?" To this, Rousseau simply affirmed, "Oh, Sir, there is no expiation for evil except good."[7] This is what God is like, that evil is indeed "expiated," as Boswell would have had it, but only by what is good. Evil does not become other than it is, the something lacking that ought to be there. The deepest struggles with God, as was already evident in the Genesis account of the Fall, deal with attempts of intelligent beings to claim this power to define by themselves alone what is evil. God responds to our evil acts, but only with something that arises out of them which

[7]*Boswell on the Grand Tour: Germany and Switzerland, 1764,* ed. Frederick A. Pottle (New York: McGraw-Hill, 1953) 254.

is itself good. We are not ultimately disarmed by our evil acts, but by God's responses to them. When we realize the kindness with which we have been treated in spite of what we have done, we begin to catch glimmerings of what God is like.

What God is like will have to include all objections arising from evil and from finiteness. God is "like us," if we can put it that way. Both God and humans are spiritual beings whose knowledge is directed in different ways to *all that is*. The *what is* of each of us is the finite image by which God established each of us, in our own peculiar way, out of nothingness. This image in its human reality includes the lifetime endeavor to know the truth about God. That is what we seek in all of our searchings. The effort "to know the truth about God" was one of the highest functions that St. Thomas attributed to natural law (*ST* I–II, 94, 2). Also, it was one of the elements that Plato in *The Republic* saw as part of his first and most obvious definition of justice, simply to know the truth (331d). To know the truth about God and to do his will are the basic questions to which we have to address ourselves in the years of our particular lives, years only we ourselves see from inside, in the stories of our passing through this life.

Often we do not want to look at the real "story" of our lives, ever a choice between living and dying, even when we believe in life everlasting. Our life is a series of choices, a record of choices, of the things that proceed out of us, not someone else. If we are Christians, we believe that we are to account for our souls. We want to know about saving our souls in that sense in which we are told to seek first the kingdom of God. Our very living insists that we attend to what is highest in us. Yet, it is easy for us to talk of anything else but of how we stand before God. The priesthood, as Christ instituted it, exists primarily to talk to us of this standing, this saving. But what happens when priests do not act for their own purpose, when their focus is elsewhere? What happens when no attentive healers of souls are to be found within the priesthood but only those who discuss merely the issues of this world?

Allan Bloom, in his *The Closing of the American Mind*, says something strikingly similar, namely, that the emptiest souls in our society are those of the young students in the twenty best universities.[8] Not only priests but professors neglect our souls. Plato was right when he taught us that the struggle over the souls of the young potential philosophers was constitutive of the central life of any city. The condition of our souls directly reflects on the quality of our public lives. Reform of society begins in reform of soul. Even the best constituted societies will wither if souls are disordered.

No one has put this point better than Margaret Thatcher, the former British Prime Minister. In an address to the General Assembly of the Church of Scotland, she said:

> Most Christians would regard it as their personal duty to help their fellow men and women. They would regard the lives of children as a precious trust. These duties come not from any secular legislation passed by Parliament, but from being a Christian. . . .
>
> What, then, are the distinctive marks of Christianity? . . . I would identify three beliefs in particular: First, that from the beginning man has been endowed by God with the fundamental right to choose between good and evil. Second, that we were made in God's own image and therefore we are expected to use all our own power of thought and judgment in exercising that choice; and further, if we open our hearts to God, he has promised to work within us. And third, that Our Lord Jesus Christ, the Son of God, when faced with his terrible choice and lonely vigil, chose to lay down his life that our sins may be forgiven. . . .[9]

Virtue is also a public good. Vice, our vices, are directly or indirectly public vices, even when we call them legal or even simply good. The choice of evil exists; the roots of virtue need spiritual nourishment.

For Christianity, the central issue in every life, even the most apparently insignificant, is the combat for the soul of each of us, philosopher or not. This combat is over no mere tem-

[8]Allan Bloom, *The Closing of the American Mind* (New York: Simon & Schuster, 1987) 25–43.

[9]Margaret Thatcher, Address, *Observer*, May 22, 1988. Address reprinted in James V. Schall, *Religion, Wealth, and Poverty* (Vancouver, B.C.: Fraser Institute, 1990) 174–77.

poral good. Its essence is God's pursuit of us and our response to him. Raissa Maritain, to whom I shall devote more attention later (chapter 3), remarked that God, in acting, seems to care for nothing in the world except for the salvation of our souls.[10] This observation contains the profoundest truth about God.

I am reminded of the death of the Venerable Bede in England, in 735 A.D. At the end, Bede gathered his monks about him, gave away what he had left of his possessions, and said simply: "It is time to return to Him who created me and formed me out of nothing when I did not exist. I have lived a long time, and the righteous Judge has taken good care of me during my whole life. The time has come for my departure, and I long to die and be with Christ." This is what God cares about, our realization that we have come from nothing, that we come to a point at which we have lived long enough, that ultimately we come to die and live with Christ.

I read the *Daily Meditations* of Mother Teresa, a profoundly moving book. I warmly recommend it to whoever will listen to me. This book is arranged to present a brief comment or incident or reflection from Mother Teresa for each day of the year. For the Fifth Sunday of Lent, we read: "There is a great hunger for God in the world. Everywhere there is much suffering, but there is also great hunger for God and love for each other. Suffering in itself is nothing; but suffering shared with Christ's passion is a wonderful gift. Man's most beautiful gift is that he can share in the Passion of Christ. Yes, a gift and a sign of his love; because this is how his Father proved that he loved the world—by giving his Son to die for us."[11] Here is talk about "saving our souls," isn't it? It is also a description of what God is like. God's Son is given to die for us. We need to reflect on why God would do this dying for us. Why did God not choose some other way to accomplish the same purpose. What is God like? God is like a Father who asks us to seek the meaning of why the Son of God is given

[10]*Raissa's Journal*, presented by Jacques Maritain (Albany, N.Y.: Magi Books, 1974) 75.

[11]*Love, A Fruit Always in Season: Daily Meditations by Mother Teresa*, ed. Dorothy S. Hunt (San Francisco: Ignatius Press, 1987) 95.

to die for us. We are also to *think* about the giving of this Son within the context of the questions our lives present to us, questions which we can avoid asking only at the peril of our *human* being. Yet, in many ways our culture and our hearts prevent us from thinking about what it means for God to give Christ to die for us. What is there in us that might cause the Father to choose so to act in our behalf?

After I had written out some passages from this book of Mother Teresa, a friend wrote to me:

> I was quite struck with Mother Teresa's diagnosis of loneliness being the worst disease. She is so right. It is the most emaciating disease whose metastasis goes from spirit to will. I think what we respond to is Mother Teresa's ability to love. And that she loves others more than she loves herself.
>
> I really do believe that a woman's education is important only if it actualizes her ability to love. A woman's ability to love others more than she loves herself is the identifying trait that separates women from feminists, mothers from career women, wives from lovers, real Sisters from nuns who would be priests. And it is this capacity to love, generating from the very essence of woman, which motivates her to give more than she will ever receive and, in so doing, receive more than she ever realized possible. Mother Teresa is probably the greatest educator of women in the 20th Century—not because of all she knows, but because of all she loves.

God is like that too. God's is a self-surpassing love that we can, if we are fortunate, find mirrored in creatures, sometimes more frequently than we might expect, when our friends offer to us, as they do, totally, unexpectedly, a pure act of generosity. This is the doctrine of the incarnation and of the Cross.

At the end of the spring semester, 1988, a young student of mine asked me, "Father, what do you do about the problems that come up between faith and knowledge?" I replied: "I think I needed to know enough about the objections to the truth to know where they came from and enough to see how they might be resolved, to be widely enough read to go to sources knowledgeable enough to see where the problem lies." In addition to this beginning, one realizes after a time that the truths of faith actually stimulate, clarify, and order the things of reason. This is what is most uncanny about the wholeness or interrelatedness of the questions that arise from faith and reason. The questions almost insist that they arise from the same source.

On Easter Sunday, 1988, John Paul II remarked: "However, Easter Sunday continues; rather, it is now endless. It is the day of Christ's definitive victory over the devil, over sin and over death. It is the day which opens onto the temporal cycle the endless perspective of eternal life where the sacrificial Lamb still offers himself continually to the Father for us, for love of us."[12] This is what we learn when we seek to know what God is like. The victory over the devil, over sin, and over death is in truth "definitive." We do not need to find another way to achieve such a victory. Already it is won for us, but not by us. We are incipiently given that which we most hope for. The Lamb's death has to do with us. Our lives reveal why this is so. To know what God is like requires us to know first what we are like.

Along such lines I wish to approach the theme of this book, *What Is God Like?* In spite of our living in perhaps the most religious nation at least in the West, we dwell in a most skeptical age. The presuppositions of our academic theorists place relativism at the very roots of our education. Everyone will be "forced" by the new university curricula to be free by the implicit denial within them of a tradition of truth.[13] The prevailing view of relativism is that what freedom means is to be bound to no truth because there is no truth to be bound to, a position which is itself intrinsically contradictory.

Yet, our age, usually as a reaction to this established skepticism, is also dominated, consciously or unconsciously, by ideologies. These systems of ideas have no real grounding in truth but nevertheless call forth passionate followings, perhaps because they are defiantly proposed against the standards and truths of classical faith. This defiance can never be wholly innocent or blameless. It must begin in a human heart confronting reality as if it were wholly free from it. The scriptural

[12] *L'Osservatore Romano*, English edition, April 11, 1988.

[13] See Gerald Graff, "Conflicts over the Curriculum Are Here to Stay," *The Chronicle of Higher Education*, February 17, 1988, 6-7.

description of the Fall remains accurate. We human beings are tempted to "be like gods." If we do not feel the pull of that temptation to be like gods, we have not yet begun to understand the forces already at work within the world and within ourselves. Writers like Eric Voegelin have remarked that the worst ideologues in our society today are often ex-Christian believers, though they may still count themselves Christians in form. But their faith is too tenuous to believe what Christianity taught us about saving our souls, about the truths of our existence.[14]

We might expect, in thinking about "what God is like," to look for some sort of esoteric doctrine. What I will rather propose will be, if I am successful, the traditional orthodoxy of the Christian faith—creation, fall, incarnation, redemption, and eternal life. I intend to use the word "orthodoxy" consciously as Chesterton so wonderfully used it.[15] I will admit that this teaching of the central truth of Christianity is "esoteric" today. It is difficult to come by, even in churches and especially in universities. But I will argue the following: the unique truth, which Christianity did not give to itself or make up by itself, but which it received through revelation as its essential story or explanation of itself, most curiously fits in with what we might, if we thought about it, "want" God to be like.

Anyone who knows modern philosophy from Feuerbach on no doubt will initially hear this view as merely the "projection" of the human desire to substitute itself for the divinity. The effort of modernity has been to rid ourselves of this "alienation" and recover not God but ourselves from such fantastic divine dreamings. This is why atheism is frequently proposed as a pure "humanism," a view which admits of only human beings. The trouble with recovering only ourselves is that, again if we have any inner insight, we know what we are like. We know that we are also *not* like God, however much we are created in his image.

[14]Eric Voegelin, *Science, Politics, and Gnosticism* (Chicago: Regnery-Gateway, 1968) 106–14.

[15]G. K. Chesterton, *Orthodoxy*, in *The Collected Works of G. K. Chesterton*, Vol. 1 (San Francisco: Ignatius Press, 1986).

Peter Kreeft remarked that "really to ask a question is harder than to answer it, for once the question is asked with all the passion of your being, it will be answered. All real seekers find. The universe is a great Answer Man; but it answers only questioners."[16] God is like this, I think. All real seekers find. Why is it we seek so half-heartedly? Psalm 119:113 echoes the same sentiment: "I have no love for half-hearted men." The existence of God ("*an Deus sit?*") requires us to inquire with serious enthusiasm about *what is*. Yet we cannot by ourselves, even if we try, answer all the ultimate questions life poses to us in our very uniqueness.

Nietzsche, to be sure, wanted to understand Christianity as an "acting" religion, not one that worried about repentance or faith or sin. "The Christian *acts*; he is distinguished by acting differently."[17] But sometimes we Christians do not act differently, so that the Nietzschean removal of sin and forgiveness from the realm of our actions deprives us of what our actions ultimately need. Hannah Arendt said that it is forgiveness that stops our evil actions; hence this is Christ's most important civil doctrine. To deprive our actions of their possibility of forgiveness or of ultimate damnation for that matter makes doing or acting simply itself, with no further meaning. This simple isolation of human action was what Nietzsche wanted.[18] Once we had put our actions forth in the world, nothing more could be said about them. Our deeds, in his view, stood under no judgment.

God did create us to act, but also we are created free and capable of acting wrongly. "There is no doctrine more appropriate to man," Pascal wrote, "than this, which teaches him his double capacity of receiving and of losing grace, because of the double peril to which he is exposed, of despair or of pride."[19] God, nevertheless, is not like someone who deals

[16]Peter Kreeft, *A Turn of the Clock: A Book of Modern Proverbs* (San Francisco: Ignatius Press, 1987) 10-11.

[17]*The Anti-Christ* no. 33, in *The Portable Nietzsche*, ed. Walter Kaufmann (Harmondsworth: Penguin, 1978) 606.

[18]Hannah Arendt, *The Human Condition* (Garden City, N. Y.: Doubleday Anchor, 1959) 212–19.

[19]Blaise Pascal, *Pensées* (New York: Modern Library, 1941) no. 523.

only in justice. Pascal was right to speak of grace and the two actual alternatives to it in each life—despair and pride. The belief that God is primarily a "justice-dealer" is perhaps the greatest heresy of our era. If God were merely justice, we would still remain in our sins. Near the end of C. S. Lewis' wonderful book, *Till We Have Faces,* he says, "This age of ours will one day be the distant past. And the Divine Nature can change the past. Nothing is yet in its true form."[20] At first, this idea sounds like a contradiction, the notion that the past can be changed. Nonetheless, it is true. Nothing is yet in its true, complete form, in which the past, with both its awfulness and its hints of glory, will finally be sorted out.

"If religion has any validity at all," Walker Percy remarked in an interview, "then the quest for the self is nonsense, you know. It's the quest for God, or as Kierkegaard, I think, said: the only way the self can become the self is by becoming itself transparently before God."[21] God is like someone who searches for us, not at all like those who think that the discovery of one's own self is the highest quest. In our search we realize that in ourselves we are incapable of learning fully about ourselves by knowing only ourselves.[22] Yet, we are to know ourselves. The incarnation is a doctrine that implies that God, though infinitely beyond us, is like us, like unto us in all things but sin, as St. Paul said. The fact that God is not like us in our sins is the great teaching of the incarnation. "Do not sin," John said in his First Epistle, "but if you do sin, you have an Advocate with the Father" (2:1) This is what God is like.

The incarnation is the bridge between God and humans. God "emptied Himself out" to become human, as St. Paul intimated. What this meant was that the condition of humanity, its frailness, its fragility was in the incarnation attributed to God. The experience of the creature was no longer merely lodged in a theoretic knowledge of God, though that knowl-

[20]C. S. Lewis, *Till We Have Faces* (Grand Rapids, Mich.: Eerdmans, 1970) 305.

[21]*Conversations with Walker Percy,* ed. Lewis A. Lawson and Victor A. Kramer (Jackson: University Press of Mississippi, 1985) 49.

[22]See *The Whole Truth About Man: John Paul II to University Students and Faculties,* ed. James V. Schall (Boston: St. Paul Editions, 1981).

edge was even more profound than the creature suspected. The fact of the incarnation meant that the question of what God is like had a basis in something within humanity itself. The temptation of identifying human experience as the highest value or reality and calling it God is not unknown to human thought. But the presence within the human race of the incarnate God means that words and deeds within this world, ones we can hear or see, do reveal what God is like by how he acted and spoke among us. The meditative life of Christians rightly is a careful looking at the life of Jesus as it has come down to us. This life reveals its origins in God. We know of God by how he acts with us. And he acts with us in the conditions of frailty in which we are found, in all our deeds and words, in our life itself.

Chapter II

Frailty

Flannery O'Connor, on October 19, 1958, wrote to Dr. T. R. Spivey about the difficulty moderns have with the Holy Spirit. Since the eighteenth century, she reflected, the religious sense has been bred out of us, especially now when, in her remarkable phrase, we confront "the religious substitutes for religion." We have no place to begin because no one believes that God has the power to do "certain things." "There is no sense of the power of God that could produce the Incarnation and the Resurrection. They (philosophic moderns) were all so busy explaining away the virgin birth and such things, reducing everything to human proportions that in time they lose even the sense of the human itself, what they were aiming to reduce everything to."[1] The content of the belief about God is fleeting; religio-political terminology substitutes for religion or revelation itself. Because of this situation, we may not confront what God is really like even within the confines of religion.

The incarnation meant that the Word was made flesh and dwelt amongst us. Christ became man as a child. When Herod sought to kill this child, he sought to kill the human being in its most frail condition. Frailty was a significant theme in the thought of Hannah Arendt.[2] The word "frailty" recalls those early twentieth century novels describing wan and delicate

[1]Flannery O'Connor, *The Habit of Being* (New York: Vintage, 1979) 300.

[2]Hannah Arendt, *The Human Condition* (Garden City: Doubleday Anchor, 1959) 167–71.

health, often the result of tuberculosis. I think especially of Thomas Mann. The astonishing weakness of the human condition itself has, however, seemed evident to most people in most eras. We are aware that one generation awaits its turn to replace another, that we can stay in this world too long. We are to die. Yet the ancients, Plato and Cicero especially, reminded us that old age should be the climax of our wisdom, not its defeat. Socrates said that death is not the worst evil. We ought not avoid it at all costs. Something may be worse. The existence of God stands for this truth that something indeed can be worse than death.

The ease with which we can be wiped out by disease, crime, or accident, not to mention eventually by old age, no doubt forbids us to expect our own durability. Yet we do not want merely to be "durable," like some sort of sturdy household goods. We are both frail and fragile because of the complexity and flexibility required to permit us to exist. The frailness or softness in our physical make-up makes it possible that such beings as we have a chance to live at all.

I am aware that there are philosophical and theological systems that wonder whether we should even exist. No doubt, were we somehow given the power, we should never have created precisely ourselves. One of the recurring charges against God is that he created us subject to frailty and, yes, to evil. These charges suggest that it would be better, therefore, not to be. Whenever this preference for non-existence appears in the logic of our argument, we should be more than cautious. Igor Shafarevich pointed out that the modern person has a death wish, a desire almost to reject the given reality placed upon his or her shoulders for the very reason that it does not come from the person.[3] God, however, is like someone who created us because he saw that we were good, though frail.

Another philosophy holds that whatever we might think of the possibility of our not being, we are, nonetheless, definitely in being. We exist and we know it. This existence, however, is said to make no ultimate difference whatsoever.

[3]Igor Shafarevich, *The Socialist Phenomenon* (New York: Harper, 1980) 281–85.

In 1977, Malcolm Muggeridge had a discussion with Professor William H. Nolte of the University of South Carolina on this very question.

> *Muggeridge*: "You (Nolte) say, there is this universe and in some way or another—we don't know how—man came into it. Then man lives in it for so many billions or whatever it may be of years. During that time he produces art, literature, geniuses of all kinds, he speculates, measures his strength, delves into what that wonderful anonymous work of 14th century Europe calls 'the cloud of unknowing'—all these things happened, and then, finished. He's gone, and all he achieved has gone, and it has made absolutely no difference."
>
> *Nolte*: "To whom could it have made any difference? Except to himself?"
>
> *Muggeridge*: "To anyone who has, through faith, grasped this transcendental dimension of life it makes an enormous difference. . . ."[4]

This intellectual sense of the meaninglessness not only of the individual human person but of the whole human race over time indicates the potential depth of our frailty. But it also makes us wonder whether our frailty is not also our strength.

We are even more frail than our physical selves when it comes to our words and accomplishments. Not too many of us, after all, will ever be particularly famous, however important it is that at least some of us should live recognizably noble lives. Most of us, in spite of the so-called "new social historians" who praise only ordinariness, will not achieve the "immortality" of fame in the city.[5] One of the earthly missions of the human race, no doubt, is to keep alive what it has best thought and done. This is why we have books and monuments and polities.[6] But even ancient monuments and shrines are frail. We chip away at them, as do the weather and natural

[4]"A Question of Faith: A Conversation Between Malcolm Muggeridge and William H. Nolte," *Catholic Mind* 76 (April, 1978) 17.

[5]See Gertrude Himmelfarb, "History with the Politics Left Out," *The New History and the Old: Critical Essays and Reappraisals* (Cambridge: Harvard, 1987) 13–32.

[6]See Arendt, *The Human Condition*, 119–55.

forces of disintegration. Books almost have to be taken out of circulation if we are to keep them for a long time. Civilizations also perish and not just ancient ones.

The Nature Conservancy worries about preserving thousands of "species" of plants and animals which are said to be disappearing like the dinosaur and the passenger pigeon once did. We panic when some bug disappears, though we know that perhaps millions of species of plant and animal life have already vanished by the action of nature, not us. We suspect sometimes that this might be a good thing, at least for us. We try to eradicate disease-bearing plants or insects. We should at times, I suppose, shoot rattlesnakes and stomp on spiders, even though we would hate to see all of these dangerous creatures eliminated.[7]

Many wonder about the worth of our own human being in the world, the passingness and dubiousness of our own existence. The Book of Job reveals this mood to us: "Man, born of woman, has a short life yet has his fill of sorrow. He blossoms, and he withers, like a flower; fleeting as a shadow, transient. And is this what you deign to turn your gaze on, him that you would bring before you to be judged?" (14:1-4). Scripture brings this fleetingness to our consciousness, almost as though, without a reminder of it, even God is skeptical that we would attend to our actual condition.

A *New Yorker* cartoon (July 27, 1987) showed a Michelangelo-type scene, with the finger of God flashing out of the dark clouds toward two Adam and Eve-like beings walking forlornly on the rather barren earth. Two obviously perplexed angels, hovering midway in the air between earth and heaven, watched this scene of the two human beings walking away from God. One angel remarked to the other, "Frankly, I think we'll regret introducing these organisms into the environment." What is God like? He definitely introduced "these organisms," these human beings, into the environment anyhow, to reveal the great doctrines of original sin and redemp-

[7]See James V. Schall, "On the Christian Love of Animals," *The Praise of 'Sons of Bitches': On the Worship of God by Fallen Men* (Slough, England: St. Paul Publications, 1978) 36–52.

tion. Even the plans of God, as far as we can tell, seem to go awry.

Towns in the West of the United States, ghost towns we call them, have disappeared. We only know of their existence because they had a railroad station or because someone published a newspaper there for a few years, a copy of which has been found here or there in some old trunk or loft. Pompeii is a familiar place by comparison, but only because of the dramatic way in which it disappeared. Towns and cities once important now are merely insignificant provincial centers.

We ourselves are disappearing every day in what we say and do. Psalm 94 reads, "The Lord knows the thoughts of men. He knows they are no more than a breath." We too, each of us, are "words" made flesh. Our individual existences are our own and no one else's. We are not interchangeable, nor are we repeatable. Our words, nevertheless, are fleeting and do not last until we put them in a permanent form in which they can be remembered. Even if we become famous, our words and deeds which are recorded in books and other works of human hands are easily forgotten. Perhaps we wrote or spoke in a language no one any longer reads or cares about. We may have written a novel or an essay in an era when everyone insists on watching television. We must strive to keep whatever we have put into reality, or else it too will soon be gone. Lost cities, lost nations, lost species, lost books, lost dramas, lost records—these too are part of the account of our frail existence.

Is it the "vanity of vanities" of the Old Testament that we think everything any human being said at any time or in any place is worth preserving? Some things, perhaps, we ought to forget. This proposition, that we keep what we say, has certain theological overtones we should not overlook about the ultimate importance of each individual who has ever existed. Scripture tells us that every hair of our heads is numbered, and what is spoken in secret will be heard in the housetops. This warning would suggest that although our lives, words, and actions seem frail, still they are known, heard, and accounted for as if they were of ultimate importance.

I myself have seen the Colosseum, the Taj Mahal, the temples in Kyoto, the Great Pyramid, and Mount St. Michel. Any such monument to human greatness can be destroyed in an instant, even while it is being eroded by time. The Golden Gate Bridge, which I have seen often, requires continual painting if it is not to erode. A man tried to blow up the Washington Monument several years ago. The famous Parthenon in Athens was partly destroyed because military supplies were stored there during a Turkish war.

Nothing lasts unless we want it to last, except perhaps for accidental fragments of what is not yet naturally disintegrated. Our museums and libraries grow because we have so much to keep, with a desire and budgets to keep it. They say if we put things in a pure vacuum, nothing will change. Possibly the moon or some planet or Antarctica will be our storehouse of what we said and did. But we must decide what it is we shall save. We would hesitate to leave this decision to our politicians, even less to our academics. Yet, who else will do it? One of the civilizing functions of medieval monks was, ironically, simply to preserve the works of antiquity.

We each need our own history, our own memory. St. Augustine was right. In *The Confessions,* he wrote: "I am become a troublesome soil that requires overmuch labor. For we are not now searching out the tracts of heaven, or measuring the distance of the stars, or inquiring about the weight of the earth. It is I myself, I, the mind—who remembers. It is not much to be wondered at, if, what I myself am not, be far from me. But what is nearer to me than myself? And, behold, I am not able to comprehend the force of my own memory, though I cannot name myself without it" (X, 16). St. Augustine, to whom I will return (chapter 11), understood the true location of human existence. Compared to the drama of our own lives before God, the tracts of heaven, the distance of the stars, and the weight of the earth are insignificant. We can recognize the human drama without ever denying the intrinsic fascination of natural wonders, without our neglecting the fact that such natural things are becoming more known every day and that it is worth knowing them.

St. Augustine emphasized that we could not even name ourselves without memory. Josef Pieper wrote a short essay entitled "What Is My Real Name?" in which he said that the names by which we designate things "do not penetrate to their core."[8] Pieper recalled his own mother in her old age asking him what her "real" name was. He answered with her first or Christian name, but she knew that name. She could not recall her father's name, which she bore as a youngster. Pieper reflected that names are intended to indicate the core of our being. The liturgy of the dead addresses the person by his or her first name. Pieper recalled being once in a Japanese monastery where a new name is given to each one after death. Isaiah talks of God addressing us by our real name (43:1). Pieper concluded that the name which truly designates what and who we are is this name that God gives us. We wish to be called and remembered by this name.

"Salvation of the soul," that great philosophical and religious theme from the very origins of our culture, relates to the permanence of what we are. The existence of God causes us to wonder about our own existence, its seeming transcience, its hope of permanence. Socrates on his last day did not talk idly of the soul's immortality. The soul remains a true intellectual battleground because we sense that without the soul's abidingness, we are indeed ultimately lost. Even the permanent seems slightly transient.

Aristotle observed that our polities often outlast our own individual lives. Our polities choose their future when they choose what past they will keep. Cities are places where we either remember our gods, or where we consign them to oblivion. The past can be retained when we see what went on within history. Who can forget the account in Thucydides of the destruction of the little town of Platea, caught between its neighbors Athens, Thebes, and Sparta?

> They [the Spartans] therefore brought the Plateans before them again one by one and asked each of them the same question. "Have you done anything to help the Spartans and their allies in the war?" As each man replied, "No," he was taken away and put to death, no exceptions being

[8]Josef Pieper, "What Is My Real Name?" *Problems of Modern Faith: Essays and Addresses* (Chicago: Franciscan Herald Press, 1985) 293.

> made. . . . Afterwards they razed it (Platea) to the ground from its very foundations. . . . The land they confiscated and let it out on ten-year leases to the Thebans. . . . This was the end of Platea, in the ninety-third year after she became the ally of Athens (III, ch. 4).

These words of the Greek historian suggest not merely our frailty and that of our cities, but also frailty of the justice in this life, the question of whether it was worthwhile for a Platean to have existed at all. Thucydides seems to suggest that Platea was worthwhile. We can read about it in his book, and we cannot forget it. In this book, Platea lives so long as there are frail books.

On October 18, 1773, Samuel Johnson wrote in a famous passage of an old monastic island no more than a mile long in the Hebrides: "That man is little to be envied, whose patriotism would not gain force upon the plain of Marathon, or whose piety would not grow warmer among the ruins of Iona."[9] Such nobility and beauty of word take us out of ourselves. I was once at the great Abbey of Monte Cassino, which had been rebuilt from ruins after World War II bombing. The Abbey was beautiful in its restored state, and, I am sure, more comfortable. Still there was something poignant about the fact that this building was not the ancient one stretching back even to St. Benedict's time in the sixth century. We think of the great Abbey Church of Cluny destroyed during the French Revolution, never to be rebuilt. Our most noble of buildings are themselves fragile.

Do our words remain? Even if we wanted to record exactly what we did or thought in one day, it would take volumes and volumes to get us through just one year. Besides, if we spend our lives paying attention to the preservation of what we say or do, eventually we only repeat what we already said. Introspection of this sort can mean that nothing ever happens to us. We can be always too busy looking back over our shoulders to see how we have performed. Thus, we never really

[9]Samuel Johnson, *Journey to the Western Islands* (Boston: Houghton Mifflin, 1965) 111.

"do" anything. We only watch ourselves. We are too busy observing ourselves to be concerned with what is not ourselves. Is it any wonder that Aquinas remarked that we cannot know ourselves until we first know what is not ourselves?

Many a Gettysburg Address, that no one ever recorded, or even heard, may have been uttered around the cemeteries of world history. "The world will little note, nor long remember what we say here," Lincoln himself remarked at this same Gettysburg. Anyone with a computer knows how frail our words seem to be. Yet "on-line" we can find a reference to and location for almost everything ever written in books or seen on video or film, provided we have the technology. Will we always have this technology? We have books preserved in a language we do not know. Will we some day have millions of video cassettes whose reproduction facilities are lost? Technology changes faster than our capacity to preserve the very instruments that preserve what we say and do.

Our frailty includes the overwhelming abundance that derives from our inventiveness and entrepreneurship. No one person can know or use everything. Aristotle defined our intellects as powers capable of "knowing all things." He held that there was a correspondence between the structure of the world and the structure of our minds. We seem to have been given this capacity to know all things but not enough time, even in a lifetime, to activate it all. Was something created "in vain"? We find in ourselves a natural call to enlightenment that is mocked by our frailty, by the fact that we die with so much still to know.

In his book, *New Elucidations,* Hans Urs von Balthasar wrote an essay entitled "Flight Into Community."[10] His argument was a subtle but important one. He acknowledged the important truth contained in Aristotle's idea that a person is by nature a social and political being. But Aristotle, and Aquinas following him, had recognized that real being is contained in each one of us. The polity exists only if we exist.[11]

[10]Hans Urs von Balthasar, *New Elucidations* (San Francisco: Ignatius Press, 1986) 104–11.

[11]See James V. Schall, "The Reality of Society according to St. Thomas," *The Politics of Heaven and Hell: Christian Themes from Classical, Medieval, and*

The meaning of all else depends on the meaning of our own existence, on why we are rather than are not. The polity is limited by what we are. Human destiny is itself the end of the polity. At least some things are not political.

What von Balthasar underscored is the failure of modern theory to attend to the transcendent nature of each person, who can by prayer or meditation reach the heart of being itself. The ultimate aloneness which grounds the frailty of each of us is, in the newer theories, presumably to be replaced by community. Even in modern religion we see the "collective" aspect emphasized. The "we" replaces the "I" in our prayers and affirmation. The individual person, asked to stand for nothing, is absorbed into some group. "It is deeply alarming," von Balthasar wrote, "to see a real flight from personal intimacy with God into the security of the community taking place in a great number of modern movements."[12] The demand that community take total responsibility for our ethical condition is related to our doubt about the status of our own existence.

What can substitute for God most easily is ironically a collectivity of some sort. God is Trinity, a many in one, so the temptation to replace our individual being with a collective one is subtle (see below, chapter 9).[13] The burden of our frailness is somehow to be compensated for not by God's plan for us, but by what appears to be more lasting, more "lightsome," wherein what we do contributes to some "good" down the ages. We can, in such a view, find no other good worthy of our sacrifices or our lives. But the good down the ages is not our personal good except indirectly. Our frailness does not permit us even to hope that the "this-ness" of our individual being has a claim on permanence. "Realism" is said to face this fact. A stark nobility claims that we are, in the end, nothing.

"The frailty of human institutions and laws and, generally, of all matters pertaining to men's living together,"

Modern Political Philosophy (Lanham, Md.: University Press of America, 1984) 235–52.

[12]Balthasar, *New Elucidations*, 108.

[13]See James V. Schall, "The Trinity: God Is Not Alone," *Redeeming the Time* (New York: Sheed & Ward, 1968), 65–96; "Trinitarian Transcendence in Ignatian Spirituality," *The Distinctiveness of Christianity* (San Francisco: Ignatius Press, 1982) 114–25.

Hannah Arendt wrote, "arises from the human condition of natality and is quite independent of the frailty of human nature."[14] Our physical existence is precarious. Even more precarious is the fact that ideas and things must be passed on to specific individuals who must choose, on their coming of age, to receive into their minds and into their continuing polities, even into their technology, what was known, spoken, and done before their time. The great barbarians of the future may well be those in charge of the latest version of recording machinery.

A change of religion or worldview by conquest or conviction contributes every bit as much to the frailty of human enterprise as the earthquake or the flood does to human artifacts. We are born with minds on which there is nothing yet written, as the ancients told us. The very power of our newness, of our being born into the world, implies not merely a repetition of what went before, but something new with each birth, something radically new for either good or evil.

Our frailty is the most curious thing about us. Finite, frail beings we are who seek by words and deeds to keep signs of our having existed at all before those who follow us. Frailness we can indeed understand. But our endeavors to counteract our frailness—this is something else, a sign that, as Chesterton said at the end of *Orthodoxy*, we can be homesick even while we are at home. And yet, it is true: neither we nor that which we have built or spoken need have existed. Our frailty places us among those things which are for their own sakes. We exist in some order of superabundance and newness which gently mocks us when we are tempted to conclude that our lives, our cosmos, in the end have "made absolutely no difference."

Yet, our frailness is itself a call to what is not frail, but to what, nevertheless, *is*. The weakest thing especially does not explain itself; its very being incites us to ask why it does exist, why it stands in its own particular way out of nothingness here and now, before us. The reality of contingent beings, those beings which are by nature most frail, demands in particular, as St. Thomas held (*ST* I, 2, 3), the being of what is

[14]Arendt, *The Human Condition*, 170.

not contingent. If goodness must absorb justice for justice to exist at all, as Plato held (*The Republic*, Book 6), so frailty must stand in the presence of what is not frail. This is why some philosophers, while distinctly surprised, were not totally confused by those records which spoke of "the Word made flesh."

At some point frailty is overcome. "The fact that God raised him (Jesus) from the dead, never to return to corruption, is no more than what He had declared: 'To you I shall give the sure and holy things promised to David.' This is explained by another text: 'You will not allow your holy one to experience corruption' " (Acts 13:34-35). This is what God is like, someone who understands the anguish of our language, the frailness of our existence against the many hints of its permanence.

God, to recall, is a God who is "prayed to." This is what he is like. Recalling what we said about prayer while anticipating the following chapter, I remember that a friend wrote, "Jacques Maritain's insistence in his *Notebooks* that it is absolutely necessary for us to pray for ourselves and others really struck me. He indicates that prayer is not an option; it is a command and an absolute necessity." God pursues us freely. We are free; this is what it means to be created in his image. Yet we are commanded to pray, almost as if we will not bother to pray unless we are shaken enough to attend to what is most important. God deals with us gently, mysteriously. But what is also evident is that apart from God our being has no option open to it other than despair, the rejection of ourselves and others. God takes us seriously enough not to want us to miss this fundamental understanding of the beings each of us are, beings receptive to the being God is.

Chapter III

''Everything That Can Be Saved Will Be Saved''

What God ''is like'' can be approached by the philosophic treatment of St. Thomas or the more meditative treatment of the contemplative saints or the active generosity of those who have obviously been led on by God. Each of these ways reveals some new insight into this topic. Here I want to look at a particular life, that of Raissa Maritain, the famous wife of the great French philosopher Jacques Maritain, both of whom I have already cited. I want to do this because the accounts of their lives that each wrote have been of particular importance to me in understanding what God is like.

These two lives, like the lives of all those who have been given to me, I want to see, if I can, in their particularity, in their privacy. The Maritains were well-known in their time and were acquainted with many of the important cultural and religious figures of their era. Yet something touchingly private hovers about them, a kind of holiness, I think. They reveal much of themselves in their personal memoirs, which help account for me what God is like.

I am reminded of something a friend, who gave me the *Journal* of Raissa Maritain, wrote about the relation of most ordinary lives to the time and places in which they appear:

> By anybody's yardstick, I live a modest and quiet life. Nothing much happens. Only everyday things. And yet everything that happens, even little things, even things that happen to other people whom I love, I feel somehow ob-

> liged to absorb, reflect upon, meditate upon, until I have somehow come to some hazy understanding of how these things might fit into the whole picture of the world. I never am unaware of the historical nature of life. Not a day goes by that I do not think something about how profoundly we are built into time. We are both in and out of time. One foot here, one foot in heaven.

Ordinary lives both in privacy and in humor, a theme we shall take up in the following chapter, have within their very unfolding something beyond themselves.

This awareness of the depths of our lives in the odd ways and places they occur is most poignant in the life and reflections of Raissa Maritain. Her journals are the mirror or record of one who sought to understand what God was like; or, perhaps better, this is how I understood her record at a time when I wanted particularly to know what God was like. Indeed, following Schumacher, I likewise wanted to know what I was like. John Paul II frequently remarks that to know the whole truth about human beings, including ourselves, we need to know about Christ.[1] We never know who will help us to learn about Christ and about ourselves. It may be our own father, or our chance reading of a book, as in this case, or a study of Thomas Aquinas or Gilbert Chesterton, or a tragedy, or a joy that broke into the ordinariness of our lives. We do not know how God will surprise us. This too is what God is like. This is why there are, actually, no "ordinary" lives.

Raissa Maritain's notebooks were written sporadically from 1906 until 1931. In addition there were "Loose Leaves" and sundry short jottings from 1931 until she died in Paris on November 4, 1960. Her husband, Jacques Maritain, whom she married in 1904, whose parallel journals have also been published, had these reflections of his wife privately printed. Their intrinsic interest and worth resulted in a French edition in 1963. The English translation was published in Ireland in 1974.[2]

[1]See *The Whole Truth about Man: John Paul II to University Students and Faculties*, ed. James V. Schall (Boston: St. Paul Editions, 1981).

[2]*Raissa's Journal*, presented by Jacques Maritain (Albany, N.Y.: Magi Books, n. d.). The Irish edition was published by Cahill & Company; the French edition by Desclée De Brouwer. Jacques Maritain, *Notebooks*, trans. Joseph W.

Both of the Maritains are famous in Catholic intellectual and cultural circles. Their influence extends to any general discussion of philosophy and theology in the twentieth century. Both were converts, Raissa from Russian Judaism, Jacques from French Protestantism. Jacques Maritain's maternal grandfather was Jules Favre, a Third Republic political figure, "a rationalist and a Rousseauist." Jacques wrote, "I felt very vexed to have inherited certain traits from him, particularly, I had to admit, a certain detestable taste for Donquixotism and for lost causes" (J 83). After reading Shalom Asch's "beautiful, astounding book, *Le Juif aux Psaumes*," about Hassidim Jewry in Poland, Raissa wrote: "My maternal grandfather was a Hassid too. And my father's father was a great ascetic. I have all that behind me. And for me too, the Psalms ought to be a perpetual nourishment" (R 274).

1. *The Arts*

Raissa Maritain's poetry, her studies in art and her reflections on friendship are well known.[3] She sang and even wrote some music. "Artistic creativity does not imitate God's creation," she wrote in 1919, "it continues it." Art is a part of the spiritualizing process. "To civilize is to spiritualize," she maintained (R 100). Art "contributes to spiritualizing man, to making him more ready to receive the natural and supernatural contemplative life" (R 95). God gave us the world in order that it might reflect him; human artists make "nature the collaborator of His omnipotence." Raissa was critical of Catholics who did not see this civilizing function of art (R 96). She felt that

Evans (Albany, N.Y.: Magi Books, 1984). [Subsequently, in this text, *Raissa's Journal* will be cited simply as "R" and the *Notebooks* as "J"]. A comprehensive account of all the publications of Jacques and Raissa Maritain can be found in *The Achievement of Jacques and Raissa Maritain: A Bibliography, 1906–61*, ed. Donald and Idella Gallagher (Garden City, N.Y.: Doubleday, 1962). For an account of aspects of Jacques Maritain's thought, see James V. Schall, "Metaphysics, Theology, and Political Theory," *Political Science Reviewer* 11 (Fall, 1981) 1–26.

[3]Raissa Maritain, *We Have Been Friends Together*, trans. Julie Kernan (Garden City, N.Y.: Doubleday Image, 1942). For a complete listing of the books and essays of Raissa Maritain, see *Achievement*, 225–31.

Catholic thought needed to be doctrinally clear and orthodox in order to allow the artist to be what he was.

Raissa Maritain was always interested in art, music, and painting. When she was well enough, she frequently went to museums, concerts, and art galleries. She wrote, "Cocteau had reserved a box for us for the dress rehearsal of *La Machine Infernale* (April 9, 1934). . . . I am overwhelmed by Jean Cocteau's play. . . . Cocteau is certainly the only tragic author of our day" (R 234). On November 23, 1935, she noted that on the previous evening she had heard at the Salle Gaveau Igor Stravinsky's double piano Concerto played with his son. "Admirable technically, but without the slightest inwardness; it gave me no pleasure in hearing it except such as one gets from any good professional job" (R 252). Raissa had a particular love for religious music: "Religious music in some way unites the knot between body and spirit. It frees the soul, exalts it towards a more spiritual life" (R 164).

A month later, Raissa had "visited the exhibition organized by the Gazette des Beaux-Arts. Modigliani, Chagall, Utrillo, Rousseau, Soutine, Pascin, Marie Laurencin" (R 253). She did not like, even "detested" Soutines, was "disappointed" with Modigliani, "charmed" with Laurencin, "indifferent" to Pascin, and "loved" Utrillo, Chagall, and Rousseau, the latter of whom she thought "almost attains absolute perfection" with his "l'Été and le Navire" (R 254). Clearly, she was a woman who knew and responded to what she saw. "I have a mystical love of natural reason," she said of herself (R 147).

Jacques, Raissa, and her sister Vera had been in Rome in 1918, when they met Pope Benedict XV. They returned to Rome on April 25, 1945 and went to Mass at both the Chiesa Nuova and at Saint-Louis-des-Francais. Raissa wrote:

> Great beauty of the church, the altar and the singing. [The French Church has the great Caravaggio of St. Matthew.] Feeling of warm welcome, of finding myself back home again. I was sitting between Jacques and Vera. I thought: all this beauty, this profusion of gold and profusion of movement in all the carving and sculpture; these intricate rites in which everything has its symbolic meaning, all this is the

> world of love; the love which flows from the first infusion of charity into the Church. As to the artists . . . they themselves were sustained, whether they had faith or not, by the great love which keeps watch in and over the Church (R 302).

Art was something that Raissa thought about, created, and fostered.

Raissa Maritain was instrumental in having Arthur Lourie's symphonic works played in Paris. "In the evening (June 12, 1936), the first public performance of Arthur Lourie's *Concerto Spirituelle,* conducted by Munch. Conducting the choirs, Vlassov and Yvonne Gouverne, at the piano Yvonne Lefebure" (R 261). In the footnote to this entry, Jacques Maritain added: "It was Raissa who had succeeded in getting this particularly important work of Arthur Lourie's performed. To do so, she had spared herself no effort, using all the strength of her will to break down the wall of silence erected by the jealousies and clannishness of the musical world round this composer whom she regarded with good reason, as the greatest musician of our time." Lourie and his wife Ella actually lived later in the Maritain's home in Princeton. On July 6, 1951, the Maritains had heard Lourie's *Anathema* in New York, about which Raissa later wrote to him: "How moving it is, the progress of your soul, visible in the way you have chosen and put together the texts of the Scriptures for this musical work. It is your Credo wholly and entirely expressed in the words of the Holy Spirit" (R 321).

2. *Contemplative Vocation*

Throughout these journals is the presence of Raissa's sister Vera, who lived with the Maritains until her own death in Princeton on December 31, 1959. She seems to have shared the deep spirituality of Raissa and Jacques. Jacques described the two sisters, both of whom suffered from ill health most of their lives:

> The two sisters were very secret, each in her own manner. Raissa hiding her treasures and her sorrows in the brilliance of intelligence and the grace of winged words, Vera hiding

> hers in a silence in which the goodness, the princely vivacity and the dreams of a candid and adventurous spirit took refuge. The solitude of Raissa was that of a poet with incredibly sensitive and delicate fingers, lover of the beauties of the world and entered into the thickness of the Cross, wholly given up to the contemplative life and to the immolations of love; the solitude of Vera was that of a contemplative disguised as a sister of charity . . . (J 74).

The contemplative side of Raissa's life and the way she looked at and explained it in her journals are of deep significance.

While the public life of the Maritains is even yet relatively well remembered, what has been less well-known is the deep spiritual life, mystical in many ways, in Raissa. Of his wife Jacques wrote on February 17, 1910, "I have the very clear impression . . . that Raissa will never have happiness except in establishing herself in the state of contemplative souls, and in making prayer the permanent foundation of her life" (J 61). So moving and profound was this life, reflected in some part in these journals, that it seems worthwhile to recount the experience and insight the reading these journals can impart.

Raissa Maritain was, first of all, as was Jacques, very conscious that the dated events of every human life are within the providence of God. On November 26, 1914, she listed the important dates in her life: "Leon Bloy receives our first letter on the Feast of St. Barnabas, June 1905; Baptism of Jacques, Raissa and Vera: 11 June 1906, St. Barnabas; Raissa's first confession: 22 July 1906, St. Mary Magdalene; First Communion of J., R., V., at Sacré-Coeur: 3d August 1906 . . ." (R 22). In 1947, she listed the things "the Lord has done for me." She remarked that the gifts of God are universal, yet somehow very particular, "for this or that individual." These were the things she detailed: "First, God made the child Jacques Maritain be born on the 18th November 1882, in Paris. Ten Months later he made the child Raissa Oumançoff be born on 12th September in Rostoff-on-the-Don. At the date of Raissa's birth, Henri Bergson, aged 23, was writing the *Essai sur les Données immédiates de la Conscience*. Leon Bloy, born in 1846, was 37, he was then writing his book on Christopher Columbus. Père Clérissac, born in 1864, was 19, he was entering the Dominicans"

(R 311) Such dates were not mere lists. They revealed a sense of divine guidance in each life.

In a brief, undated note entitled "The True Face of God," Raissa wrote, in a passage that serves to define her spirituality: "So when a soul suffers, and suffers from this inexorable Law of transmutation of a nature into a higher nature (and this is the meaning of all human history)—God is with this nature which he has made and which is suffering—he is not against it. If he could transform that nature into his own by abolishing the law of suffering and death, he would abolish it—because he takes no pleasure in the spectacle of pain and death. But he cannot abolish any law inscribed in being" (R 390). The meaning of human history is, for Raissa, concentrated in each human life, in its particular events, in its relation to God. The dates of this life are filled with significance.

3. *Home and Friends*

I was given *Raissa's Journal* for Christmas, 1987. I had known of these journals but had never read them. The preface of this volume is by Abbé René Voillaume, who was the Prior of the Little Brothers of Jesus, the order which Jacques joined after Raissa's death. In this preface Voillaume cited a letter of Raissa, dated March 7, 1924, the Feast of St. Thomas Aquinas. Raissa remarked that "Christ, with all his merits and the merits of all the saints, will do his work deep down below the surface of the waters. *And everything that can be saved will be saved*" (R xx). This remark hints that there may be things that cannot be saved because they will not to be. The drama of this book on "What Is God Like?" must be seen in the response to this ever-present dilemma of human existence, the place of the human heart in the struggle for salvation.

As I read these moving journals, what was striking was the account of Raissa's life with God. Often I noted that these journals were filled with such remarks as: "Prolonged prayer in the morning"; "silent prayer in the train"; "intense absorption in God between 9 and midday"; "the days of anguish have returned for me"; "terrible night"; "God-given absorption does not alter the underlying base of sadness, even of sorrow, of which I have been inwardly aware for several months.'' The suffering of Raissa's life caused her to reflect on its reality in her spiritual life. She understood that ''sacrifice is an absolutely universal law for the perfecting of the creature'' (R 59). This led her to the need to understand the relation of suffering to God and the world in which we human beings exist. She knew quite well that we must have a proper understanding of God if we will have the sort of relation to him that he wishes.

But the Maritains were careful to lead a life of openness to their friends and to their family. Raissa wrote to Jacques in January, 1936: ''Go on loving me like this, I need a great deal of love in order to live and I know that I have to love 'as not loving,' in St. Paul's sense, and beyond St. Paul's sense. What a terrible vocation! It is for that God has placed your marvelous love at my side. For with whom would I have been able to live such a vocation, except with you? . . . But, Jacques, to live like this is a martyrdom . . .'' (R 255). In reading these lines, we realize that, in the midst of their own spiritual lives, the Maritains knew so many men and women that have become important in the life of Catholicism—Gilson, Péguy, Psichari. The latter two were both killed in World War I, duly noted in the journals: ''22d August 1914: Ernest Psichari killed at Virton (Belgium); 5th September 1914: Charles Péguy killed at the Marne'' (R 24). The couple also knew Gheon, Julien Green, Bergson, Bloy, Abbé Charles (later Cardinal) Journet, Marcel, Reverdy, Père Charles, Père Clerissac, Père Dehau, Père Bruno de Jesus-Marie, Mauriac, Roualt, Berdiaeff.

The Maritains knew Eric Satie and Cocteau well. Their deaths are recorded in the journals: Death of Eric Satie at the Saint-Joseph hospital (July 2, 1925). ''A few days ago, on June 29th, Jacques saw Satie for the last time. When Satie fell asleep, Jacques stayed beside him, praying under his breath. Then Satie woke up and said these very sweet words to Jacques: 'It's good to be together like this, without saying anything, especially when one thinks alike' '' (R 184). The Maritains were at the baptism of children of friends, often godchildren; they were instrumental in several vocations; they organized retreats and had a chapel in their home.

When their young friend Charles du Bos died in 1939, Jacques went to the funeral. Raissa wrote: "We have lost a great friend. But the heart is wrung above all by the thought of what this man suffered, especially in the last three years. He died prematurely. . . . Whenever a friend dies, it is difficult not to tell oneself that one didn't love him enough, or rather that one was negligent in showing friendship and esteem and admiration" (R 275).

The Maritains were never far from the sacraments. Mass was said by Abbé Journet, by Père Lamay, by their friend Père Garrigou-Lagrange, and a large number of other priest visitors. They were concerned about confession and even sought out Père Charles to assist Cocteau (R 182). What is striking about this brilliant couple is their zeal and piety about the basic things of the faith. For them, it was the sacramental life that had to be central, however much this followed upon and, more, contributed to any intellectual life.

Jacques Maritain spent a significant part of his academic life discussing the proper human public and economic life, in genuine philosophic and theoretical analysis. What is startling in these journals, however, is to realize that practically every thought and search after the truth in the Maritains' life was discussed between them, and not merely discussed but prayed over. Raissa wrote on April 12, 1934: "Everything that is in Jacques' work we have first lived in the form of a vital difficulty, in the form of experience—problems of art and morality, of philosophy, of faith, of prayer, of contemplation" (R 235). Jacques reflected the same thought from Paris on June 10, 1908:

> My beloved Raissa! I will know only in Paradise all I owe to her. Every good comes from God. But as earthly intermediary, *everything* has come to me through her, from her heart, from her reason, from her prayers, from her counsels, from her example, from her sufferings, from her virtues, from her love for God and from her tender love for miserable me.
>
> This is what I wrote at Heidelberg the 19th of March, and I recopy it in Paris [and forty-six years later I recopy it in Princeton, because I have thought that all the days of my life] (J 48).

The intensity of the spiritual life in the various homes of the Maritains, in Heidelberg, in Kolbsheim, in Meudon, in Versailles, in Paris, in Toronto, in Rome and in Princeton comes as a surprise to anyone who might think that their interest in the intellectual life overshadowed their spiritual life. But they never thought of these lives as separate or even distinct.

4. *Primacy of God's Love*

In these journals, what becomes clear is that the primary relationship that must exist in the world is not that between people but between each person and God. Raissa noted "the illness and death of our beloved godfather, Leon Bloy," on October 3, 1917. She wrote to the Father Abbot of Saint-Paul: "The Fatherland, the one where we will love each other! How can one not long for it ardently? Here below men have claimed to be dispensed from loving God (who, they say, does not need our love) and to make the human race happy by philanthropy alone—and God, abandoning them to themselves, shows them that, without love of Him, love of one's neighbor cannot be realized on earth. But who wants to understand this?" (R 63). This position will come as something of a scandal to our era, but it is refreshing to follow Raissa Maritain in her life with her husband, her sister, her many friends, her God, to be reminded of what is central.

Christianity has never been a religion that was free to neglect the world, because of its incarnational grounding in the life of Christ. But something disturbs our complacency in reading Raissa's continual insistence that what counts is our relation to God, that this is why the world was created, almost as if whether we produce a perfect order or not is relatively indifferent. "All that can be saved will be saved." To be saved requires first that we will to be saved, will to love God first. Raissa reflected on St. Thomas' teaching on the proper order of creation. From Versailles on October 19, 1921, she wrote: "Jacques is thinking of forming a society of the people who meet every month at our house to study with him this or that point of Thomist teaching. I propose that all those who join it should make a vow of *oraison,* so as to emphasize the necessity of the spiritual life for those who serve God by intellectual work" (R 126–27). Phrases from St. Thomas are often found in Raissa's comments.

5. *Women*

Raissa Maritain was most insightful about the nature of the intellectual and spiritual life for a woman. "These poor intellectual women! How people mistrust them!" she mildly reflected (R 134). "The realism and the faculty of disinterested contemplation proper to women make them lovers of metaphysics when they study philosophy" (R 109). She was most insistent that women had to develop their metaphysical sense, that their capacity to do so was in fact deeper because they were women. She was quite concerned about the intelligence of women, although she was the opposite of a modern feminist. She could get annoyed, however: "A great theologian preaches Love to women, but teaches Intelligence to his disciples. The two ought to be preached and taught simultaneously" (R 170). Raissa thought that metaphysics was the most proper subject for "a feminine mind with a gift for abstraction. I am not saying that women are gifted for cutting a figure as great philosophers—but only for understanding and assimilating the philosophy of great philosophers" (R 111). Indeed, she thought that both sexes should "be taught true philosophy." She did not think that women "as a rule" excelled "either in the arts or in the sciences," but they possess "keenness of intellectual vision." Metaphysics is difficult for everyone, but "woman's realism delights in the knowledge of ultimate realities." She continued: "Her sense of order—'she would tidy up God himself', Péguy said—is satisfied by being able to order her whole being in the light of intelligence. Her powers of contemplation enable her to love the truth she knows more intensely and, in certain cases, to increase her range of knowledge through the very love that she bears the Truth. Her great capacity for loving attaches her more strongly to the truth and induces her to dedicate herself to it" (R 112). Young women who want to have an intellectual life will be more profound if they frequent the truths of faith rather than "the world.'' Those young women who are easily discouraged ought not to take up philosophy, ''but those who seek to please God, if they have the taste for abstract truths, ought to cultivate their intellect humbly and fearlessly, for knowledge can only increase their charity'' (R 111).

Twice in these journals did Raissa Maritain seem to be particularly annoyed, both instances having to do with ''modern'' theologians discussing women. She wrote to her friend Antoinette Grunelius, from Rome, in 1946, on religious psychology. ''Married people make their own psychology and unmarried people are out of their depth in it,'' she thought (R 309). Raissa considered it particularly dangerous to ''give as essential properties of marriage ones which only belong to marriage fulfilled in exceptional conditions of love, harmony, happiness, delicacy, and intelligence. These theologians appear to forget that marriage is a sacrament, even if it is not happy, even if it is not a love marriage, even if it is only a 'marriage of convenience.''' To this doctrine of the unbreakable sacramental nature of marriage, she added with some irony, ''When one sees the number of celibate analysts who devote themselves to the problem of marriage, one has the feeling that it is the analysts most of all who would need to get married'' (R 310).

On October 11, 1950, we find Raissa, Vera, and Jacques going to see their friends, the Benedictine nuns of Regina Laudis. Raissa remarked: ''A Sister I know particularly well is none too happy, she cannot get accustomed to this foundress' life. And besides she is perturbed by the influence of certain thinkers and theologians'' (R 319). The relation of spiritual life and Christian intelligence was of great concern to Raissa Maritain. She understood, however, that our vocations in life come in obedience to God: ''What we have to do is not determined by truth alone but by the particular purpose of the providential government of mankind. There are many things we do not know concerning the pattern of life of other peoples according to God's purpose'' (R 222). She meant by this that God is not ultimately defeated by falsehood or sin, even though the upholding of truth is a necessity for the Church, for the philosopher, and for the religious.

6. *The Essential Relations*

The heart of what Raissa Maritain lived had to do with the truth about God's ways. However much she was interested in the intellectual, social, and artistic life as necessary for Christianity and for modern culture, she understood that the real drama of creation was the relation of a person to God. "God and souls, there is no other interest in life," she exclaimed on May 17, 1922. In these reflections there is never any of modernity's proposition that until the world is restructured, faith is not possible. Quite the opposite, the central thought is one's personal relation to God. Until this is rightly ordered, civilization will become increasingly disordered. "Since the advent of Christianity, there is no true civilization except that which, through the earthly city, *aspires* to the heavenly city" (R 108).

Raissa Maritain's prayer life did concern itself with the world, with reparation for sin, with conversion (including that of her own people, the Jews), with the ravages of war. But she did not think the causes of the evils in the world, at bottom, were political or military or economic. This is why the gospel also had to be preached to everyone:

> Since every man of good faith and pure morals can receive divine grace and the grace of final perseverance without visibly belonging to the Church, why the preaching of the Gospel? Why not preach only the existence of God, good faith and purity, which is accessible to every conscience?
>
> Can we not say that souls which are saved in this way do not collaborate actively in the salvation of the world? They are saved but they do not save. . . . In any case, preaching of the Gospel is necessary in order to afford souls a normal state with regard to salvation (October 15, 1931, R 207–08).

She understood, with Aquinas, that for most people the normal condition required for salvation includes the gospel, so its being preached and practiced are important.

Raissa Maritain did not think that God cares primarily about the things of the world, however important they might be secondarily. She understood that because of human freedom God's choice of creating this world might entail profound disorders. But the reparation for the wrongs chosen in freedom also have to arise out of freedom, out of prayer, out of sacrifice and suffering. This is a doctrine that we no longer delight to hear, since it goes against the grain of modernity, which has practically eliminated interior life by calling it a mere superstructure of society.

Raissa Maritain thought that the contemplative life kept the world together and guided it to its primary mission. She was content to live her life most directly in prayer and sacrifice. She held that eternity had already begun in the souls of the contemplatives—of whom there were not so many, but this did not matter. ''They [contemplatives] are face to face with God, alone with Him, not yet in the evidence of Vision but in the union of friendship. And God appears to care about nothing in the world but their love and faithfulness. . . . In the love of this great One sheltered in God, this contemplative Mother that, in her essence, the Church is, incentives to all forms of human justice and human prosperity are contained—it is the immense *surplus*—if only men wanted to know, or at least seek the Kingdom of God'' (R 267). She remarked that the ages in which many mystics flourished were often ages in which ''the level of the world and even of the clergy'' was very low. She concluded, ''to be sanctified and pacified, society too must begin by being faithful. Grace is not hereditary; it is not the patrimony of any one people'' (R 268).

Raissa herself was often astonished at this teaching that what God wants is our prayers, our attention, our lives, not our politics. She wrote on June 18, 1918: ''I marvel at the possibility which has been given me to rest in silence with God and experience true peace. It astonishes me to think of the value the Lord attaches to our poor love. One would really think that possessing our hearts is the end he proposed to himself in creating us; and he seriously pursues what he has proposed to attain. . . . Uncreated love, in pouring itself out on creatures, remains love and consequently is not satisfied unless another expansion responds to its expansion and makes union possible'' (R 75–76). This passage, in summary, contains the extraordinarily important teaching of Raissa Maritain. She understood the right order of our relation to God. But she realized that politics are not God's primary interest in us. This conclusion led to what she had to say about suffering and evil.

7. *Suffering*

Raissa Maritain wondered: why there is suffering in the world at all? She was aware with St. Thomas that suffering together with the question of evil were the two arguments against God: "To deny God because all nature groans and travails is only to relieve God of the responsibility of a creation of such a kind that it inevitably involves suffering" (R 228). God was not prevented from creating because of a foreknowledge that suffering might happen. This meant that God's purpose in creation was such that whether we suffered or not was not the first consideration of the divine action. God had some other fundamental purpose in mind. Raissa saw here the divine need of human beings in the providence of God.

Raissa Maritain wrote reflectively about the nature of suffering in the Christian tradition: "There is also a *fulfillment* of the Passion which can be given only by fallible creatures, and that is the struggle against the fall, against the attraction of *this world* as such, against the attraction of so many sins which represent human happiness. That gift Jesus could not make to the Father: only we can do it. It involves a manner of redeeming the world, and of suffering, which is accessible only to sinners" (R 247). After World War II, Raissa observed that, even though she hoped France and England would win this war, still following this great disaster, it was necessary that there be a "general rectification of men's minds, the return to certain fundamental truths without which a good human life and a lasting peace are impossible" (R 284).

Raissa Maritain had a special place in her thought for Mary. "The Blessed Virgin is the spoilt child of the Blessed Trinity. She knows no law. Everything yields to her in heaven and on earth. The whole of heaven gazes on her with delight" (R 36). The Maritains had a great devotion to Our Lady of La Salette (J 81–98). They attributed Raissa's recovery from a serious illness to her intercession at the time of receiving the Last Sacraments. Jacques Maritain wrote: "Anointing of the Sick and cure of Raissa, 17th of January 1907. Consecration to Mary (according to Grignion de Montfort) 25th of March 1907. Confirmation of the three of us (Jacques, Raissa, and Vera) at Grenoble, 6th of July (after first pilgrimage to La Salette)" (J 77).

8. *Sin*

Since "all created things have been rendered bitter by sins" (R 72), it follows, Raissa Maritain held, that the essential drama of life has to do with sins and the way God has of combating them. On March 24, 1919, Raissa wrote a prayer in her journals about the way God works with sinners: "You will that the saints should constitute a great capital of merits and love. . . . You let sinners go their own way, you stir up the just to love you more—and you levy in advance the share of the poor people who only recognize you when they are dying. This is the way the world goes, and you show that your kingdom is not of this world. This is how saints grow. This is how the Redemption is accomplished" (R 96). Raissa wrote to her friend Catherine van Rees that the key to this response of God to sinners was in the "redemptive suffering" of the saints, of the people who loved God (R 116).

To Maurice Sachs, another young friend, Raissa wrote concerning the question of human suffering, that this was not a new question, the problem was as old as Job, as recent as Dostoevsky and ourselves. "But God does not leave it unanswered. There is first and foremost the answer addressed to all which is the Passion of the Son of God. Does it not signify, first, the gravity of sin which calls for such an expiation? Then, that suffering united to love is the way to eternal life? And suffering comes from sin, or from the world; and love comes from God" (R 284).

Her spiritual advice was ever "Avoid sin, humble oneself because of sin, never be discouraged. Love God, love, love" (July 13, 1921, R 126). Sin, the Passion, love, suffering, each is related to the others, each must be distinguished and set in the order in which God has responded to them.

Raissa spoke of two sorts of people: one sort, like Dostoevsky's characters, "are capable of assimilating sin, of living with sin, almost of living on it, of drawing from it useful experience, a certain human enrichment, a development, even a perfecting, in the order of mercy and humility—of arriving finally, at the knowledge of God, at a certain theodicy, through extreme experience of the misery of the sinner" (R 245). The other sort of person cannot rest until the sin is gotten rid of "by contrition and confession. These are called to be assimilated to Christ. They can accept or refuse. It is a redoubtable moment when they hear that call—it is the voice of Jesus himself" (R 245).

We must not hope that by diligently following God's laws, the earth will automatically become better. "One must stop considering the observation of religious laws, faith and even charity as guarantees of a happy life on earth" (R 248). She added, "The only assurance of privilege that we have is that 'all things work together for the good of them that love God' (St. Paul); but that *all* includes all calamities and all tribulations" (R 248). The purpose of redemption is not directly to stop all sins and disorders. Rather it is to bring men and women to God through their freedom, even when they abuse it. The suffering of contemplatives and saints becomes crucial to the final recognition of God's love for sinners; in God's grace we are connected with one another. She wrote on April 16, 1946, "There is a sanctity for each one of us, proportioned to our destiny and which God proposes to obtain by means which are not catalogued in any manual of perfection" (R 305).

9. *God and Suffering*

On November 11, 1939, Raissa wrote a long, important letter, again to Maurice Sachs, in which she discussed with him the problem of God and suffering. "You are not to reproach me, Maurice," she chided him with some alacrity, "for worrying about one person when so many men are suffering and in danger of death. It is right and natural that we should worry first of all about those we love; and even those whom we only know by name are already closer to us by that very fact" (R 283). Besides, suffering with love is the way to eternal life. She realized that proof for the existence of God was not easily followed by many people, but all knew and considered suffering.

Raissa Maritain was not someone who thought everyone was a philosopher. But she was certain that faith did have the only answer to suffering.

> Every act eternally unfolds its consequences. The relations of God with men are not something vague and confused in which anything at all might happen in a haphazard way. They take place in an atmosphere of exactitude and light. Mercy will have the last word. But this is because truth and charity will have first entered men's hearts by ways which, on account of our obduracy, are often difficult; and, sometimes, as today, bloodstained.
>
> You will tell me no doubt that all this is coherent within the whole framework of Catholic doctrine but that this doctrine presupposes just what you question—the very existence of God, which is incompatible in your eyes with human suffering.
>
> But this is because Catholic doctrine is, among all religious doctrines, the one that best integrates the existence of evil and suffering; the one that gives the best account of the causes of our misery and of the remedies for it (R 285).

These remedies are not political or medical, but spiritual.

In 1959, Raissa wrote on this point again: ''Suffering is necessary in this world—as God has made it. There are perhaps other worlds, answering to other ideas of the Creator. Under a tragic sign is our life in this world. God gave this world—before the fall of the Angels, before the fall of the parent stem of humanity: the first couple, Adam and Eve—to that great Archangel who, once fallen, became the dark Prince of this world. And after that, humanity had to be redeemed, the time of this world had to be redeemed'' (R 331). This redemption was the work of God, not humanity. We are first to understand ''the world as God made it'' before we can understand either our dignity or our tragedy, before we can understand how suffering relates to God's response to both.

10. *Intelligence and Evil*

In the area of religious intelligence Raissa Maritain was a sharp debater. To an unnamed young skeptic (P. H.) who had written to her she responded that she respected his search for absolute love. She warned him, however, about attaching himself to this world ''as if it were our final end.'' But we must not completely disassociate ourselves from the world either.

"It is not in Paradise that we will have to be just and pure, this is demanded of us *today*." She knew that he "wanted to construct a world without God." But she insisted: "I *know* now that there are laws and precepts which are part of the nature of things; such is the Decalogue. I know that human life has its fullness elsewhere" (R 343).

The fact of evil in the world is not easily comprehended. Raissa came to the conclusion, as she wrote in a brief fragment, that "*God knows what he permits*." Her explanation of this passage is moving:

> He is not like a man who regretfully permits what he cannot prevent. He has let men go their own way armed with their freedom—and they go it. They go, gamble and work, risk everything—win more or less, and perhaps will end by winning everything. God has simply reserved for himself in humanity one Man who is his Son. And this Man-God calls to himself, for his own work—which he also has to do with men's freedom—calls a small number of men—a handful in each century to work in his own way . . . and that is sufficient (R 365).

Here are the familiar themes of Raissa Maritain: that freedom must be met with freedom, that God will respond to those who first search for him, that God's relation to each person is the central drama of existence, that "God knows what he permits."

11. *Conclusion*

The first spiritual father Raissa had was the famous Father Clérissac. He told her that she should discipline her time of prayer to conform to her household and official duties. This advice proved to be unsettling to her, as she was not at all sure what God was teaching her. When she met Father Dehau, who later became her director for many years, she was more content with what she was to do and how she was to pray. Jacques recorded this matter:

> Ever since these first meetings, Father Dehau became a providential guide for us. He understood Raissa's vocation

> at once. I remember that at this time she was very troubled, not knowing what God wanted of her and why He pursued her, wondering even if she ought not to throw herself into external works. Father Dehau said to her: "When you feel an interior call to recollection, never resist. Let yourself be led at the very instant. And remain with God as long as it pleases Him, without yourself interruption (unless you are obliged to do so by a duty of charity or some other necessity)." Raissa was delivered, she had found her way (J 78).

She realized that in the spiritual life "one has simultaneously to act and to let God act as he pleases. Above all, docility to let him act; not to try too hard to know" (R 263).

In January, 1924, from her home in Meudon, Raissa Maritain recalled the beautiful words of St. Ambrose: "As He took my will, so He took my sadness." She remarked that St. Ambrose spoke "magnificently" here. And why? Her words seem to sum up, better than any others, her spiritual experience: "Jesus knew sadness, and sadness was repugnant to his human will." She knew sadness, its repugnance, but she also knew that if sadness is to have a place in our lives, we must not simply reject it but respond as Christ did.

God knows what he permits.

God is with this created nature that is suffering—God is not against it.

"As He took our wills, so He took our sadness."

One would really think that possessing our hearts is the end that God proposed and pondered in the divine mind in creating us.

And everything that can be saved will be saved.

Chapter IV

On "Really Not Talking to Machines": God and Laughter

"Everything that can be saved will be saved"—these graphic words from Raissa Maritain can apply, perhaps most of all, to our laughter. Though I remember how a friend could be quite sober and serious, I remember her as mostly laughing. As I think of it, this combination of laughter and seriousness exemplified for me that in the highest things, the distance between seriousness and laughter often appears to be quite small.

> I just had some fun. The phone rings. A computer tells me that it wants to give me a lot of money if I buy some magazine. I do not *really* talk to machines, but I take the challenge! After I am told what I can win if I listen to the spiel, the machine asks me what magazines I get. I say to it, "I receive no magazines." It says back, "What magazines would you like to receive that you do not now get?" I say to the machine, "I am blind, and I do not read magazines." The machine says, "One of our representatives will call you tomorrow." I *can't* wait for that call, which will not ever come. Can I sue them because they broke their A.T.&T. contract with me?

When I first read this account, I just laughed at the thought of someone, quickly pretending to be blind, talking back to a computer that was using the phone to sell dumb magazines.

The subject of knowing ourselves, the classic question from Socrates, by talking or not talking to machines, is an interesting one. No one has put the problem better or with more delight than the late Walker Percy. "Why is it possible to learn more in ten minutes about the Crab Nebula in Taurus, which is 6,000 light-years away, than you presently know about yourself, even though you've been stuck with yourself all your life?"[1] What is amusing about Percy's question is not merely the suspicion that those who study humans do not themselves know much about us, but that we do not know much about ourselves, even though we have been right there in front of ourselves all our lives. Comparing the Crab Nebula to ourselves, with ourselves coming out on the short end, this amuses us.

Why do we laugh? I have a *New Yorker* cartoon in front of me, by Modell. The scene is morning on a New York subway platform. Five men, all in business suits, all obviously high-powered executives, stand there each reading the *New York Times*. Four of the men are clustered to one side. All four have a very angry-provoked-annoyed-ticked-off frown on their faces. What are they glowering at? They are staring down the fifth man who, reading the very same *New York Times*, on the very same subway platform, is roaring with laughter. How odd! One man finds the *Times* enormously humorous, whereas the other four have seen nothing funny about it at all.

I want to talk about God and humor. This topic, like so many, can begin with Nietzsche. In the fourth part of *Thus Spoke Zarathustra* Nietzsche wrote: "What has so far been the greatest sin here on earth? Was it not the word of him who said, 'Woe unto those who laugh here?' Did he himself find no reasons on earth for laughing? Then he searched very badly. Even a child could find reasons here. He did not love enough: else he would also have loved us who laugh. But he hated and mocked us: howling and gnashing of teeth he promised us."[2] This is a not an uncommon position, never more graphically stated. If we take Nietzsche at face value, the fact that Christ did not laugh meant that he did not love, that he lacked a very simple human experience. This lack evidently disproves his mission among the beings who laugh.

[1]Walker Percy, *Lost in the Cosmos* (New York: Simon & Schuster Pocket Books, 1984) 7.

[2]Friedrich Nietzsche, *Thus Spoke Zarathustra*, IV, 16, in *The Portable Nietzsche*, ed. Walter Kaufmann (Harmondsworth: Penguin, 1955) 405.

At the end of *Orthodoxy*, almost as if to respond directly to Nietzsche, which he did rather frequently, Chesterton surmised that there was only one thing that God did not reveal to us. Christ showed anger, pathos, logic, tears, and warmth. But, Chesterton concluded: "There was something that He hid from all men when He went up a mountain to pray. There was something that He covered constantly by abrupt silence or impetuous isolation. There was some one thing that was too great for God to show us when He walked upon our earth; and I have sometimes fancied that it was His mirth."[3] The reason God did not reveal more fully his deep inner happiness, Chesterton felt, was that we mortals would be unable for now to bear the utter joy of the Deity. God's mirth was something we could only sustain in eternity, however much it pervaded our very lives. We were promised eternal life. But it was impossible to get across much of what eternal life was like. Our condition is also one of faith and waiting.

Merriment in God reminds me of something else that was written to me. Evidently, as is my wont, I had once cited a remark of Chesterton to the effect that God would be astonished "at what He had created." This was the response that I have often pondered: "And Chesterton thinks that God would be astonished at what He has made?—interesting thought, God being astonished. I rather see Him with a smile and Head shaking." As I think about it, this image of God seems theologically quite right. God is astonished, as if something might indeed pique his attention. God might well wonder at our deeds, with a smile and head shake. We human beings display astonishment in not comprehending God's astonishment. But the kindly bemusement at knowing us well enough is God's freedom.

I would like to treat God and laughter in a specific, no doubt odd, way. One evening, I was thumbing through John McKenzie's *Dictionary of the Bible*, looking for something else, when I came across the entry on "laughter." It addressed itself to the same problem that Chesterton had commented on,

[3]Chesterton, *Orthodoxy*, in *The Collected Works of G. K. Chesterton*, Vol. 1 (San Francisco: Ignatius Press, 1986) 365–66.

namely, how laughter appears, or does not appear, in Scripture, how humor and the Deity are related.

> Laughter is presented rather unfavorably in the Bible. The word sometimes means to be merry or to make merry or to play. . . . Most frequently laughter expresses one's gladness at the downfall of an enemy or indeed of anyone who is cast down from eminence or success. . . . It has sometimes been remarked that Jesus never laughs in the New Testament. Neither does anyone else; the only people in the entire New Testament who laugh are the mourners in the house of Jairus who laugh in disbelief at Jesus' promise to revive the girl (*Mt.* 9:24). One of the beatitudes of Luke (6:21) promises the laughter of gladness to those who mourn, and one of the woes promises mourning to those who now laugh, where laughter is a sign of frivolity.[4]

For someone who would like to suggest that Christianity is a religion of joy, of mirth, this is not a propitious beginning. Perhaps Nietzsche was right.

Laughter presupposes a metaphysics, perhaps even a revelation. Aristotle had observed that wit is a sign of intelligence. It is based on the ability to see the relations between things. Curiously, the Persons in the Trinity are usually placed in the category of "relation" in Christian philosophy, almost as if to confirm Aristotle's insight about wit and relation. Yet the possibility of ultimate joy requires that God is, as such, a being standing in delight and deep happiness. God must be like this, however difficult it is to understand fully what this might entail. It also suggests that we cannot be another kind of being than the specific, rather comical one we are most of the time. God's internal joy cannot depend on something we give to him, however much he might give to us. Yet we would hope to make God glad because of our deeds. Creation is capable of admitting that something other than God exists and causes delight even to God; this is, after all, the orthodox view. Joy is something God gives to us. Even when we think we know by ourselves what it is that we might ultimately want,

[4]John L. McKenzie, *Dictionary of the Bible* (New York: Macmillan, 1965) 494-95.

we still must admit that joy is something that comes to us from the very structure of the world. We do not really make it. Revelation teaches us to dare to want what we really want. We come to a point when we realize that we define our joys too narrowly. Ironically, the fundamental objection to God lies in our being promised too much, not too little.

A description of God's relation to us as that of someone who smiles and shakes his head over our actions is probably close to the truth. In our joy, there remains a hint of sadness. We cannot have lived very long without having noticed it. And if we have not so noted, we have been inattentive. Flannery O'Connor even saw a relation between "the comic and the terrible." Writing of her impressions of the famous French writer Simone Weil on September 24, 1955, O'Connor wrote: "In my own experience, everything funny I have written is more terrible than it is funny, or only funny because it is terrible. Well, Simone Weil's life is the most comical life I have ever read about and the most truly tragic and terrible. If I were to live long enough . . . I would like to write a comic novel about a woman—and what is more comic and terrible than the angular intellectual proud woman approaching God inch by inch with ground teeth?"[5] When questioned by a respondent about this odd juxtaposition of the comic and the terrible, O'Connor remarked that she was "paying her [Simone Weil] the highest tribute I can, short of calling her a saint, which I don't believe she was. Possibly I have a higher opinion of the comic and the terrible than you do."[6] Laughter and sadness, laughter and terribleness exist not in two separate worlds but in the same one. Any hint that they do not is a Manichean position that would separate what are found together. Yet they are not the same. This is the mystery.

All comedians somehow seem, in their personal depths, to have a touch of heartache about them. Is it because they are struck by the fact that the joy they create is so fleeting? Or is it because their laughter seems to cover an emptiness in being they do not want to face? Scripture was right to remind

[5]Flannery O'Connor, *The Habit of Being*, ed. Sally Fitzgerald (New York: Vintage, 1979) 105-06.

[6]Ibid., 106.

us of the darker side of laughter, that it can be mocking and hurtful. "There is a great difference," Boswell said at Yverdon on December 18, 1764, "between intemperance of mirth and a cheerful glass of gladness."[7] But this darker aspect, while it must be accounted for, does not seem to penetrate to the most important thing about laughter. Laughter is for us always tinged with poignancy, with a sense of incompleteness even in the deepest human joy.

Several years ago, at a book sale someplace in Washington or San Francisco, I bought a copy of Bob and Ray's *Write If You Get Work.*[8] This particular edition had a foreword by Kurt Vonnegut, Jr., that seemed to understand my problem about laughter. Vonnegut began his reflections on the humor of Bob and Ray in this way: "It is the truth: Comedians and jazz musicians have been more comforting and enlightening to me than preachers or politicians or philosophers or poets or painters or novelists of my time. Historians in the future, in my opinion, will congratulate us on very little other than our clowning and our jazz."[9] Clowning and perhaps preaching are, no doubt, part of our being. St. Paul said that we would appear "foolish" before men, almost as if they could not get the joke of what we were about (1 Cor 1:21).[10]

God is "like" both humor and music, both laughter and even dancing. C. S. Lewis thought that the Great Dance was the most apt symbol of what God had created. "The Great Dance does not wait to be perfect until the peoples of the Low Worlds are gathered into it. . . . The dance which we dance is at the centre and for the dance all things were made. Blessed be He."[11] This too is most suggestive of what God is like.

[7]James Boswell, *On the Grand Tour: Germany and Switzerland*, ed. Frederick A. Pottle (New York: McGraw-Hill, 1953) 270.

[8]Bob Elliott and Ray Goulding, *Write If You Get Work* (New York: Random House, 1975).

[9]Ibid., v.

[10]See James V. Schall, "On Playing," *The Praise of "Sons of Bitches": On the Worship of God by Fallen Man* (Slough, England: St. Paul Publications, 1978) 123–36.

[11]C. S. Lewis, *Perelandra* (New York: Macmillan, 1965) 214-215. See James V. Schall, *Far Too Easily Pleased: A Theology of Play, Contemplation, and Festivity* (Los Angeles: Benziger-Macmillan, 1976).

Vonnegut had spoken with Bob and Ray one day in a most delightful exchange. They were very funny, and he had enjoyed their banter. But something bothered Vonnegut about the experience. "I was puzzled that day by Bob's and Ray's melancholy," he reflected. "It seemed to me that they should be the happiest people on earth, but looks of sleepy ruefulness crossed their faces like clouds from time to time. I have seen those same clouds at subsequent encounters—and only now do I have a theory to explain them."[12] Vonnegut surmised that though Bob and Ray could go on being funny "almost indefinitely," still this abiding merriment could become "profoundly pooping by and by." Yet, the humor of Bob and Ray had a kind of innocence to it. "Man is not evil, they seem to say. He is simply too hilariously stupid to survive." To this Vonnegut added, "And this I believe. Cheers."

We find this curious propinquity of laughter and evil requiring some separation. If we are too hilariously stupid to survive, can the world be rooted in joy? Joy wants nothing more than to survive, not for survival's sake, to be sure, but for joy's sake. And if we are not evil, certainly we have the possibility of doing evil. Can this be ignored?

Another *New Yorker* cartoon put us in an elegant party. Folks were standing about drinking and conversing. On a couch sat a beautiful young woman, long formal dress, very long, dark hair. She was listening with just a slight hint of doubt to a very innocent young man, who was sitting on the edge of the sofa with his hands folded on his knee. The earnest young man told her: "I operate under the assumption that man is basically good" (Weber, April 27, 1987). We smile a bit, knowing in our hearts that the world is not really this way, in spite of such Rousseauistic views in our young. The young woman is totally impervious before this naiveté. So there is hope.

Many a philosopher has used the reality of evil to dampen our spirits, to smother our belief. The laughter described in Scripture was often a mocking laughter, one which saw man not so much as humorous but as prideful or boast-

[12]Ibid., vii. See James V. Schall, "On Sadness and Laughter," *The Praise of "Sons of Bitches,"* 113–24.

ful. Yet we do not want to locate laughter, humor, and joy—which are not the same things, but closely related—in our deficiencies or in our sins. But we do not want to deny what we have done, even if it is evil, perhaps especially if it is evil. We realize that our past can somehow be changed when we acknowledge the record of our actions against the smile of the Divinity.

We assume, I think, that tragedy is more profound than comedy. That this is not the case needs some attention. Joseph Epstein asked in a wonderful essay why after meeting and laughing with old school friends, why "for all our laughter, for all the joy in these meetings, when they are over and I drive home, usually alone, I tend to feel a tinge of sadness. . . . Why this sadness?"[13] He went on: "For happiness not only cannot be recaptured, it can scarcely be described, let alone analyzed. Unhappiness, on the other hand, analyzes beautifully. Perhaps this is why so many intellectuals are drawn to it. Sadness, too, implies a criticism of the world. Happiness is an expression of joy in it."[14] The relation of happiness and sadness, of laughter and tears, bears out the truth that joy and laughter are the more mysterious realities.

The tragic hero is too exalted directly to represent most of us, even when we are called upon to be heroic. Aquinas saw the deeper profundity in God's efforts to save everyone, even the ordinary, through revelation (*ST* I–II, 91, 4). The explanation of our joy and laughter is ever more difficult than the explanation of our defeats and sins. God as a "punisher of our evils" is much more comprehensible to us than God as the final source of our delight. Our delights are realities, the cause of which we cannot wholly attribute to ourselves. Yet we know that they are meant for us.

Chesterton, in his "Ballad of a White Horse," spoke of "joy without a cause." C. S. Lewis entitled his own autobiography "Surprised by Joy." Joy has something of the unexpected about it, something essentially given to us for no reason of our own, like our very existence. Yet it has also about it the

[13]Joseph Epstein, "The Crime of a Happy Childhood," *The Middle of My Tether* (New York: Norton, 1983) 226.

[14]Ibid., 235.

feeling that it is indeed intended for us, for us in our particularity. Much philosophy seeks to explain how this joy is quite impossible. Our minds batter against our suspicions. We have to attend to our philosophies. Many would exclude *all that is*.

I once was given a present. Solemnly, I was told that it would be a present "of something about which I had written that I did not much like," though, I was assured, I would like this gift. However much I tried, I could not recall what I had written about not liking, though I had written about things that others did not like about me, such as my illegible handwriting or my views on dogs and cats.[15] The giver of this particular gift implied that I might not really know what I would like, even when I thought I knew what I did not like. The great sin may indeed consist in choosing to consider too little.

This mystery of what I "did not like" was cleared up when I was presented with Lillian de la Torre's *Dr. Sam: Johnson, Detector*, a book I had never heard of. But that was the point. I was much surprised and astonished. Someplace I had written that I did not like detective stories. Naturally, this recollection hinted at the clarity of my friend who knew that I would be unable to resist anything about Dr. Johnson, even if Johnson himself did not actually write detective stories, which genre I did not like. In the introduction Lillian de la Torre explained just why she wrote this detective series in some sort of distant relation to Boswell and Johnson. She explained that Boswell and Johnson "lived out their joint lives in the 'full tide of human existence'—eighteenth-century London." I very much like that phrase—"the full tide of human existence." Johnson felt that London was indeed an infinite city, as it is. I have been there.[16]

Of Johnson himself Lillian de la Torre wrote that he "triumphed over loneliness by the warmth and kindness of his heart, supplying 'the vacuity of life' by warm and happy

[15]James V. Schall, "A Few Mad Words about Dogs and Cats," *The Monitor*, San Francisco (October 24, 1974) "On Elegant Handwriting," *The Monitor* (September 7, 1978).

[16]See my remarks on Belloc and London, "The Mortality of Immortal Men," *Another Sort of Learning* (San Francisco: Ignatius Press, 1988) 135–52.

friendships. He roared down sham, and laughed away nonsense."[17] The inner relationship of the full tide of human existence, loneliness, the vacuity of life, laughter, friendship, and kindness is nowhere more graphically connected. We expect that what God is like in any of these elements heals in some cases, blesses in all. We do not so much laugh away nonsense—a word I rather like—as laugh because we see the point of why something is funny "in the full tide of human existence," our particular human existence. Chesterton said that God could forgive us our sins but that no one could forgive us when, at an elegant restaurant, we spilled gravy on our tie. In this remark, he showed us how everything, even our sins and manners, could be overcome in laughter.

The melancholy, the loneliness, the vacuity of life, nonetheless, remain to make us wonder if it is joy for which we are made. Johnson was, in many ways, a very joyful man. But he was also a lonely one. Perhaps these two go together, loneliness and joyfulness, almost as if our loneliness is designed to prevent us from being content with anything but the deepest joy, which can only be given to us. Yet, as I have said, joy is much more difficult to explain both in us and in God.

What is God like, looking on smiling, shaking his Head? I have a cherished book, *The World of Wodehouse Clergy*, which two young friends gave me. I realize that laughter can be seen as the opposite of God. Baudelaire remarked that "laughter comes from the idea of men's own superiority. A satanic idea, if there ever was one."[18] I shall attend to this point. But first, to return to the sort of laughter and piety which is not "satanic," in one of Wodehouse's stories the Bishop of Stortford had a young daughter, Kathleen, whom he once caught reading a novel called *Cocktail Time*. In some horror at the potential for corruption, the good Bishop snatched the novel

[17]Lillian de la Torre, *Dr. Sam: Johnson, Detector, Being, a Light-Hearted Collection of Recently Reveal'd Episodes in the Career of the Great Lexicographer, Narrated as from the Pen of James Boswell* (New York: International Polygonics, 1983) viii-ix.

[18]Cited in W. K. Wimsatt, *The Idea of Comedy* (Englewood Cliffs, N.J.: Prentice-Hall, 1969) 287.

out of her hands and hastily read it himself to see if it was as disordered as he suspected.

> At 12:15 on the following Sunday he (the Bishop of Stortford) was in the pulpit of the church of St. Jude the Resilient, Eaton Square, delivering a sermon on the text "He that touches pitch shall be defiled" (*Ecclesiasticus*, xiii.1), which had the fashionable congregation rolling in the aisles and tearing up the pews. The burden of his address was a denunciation of the novel *Cocktail Time* in the course of which he described it as obscene, immoral, shocking, impure, corrupt, shameless, graceless and depraved, and all over the sacred edifice you could see eager men jotting the name down on their shirt cuffs, scarcely able to wait to add it to their library list.[19]

This delightful combination of piety, humor, a bit of madness, and the human condition, which Wodehouse saw, touches the amusing ordinariness of the actual lives most people live. Mirth and salvation are intimately connected, without denying that there can be a kind of diabolical laughter in what is damned.

Yet we must be cautious here. W. K. Wimsatt, in his essay on comedy, also pointed out that laughter for the Greeks had a bite to it.[20] The Scriptures and the Greeks were not too far apart in their judgment about the possible dire effects of humor and laughter. Nietzsche, who was familiar with the mockery of the sacred that often opposes the higher ends presented in faith, wrote, "Laughter.—Laughter means being *schadenfroh* ('taking a mischievous delight in the discomfort of another person') but with a good conscience."[21] Of course, there is often a bad conscience in much humor. But the suspicion that laughter and the highest things stand in opposition needs to be questioned if we are to come to the proper understanding of either.

In Umberto Eco's novel *The Name of the Rose*, the monks apparently sense a destructive power in laughter, its ability to

[19]*The World of Wodehouse Clergy* (London: Hutchinson, 1984) 236-37.

[20]Wimsatt, *The Idea of Comedy*, 1–21.

[21]Friedrich Nietzsche, *The Gay Science*, 3, no. 200, trans. Walter Kaufmann (New York: Vintage, 1974) 207.

mock rule and suppress fear. The rediscovery of laughter, symbolized by Aristotle's lost treatise on comedy, was considered to be a threat to religious control. The thesis in Eco's novel is worth reflection:

> That laughter is proper to man is a sign of our limitation, sinners that we are. But from this book [Aristotle] many corrupt minds like yours would draw the extreme syllogism, whereby laughter is man's end! Laughter, for a few moments, distracts the villain from fear. But law is imposed by fear, whose true name is fear of God. This book could strike the Luciferine spark that would set a new fire to the whole world, and laughter would be defined as the new art, unknown even to Prometheus, for cancelling fear.[22]

This "Luciferine spark" is what Baudelaire had in mind also, the sense that there is in the universe no order but our own.

In Eco's novel Christianity and laughter are not complimentary, as mutual causes. They are opposed to each other because there is no order of joy. Joy is caused, in the world of *The Name of the Rose*, by lack of order, whereas in Chesterton joy is hidden only because for now we cannot bear the fullness of its completion. Eco continued: "But if one day . . . the art of mockery were to be made acceptable, and to seem noble and liberal and no longer mechanical; if one day someone could say (and be heard), 'I laugh at the Incarnation,' then he would have no weapons to combat that blasphemy. . . ."[23] Need we point out in this regard that among the philosophers some one had already been found to laugh at the incarnation?

The following passage from Nietzsche, among others, illustrates this eventuality of laughter *at* the incarnation:

> Everything that has turned out well, everything that is proud and prankish, beauty above all, hurts its ears and eyes. Once more I recall the inestimable words of Paul: "the *weak* things of the world, the *foolish* things of the world, the *base* and *despised* things of the world hath God chosen." This was the formula: *in hoc signo* decadence triumphed.

[22]Umberto Eco, *The Name of the Rose* (New York: Harcourt, 1983) 474-75.
[23]Ibid., 476-77.

> *God on the Cross*—are the horrible secret thoughts behind this symbol not understood yet? All that suffers, all that is nailed to the cross, is *divine*. All of us are nailed to the cross, consequently *we* are divine. We alone are divine. Christianity was a victory, a nobler outlook perished of it—Christianity has been the greatest misfortune of mankind so far.[24]

The misfortune of Christianity for Eco lies in its substitution of fear for laughter, but for Nietzsche decadence followed from the Cross. The Cross mocks man's chance to achieve the superman, the man who makes his own laws.

Is there a path that might rejoin laughter and faith, joy and the Deity? In his remarkable essay "The Bias of Comedy and the Narrow Escape into Faith," Nathan Scott took up the relationship between tragedy and comedy. Wimsatt noted Scott's definition of the comic as "the art that is dedicated to telling the whole truth."[25] Humor is often merely describing what went on in our day. A friend wrote of her six-year-old: "Actually, Paul has been much better today after crying so much last night about his grandfather. He can be so funny in his honesty. At the doctor's office today, I was trying to distract him from his exam by chatting with him about his room. I asked him, 'Paul, if you could fix up your room anyway you liked, what would you do?' 'You mean anyway I like in the whole wide world?' 'Yes, any way, any design.' 'Well,' he responded, 'I think I would like it *messy*!' What is more to say?" What is more ordinary, indeed.

We can never forget that the greatest Christian drama bears the name "The Divine Comedy." Speaking of the whole tenor of the Medieval period with regard to the comic, Wimsatt wrote:

> This kind of (popular) drama was part of a much greater Medieval vision of evil as a kind of grotesque dilapidation, deformity, or deficiency of good sense and virtue which, in the long run, was *always* destined not only for defeat but to make its own special kind of contribution to the harmony of the *Divine Comedy*. . . . In his dedicatory letter to the Lord

[24]Friedrich Nietzsche, *The Anti-Christ*, no. 51, in *The Portable Nietzsche*, 624.
[25]Wimsatt, *The Idea of Comedy*, 18.

> of Verona, Can Grande della Scala, prefixed to the third and happy part of the poem . . . Dante explains that he calls his poem a "comedy" because comedy begins in adversity but ends in happiness. . . .[26]

If we recall the idea of God "shaking His head" at our condition, this notion of comedy redeems what is humorous, even perhaps what is wrong, in the human condition. It is not enough to say that God is joyful beyond the possibility of any error or disorder. What one must maintain is that God is joyful even within the world of our sins and disorders and messiness. Even a minimal understanding of what God is like must include this realization. Hans Urs von Balthasar wrote, "God could not create any angel or any human being in a definitive state of good from the outset: the spiritual being himself must decide what ought to be best for him."[27] What God is like allows for the possible choice against one's own true good, just as it allows the choice for our good, a real choice in either case, our choice.

Nathan Scott remarked that the Christian doctrine of creation implied that finite beings are possible, that they are not God. God was the creator of heaven and earth, as the Creed teaches. Scott added: "Now when, in its worship, the Church recites these words (of the Creed), its intention is to assert that 'in the fullness of time' God did really become man without ceasing to be God. It does not merely assert that through the life of Jesus the carpenter of Galilee we may come to discern what God is like: it says, rather, that Jesus Christ *is* God Himself incarnate."[28] The fact that Jesus Christ is God himself reveals to us what God is like. Scott treated the notion of comedy from this perspective. For the comic is addressed to our fallibility and humanness, to our faults and embarrassments.

"The major purpose of the comedian is to remind us of how deeply rooted we are in all the tangible things of this

[26]Ibid., 18.

[27]Hans Urs von Balthasar, *New Elucidations* (San Francisco: Ignatius Press, 1986) 262.

[28]Nathan A. Scott, Jr. *The Broken Center: Studies in the Theological Horizon of Modern Literature* (New Haven: Yale University Press, 1965) 112-13.

world . . .," Scott wrote. "The notions of comedy, to be sure, finally lead to joy, but it is to a joy that we win only after we have consented to journey through this familiar, actual world of earth which is our home and, by doing so, have had our faith in its stability and permanence restored. The joy of comedy is a great joy, but it is a joy that can sometimes come only after humiliation. . . ."[29] The fallibility and chaos of ordinary lives, which are so much the causes of our laughter, rejoin at this point the more transcendent notion of joy. Put briefly, we want ultimate joy to be our own, and the joy of others, like our own, includes the finite, particular being we each are. Indeed, it includes our relation to other finite beings in our own ken. This is why Johnson's "warm and happy friendships," although they did not eliminate a deep loneliness, nevertheless comforted.

The two facts of human being—we are finite, we are fallen—remain.[30] We are created good but limited beings. We are not exactly evil, but we can do evil acts, even the final one of losing our souls, of choosing our own "truth." Comedy rises in these two conditions. It intimates, paradoxically, a sense of abiding joy. In our deepest experiences we realize that the presence of something beyond ourselves is most vivid. This sense of transcendence is not satisfied merely by the existence of universal forms or ideas, by philosophy, which, at its best, might point us in the right direction. *Dr. Sam: Johnson, Detector,* was right in reminding us that "man's intellect has been given to him to guard against credulity."[31] But our reason was also given to us to guard against the credulity of reason itself, as Johnson also understood.

"Comedy asks us to be content with our human limitations and possibilities," Scott observed,

> and to accept our life in this world without the sentimentality either of smugness or of cynicism. And when we wish to be pure discarnate spirit or pure discarnate intellect, the comedian asks us to remember the objective, material con-

[29]Ibid., 103.
[30]Schall, ob. cit.
[31]de la Torre, *Dr. Sam,* 30.

> ditions of life with which we must make our peace if we are to retain our sanity and survive. He will not let us forget that we are men, that we are finite and conditioned creatures—not angels. In its deeply affirmative attitude toward the created orders of existence, in the profound materialism of its outlook, the comic imagination, it seems to me, summarizes an important part of the Christian testimony about the meaning of life.[32]

Comedy is particularly close to the doctrine of the resurrection of the body. If it is true that we are not just spirits but finite human beings in a given time and a definite place, it follows that the very particularity in which we experienced our joy and laughter must be related to our highest end. Comedy and resurrection are two sides of the same doctrine. The one is incomplete without the other. The salvation of our souls must include and be manifested in the resurrection of our bodies.

Charles Williams, in his study of Dante, spoke of a "stupor" that invests us when confronted with the highest reaches of being and love. Comedy brings us the question of the ordinary lives of everyone, every ordinary person, when he ends well. "There is, however, another side to the *Paradiso*," Williams wrote. "Besides being an image of the whole redeemed universe, it is also an image of the redeemed Way. It is . . . an image of a redeemed love-affair—that is, of an ordinary love-affair, if things went as they ought to go."[33] No doubt things do not usually in our world go as they ought. Nonetheless, the ordinary way, the way through finiteness and disorder, we are led to believe, because of the redemption, can arrive at the highest end, at the vision of God himself.

That things seldom go as they ought to go finds its roots in our finiteness and in our sins. Williams continued,

> Dante says, brightness is acquired by joy, just as on earth joy breaks in a smile, but "below" the spirits darken as their minds sadden. . . . "Here (above) we do not repent, but smile . . . not at the sinfulness, which does not return to

[32]Scott, *The Broken Center*, 116.

[33]Charles Williams, *The Figure of Beatrice: A Study in Dante* (New York: Farrar, Straus & Cudahy, 1961) 192.

> mind, but at the Worth that ordained and forefurnished us. . . ." This, now, is what seeing sin in God is. They remember the sin as occasion of love's potency. . . . The fault between them is a cause of joy; so only that the fault has been put by, it is possible even here to be gay in recollecting it. This natural delight is already a flash of our most courteous Lord, and the souls in heaven supernaturally return His courtesy in accepting it.[34]

The smile remains the context of the "most courteous Lord," as Williams put it. Christ's redemptive mission is not complete until the courtesy of joyful acceptance is present in us.

God, like my friend, does not talk too much to machines either. God fathoms what it is like to understand us even if we have been "stuck with ourselves all our lives." The order of the world, in the full tide of human existence, is not defeated by the disorder of our minds. Courtesy, that great medieval word, acknowledges what is given, especially when what is given is forgiveness and joy. This courtesy, as Charles Williams intimated, is something, perhaps the only thing, we can give to God. The things that cause joy can cause further joy. This is what God is like.

[34]Ibid., 203-04. See also Dorothy Sayers, "Dante and Charles Williams," *The Whimsical Christian* (New York: Macmillan, 1978) 180–204.

Chapter V

"Deprived of Grace": *The Rebel* and the Only Christ We Deserve

In wondering what God "is like," beyond the sadness and the laughter, we ask how he is seen by others. How does Christ in particular look to someone who does not believe in him? St. Thomas insists that, if we be intellectually honest, we state not merely why our faith is believable, but the principal arguments against it. How are they to be accurately understood? In the history of Western literature we possess a number of writers and thinkers who have come to consider Christ in one way or another from outside the confines of the faith, or at least how they understand Christ. A curious relation often exists between Christ and those who do not believe in him. Few have better addressed the question of what God might be like to a stranger or to a skeptic than Albert Camus, the Algerian-French novelist-philosopher, in his intellectual history, *The Rebel*.

Let me begin by citing some things from Camus which will set the stage for these reflections on his approach to God. These remarks will, I think, deepen our considerations about the reality of God. "If I were a believer," Camus wrote, "Gide's death would be a consolation. But if those believers I see do believe, what is the object of their faith? Those *deprived of grace* simply have to practice generosity among themselves."[1]

[1]Albert Camus, "Encounters with André Gide," in *Lyrical and Critical Essays*, ed. Philip Thody (New York: Vintage, 1970) 253.

In another passage, Camus set the stage for these particular reflections: ''One would therefore not be much mistaken to read *The Stranger* as the story of a man who, without any heroics, agrees to die for the truth. I also happened to say, again paradoxically, that I had tried to draw in my character *the only Christ we deserve*.''[2] Deprived of grace, the only Christ we deserve—these are the notions that I want to consider. What is God like? What sort of Christ *do* we deserve? These are questions of the greatest moment. Do we have a God that is more than we deserve? Is this what the life of Christ is about?

A pertinent cartoon in the *New Yorker* showed a rather uppity couple leaving an elegant party, with host and hostess still seen in the doorway happily waving them good-bye. Some distance down the front walk, out of ear-shot, the vexed wife turned to her obviously self-satisfied husband, to reprove him with some acerbity, ''You misquoted St. Thomas Aquinas, Albert Camus, and me.''[3] We can speculate which, in these circumstances, was the more faulty citation. But the juxtaposition of Thomas Aquinas and Albert Camus is, in the present context, fortuitous.

Camus' great work on modern intellectual history, *The Rebel*, his penetrating prophecy of Western decadence, reminds us of nothing so much as a book of perhaps Aquinas' greatest biographer: G. K. Chesterton's *Heretics* (see below, chapter 7).[4] I say that *The Rebel* reminds us of *Heretics* because in an odd sort of way both books are accounts of where erroneous intellectual positions lead, first in the mind and then in reality. The only difference is that Camus unlike Chesterton never arrived at an *Orthodoxy* or a *St. Thomas Aquinas*. Hence, Camus' world is filled with a kind of heart-rending urgency to discover a viable substitute for what is already known in faith. Yet Camus retained a quiet refusal to draw specifically revelational conclusions from his own premises. In this refusal or inability he may have been in his own terms either ungenerous or ungraced. He was never unintelligent.

[2]Albert Camus, ''Preface to *The Stranger*,'' *Lyrical and Critical Essays*, 337.

[3]*New Yorker*, October 19, 1987.

[4]G. K. Chesterton, *Heretics* (San Francisco: Ignatius Press, 1986). This is Volume 1 of the *Collected Works*, which includes *Orthodoxy; St. Thomas Aquinas*, is found in Volume 2 of the *Collected Works*, 1986.

Chesterton held that, were it not already invented, he himself would have had to fashion Christianity. For Camus, however, we only get "the Christ we deserve"—that is, the one we were historically given is not the one we deserve. We die for a truth that is not "the Truth." We practice "generosity" but we need no grace either to know what generosity might be or to realize what more than ourselves we might need to practice it.

Camus perceived the problem connected with reason and revelation. Chesterton had observed in his *St. Thomas Aquinas* that revelation was singularly "democratic" because it included the non-philosophers—the vast majority of humanity—who had neither the time, incentive, or capacity to sort out the intricacies of philosophic reasonings about God.[5] Chesterton was referring to Aquinas' famous question of whether in addition to reason, revelation was "necessary." "The Second Reason [for this necessity]," Aquinas observed, "was because of the uncertainty of human judgment, especially about contingent and particular things. There happen to be many diverse judgments about different kinds of human action, from which diverse and contrary laws can proceed. In order therefore that man might know without doubt what should be done and what avoided, it was necessary that he be directed in his proper acts by a divinely given law about which he could not err" (*ST* I-II, 91, 4). Aquinas here gave a suasive argument about why revelation is not contradictory. He did not present a rigidly logical argument about why revelation might have been "necessary." The human plight itself did not "coerce" God into making divine law certainly known so that people had no possibility of rejecting it. The gratuity of faith also implied that no intrinsic necessity caused God to act towards us. God need not have acted towards us in the way revelation describes. God chose this way, God's way.

In his review of Jean Guitton's "Portrait of a Chosen Man," Camus presented a remarkable understanding of the relation between reason and revelation. That Camus remained on the side of a reason closed to revelation, or at least on the

[5]Chesterton, *St. Thomas Aquinas, Collected Works*, vol. 2, 434–42.

side of someone who did not choose to believe, did not prevent him from understanding what was at issue. Father Pouget, a priest in one of Guitton's novels, sought the correct way in Camus' view. The priest's way was proportioned to the human, gradual way of knowing, to find a ''middle way between blind faith and a faith that knows its reason.''[6] Camus summarized the orthodox position: ''The Church gives every liberty to her theologians. She rejects only those theories which threaten the existence of the faith in their time. Revelation teaches what is, the Church rejects what is not. The task of the Church is thus to watch over the march of truth, preventing men from causing it either to hasten or to stray. Heretics, in short, are men who want to go faster than God.''[7] Camus recognized that this question was ''metaphysical'' and not one exclusively conditioned by the history of one's time.

The argument found in Guitton did not try to ''prove'' faith. Faith is left intact. Faith is not to be the result of a rational syllogism or a scientific investigation. Camus understood that reason's function is ''apologetic.'' With a penetrating observation he continued, ''Method does not try to convince people immediately. That is the task of grace.''[8] Reasons to believe that do not contradict human intelligence do exist, but ''the freedom of choice'' to believe or not remains absolute. Camus remarked that in the past century reason and science have been much too connected with each other.

In an incisive footnote, Camus added this observation: ''In fact, contemporary disbelief is no longer based on science in the way that it was at the end of the last century. It denies both science and religion. It is no longer the skepticism of reason when confronted with miracles. It is a passionate disbelief.''[9] Disbelief is choice not reason. Camus saw in this

[6]Camus, ''Portrait of a Chosen Man (1943),'' *Lyrical and Critical Essays*, 221.

[7]Ibid., 223.

[8]Ibid., 224. See James V. Schall, *Reason, Revelation, and the Foundations of Political Philosophy* (Baton Rouge: Louisiana State University Press, 1987).

[9]Camus, *Lyrical and Critical Essays*, 225. See also on this point, Stanley L. Jaki, *The Road of Science and the Ways to God* (Chicago: University of Chicago Press, 1978).

analysis of Guitton a means to ''restore prestige to grace'' by clarifying the exact role of reason.

Yet Camus himself did not accept this alternative of grace. He was constrained in his philosophic thinking to account for justice without charity or mercy because this latter option, which originated from revelation, was not open to him. The pursuit of reason closed off from grace, with neither God nor the abstract substitutes for him such as justice and order available to it, requires a steady heart and an artistic imagination[10]. To pursue this alternative of a reason without grace is why Camus wrote novels and stories. He knew where the ideologies lead, that is, to the totalitarian states, though it often took great courage to confess it. *The Rebel* was an effort to see if there was any alternative between ideologies and faith, if there was a true philosophy uninspired by faith.

The Rebel is by any standard a great book. It is a book about the need for limits, for moderation, a basic theme of the Greek classics in political philosophy. The classics originally embodied this theme of moderation and discipline as essential aspects of the very condition of man on this earth. Camus wrote:

> Far from demanding general independence, the rebel [as opposed, in Camus' terms, to the revolutionary] wants it to be recognized that freedom has its limits everywhere that a human being is to be found—the limit being precisely that human being's power to rebel. The most profound reason for rebellious intransigence is to be found here. The more aware rebellion is of demanding a just limit, the more inflexible it becomes. The rebel undoubtedly demands a certain degree of freedom for himself; but in no case, if he is consistent, does he demand the right to destroy the existence and freedom of others.[11]

Camus was aware of the dangerous paradox of a freedom that claims no limits but those of its own making. ''Absolute freedom mocks justice. Absolute justice denies freedom.''[12]

[10]Camus, *The Rebel: An Essay on Man in Revolt*, trans. Anthony Bower (New York: Vintage, 1956) 279-80.

[11]Camus, *The Rebel*, 284.

[12]Ibid., 291.

Yet Camus also understood that the absolute refusal to do anything against those claiming unlimited freedom, in effect, yields complete power to these claimants. This absolute power, because of the theoretic claim to unlimited freedom, became a moral claim. "If rebellion exists, it is because falsehood, injustice, and violence are part of the rebel's condition. He cannot, therefore, absolutely claim not to kill or lie, without renouncing his rebellion, and accepting, once and for all, evil and murder."[13] This is why the theme of murder is so central to the discussion in *The Rebel*, because absolute freedom must eventually challenge the fifth commandment, the prohibition of murder.[14] Indeed, *The Rebel* is a history of man's effort to "make himself" independent of any commandments as this notion from roots both in philosophy and theology has worked itself out in modern political thought and practice. The instant we doubt that there are already definite limits in being or in human nature, the minute we claim the right to assume that all limits are relative to us, that same moment there begins an intellectual process that must end in the destruction of any tolerable, natural human order. To his credit Camus understood this logic and intellectually pursued its consequences to their bitter end, to the end of modern totalitarian tyranny. This modern version is not like ancient tyranny merely an aberration of one man, but aberration in the order of being itself.[15]

Camus began his study with the notorious Marquis de Sade as a kind of prototype of the modern mind's eventual direction. "Sade's success in our day is explained by the dream that he had in common with contemporary thought: the demand for total freedom, and dehumanization coldly planned by the intelligence."[16] Camus recognized that the thought of the two centuries he recounted beginning with the French Revolution was "spiritual" in its origins. "The astounding history evoked here is the history of European pride."[17] Again

[13]Ibid., 285. On this point, see Jacques Maritain, *Man and the State* (Chicago: University of Chicago Press, 1951) 71–75.

[14]Camus, *The Rebel*, 279–93.

[15]Ibid., 251.

[16]Ibid., 46; on Sade, ibid., 37–46.

[17]Ibid., 11.

a word, rich in classical and revelational overtones, must be used adequately to account for what is at issue. That word is, exactly, *hubris*, or better, *superbia*, pride, the claim first heard with Prometheus and especially in Genesis, that we ourselves are the causes not the discoverers of the distinction of good and evil in things. "The history of rebellion, as we are experiencing it today, has far more to do with the children of Cain than with the disciples of Prometheus. In this sense it is the God of the Old Testament who is primarily responsible for mobilizing the forces of rebellion."[18]

This claim of absolute autonomy is the ultimate root of the accusation against God made in the name of justice, the accusation that this world is not well made. Implicitly, some of our kind claim to be able to make the world and mankind better. Eventually this claim implies not merely the solitary complacence of a Lucifer but the active attempt to fashion all of reality into those forms developed by the human intellect which claims that all is relative so that nothing is limited by *what is*.

In Camus' short story "The Renegade" the priest who embraced the Fetish that rejects everything his faith had stood for shouted, "I have something to settle with him, and with his teacher, with my teacher who deceived me, with the whole of lousy Europe, everybody deceived me."[19] The exile, the kingdom, the Fall, the Republic, the City of God, the deception of the whole intellectual heritage of Europe, the history of pride—Camus was ever aware that our own deceptions are likewise self-inflicted. When these deceptions are firmly held, we seek to erect a plausible surrogate reality for them, not to imitate *what is*. This substitute reality will look to the artist in us to supply the outlines of the alternate world we seek to put in place of the being *that is*, the reality that God created.

Even at the end Camus had not resolved this relationship of pride, suffering, and faith. He sided with the artist in us and not with the Divine Artist to whom an Aquinas so often looked when confronting the same problem (*CG*, II, 45). Camus

[18]Ibid., 32.

[19]Albert Camus, "The Renegade," *Exile and the Kingdom*, trans. Justin O'Brien (New York: Vintage, 1958) 36.

wrote: "Even by his greatest effort man can only propose to diminish arithmetically the sufferings of the world. But the injustice and the suffering of the world will remain and, no matter how limited they are, they will not cease to be an outrage. Dimitri Karamazov's cry of 'Why?' will continue to resound; art and rebellion will die only with the last man."[20] For all his complaint of limits Camus insisted that the answer to his transcendent problem be solved in the existing, limited world.

This insistence is the root of Camus' rejection both of Christianity and of modern materialism. Neither could solve his question in his own terms.

> Historical Christianity postpones to a point beyond the span of history the cure of evil and murder, which are nevertheless experienced within the span of history. Contemporary materialism also believes that it can answer all questions. But, as a slave to history, it increases the domain of historic murder and at the same time leaves it without any justification, except in the future—which again demands faith. In both cases one must wait, and meanwhile the innocent continue to die. For twenty centuries the sum total of evil has not diminished in the world. No paradise, whether divine or revolutionary has been realized.[21]

If we understand Camus correctly, the human philosophical artist within time has only the alternative of a kind of creative solution to suffering, which suffering itself remains somehow identified with evil and not with its being caused by the human will.[22] Camus' famous choice of "action" over contemplation and revelation to create a limited decency is the consequence of a theoretic impasse.[23]

We can better understand the implications of this impasse if we recall that in his classic discussion St. Augustine placed evil not in things or in suffering but in the will, in the

[20]Camus, *The Rebel*, 302.

[21]Ibid., 303-04.

[22]See James V. Schall, "The Nature of Evil," *Claremont Review of Books* 5 (Spring, 1986) 10-11.

[23]Camus, *The Rebel*, 301.

very will that chose to reject given order. On the issue of suffering and injustice St. Augustine did not see that the conditions of earthly life would get better as time went on, but in fact worse (see below, chapter 11).[24] This is why Augustine is perhaps much more relevant to the twentieth century than any other philosopher, because it is in the twentieth century that the horrors about which Camus tried to account for have occurred.[25] "The nineteenth and twentieth centuries, in their most profound manifestations, are centuries that have tried to live without transcendence," Camus wrote.[26] St. Augustine would have found no incongruity between the effort to live without transcendence and the horrible results for which Camus sought to account apart from faith or modern materialism. For Camus these results were caused by religion and materialism.

St. Augustine saw a direct relation between the individuals in this life and those in the next—the members of both the City of God and the City of Man were exactly ourselves. Camus' premises, however, did not presuppose that there could be a continuity between those who actually suffer and those who reach beyond this life. Camus' ultimate problem was not with suffering itself but rather, as for the young men in *The Republic,* with immortality (608c). "[Interviewer] 'You once wrote: "Secret of my universe: imagine God without the immortality of the soul. 'Can you define more exactly what you mean?' [Camus] 'Yes, I have a sense of the sacred and I do not believe in a future life, that's all.' "[27] The earnest desire to reduce or eliminate suffering cannot, at the expense of freedom itself, be avoided. So the problem must return to the Divinity, to the reason why there is something rather than nothing. This alternative Camus could not accept according to his own understanding of freedom. His own philosophy is, likewise, an artistic alternative to *what is* and its causes.

[24]See Herbert Deane, *Political and Social Ideas of St. Augustine* (New York: Columbia University Press, 1963) 38.

[25]See John East, "The Political Relevance of St. Augustine," *Modern Age,* 16 (Spring, 1972) 167–81.

[26]Camus, *The Rebel,* 142.

[27]"Replies to Jean-Claude Brisville," in Camus, *Lyrical and Critical Essays,* 364.

Camus understood that revolution seeks metaphysics, and metaphysics grounds any action that flows from this understanding of its own world. There is a ''metaphysical rebellion'' and an ''historical rebellion,'' as if to suggest that being and action in modern philosophy originate in thought but end in reality. This is the history of precisely ''European pride'' because, as Leo Strauss wrote, this civilization is the universal civilization. This civilization claims to aim at, to reach truth itself and not merely the truth of one's own culture or nation. The crisis of this civilization arises not from the claim that there *is* a truth but from the claim that there is *not.*[28]

''The revolution of the twentieth century,'' Camus perceptively wrote, ''believes that it can avoid nihilism and remain faithful to true rebellion, by replacing God by history. In reality, it fortifies the former and betrays the latter. History in its pure form furnishes no value by itself. Therefore one must live by the principles of immediate expediency or keep silent or tell lies.''[29] Both positivism and historicism are based on an inescapable relativism, something Camus clearly understood. But he was unwilling to admit the need of any ''absolute'' principles as an alternative to avoid the dangerous consequences he saw so clearly flowing from this same relativism.

The consequences of the claim that there is no ultimate truth are what Camus tried to think his way through to some alternative other than the classic truths of this universal theodicy and civilization. On the way Camus had to reject those ideological philosophies proposed by the modern artist-philosopher who set out to establish his or her own truth in this world, presupposing no limits. From his study Camus apparently concluded that any claim to truth was dangerous even if it was to that higher truth which is not rooted in purely human intellect. In Camus' analysis, ''Marxism is only scientific today in defiance of Heisenberg, Bohr, Einstein, and all the greatest minds of our time. After all, there is really nothing mysterious about the principle that consists in using scientific reasoning to the advantage of prophecy. This has already

[28]Leo Strauss, *City and Man* (Chicago: University of Chicago Press, 1964) 3.

[29]Camus, *The Rebel*, 288-89.

been named the principle of authority, and it is this that guides the Churches when they wish to subject living reason to dead faith and freedom of the intellect to the maintenance of temporal power."[30] The problem of freedom of intellect over against temporal power was present in *The Apology* of Socrates and at the death of Christ. It remains an open question whether over a long period of time a living reason can exist without a living faith. This latter, the living faith, is where Camus himself had understood the reality of grace to be at issue even though he felt himself to be "deprived" of this very grace because he could not see any "object of faith." Further, he insisted on the "Christ we deserve" because he held that the scope of human suffering is related only to the sufferers and not through them to the Passion of Christ.

Camus could not accept, because of his position on the object of faith or metaphysics (First Mover), that there was a proper locus for the Absolute. This removal of God left Camus with the sole alternative of what might be called "absolute limits," that could be little other than another act of faith. "If . . . rebellion could found a philosophy it would be a philosophy of limits, of calculated ignorance, and of risk. He who does not know everything cannot kill everything. The rebel, far from making an absolute of history, rejects and disputes it, in the name of a concept that he has of his own nature."[31] Camus remained within the discussion of human finitude and moderation that was located in the classical discussion of ethics and politics. These were the areas in which evil and suffering existed as intellectual and moral problems.

Camus understood that thought deprived of a transcendent object turned on itself to seek to explain all things as if human reason itself were sufficient. In this case "metaphysics is replaced by myth."[32] The world of the "sacred" does not initially leave the world of reason closed in on itself. But the modern person demands "a human situation in which all answers are human." This alternative means that everything is either "an act of grace" or "an act of rebellion." For Camus

[30] Ibid., 222.
[31] Ibid., 289.
[32] Ibid., 21.

rebellion is identified with a human reason which cannot accept that suffering and evil can be dimensions of the reality we have been asked to dwell in. The very act of human reason in knowing this reality includes the fact of knowing its injustice which makes intellect by definition rebellious. Camus' worry follows: "Is it possible to find a rule of conduct outside the realm of religion and its absolute values?"[33]

The rejection of the alternative proposed by grace, Camus quickly realized, involved the claim to be free from the norms said to derive from God and, eventually, from a nature dependent on God. "If there is no human nature, then the malleability of man is, in fact, infinite."[34] Humanity was poorly made; since nothing prevented it, the modern project was to refashion the person over against the world in which anyone suffered. Camus saw that modern absolutism began in a kind of act of charity but was to end in a tyranny worse than even the brightest of the ancients could have imagined. *The Rebel* is the record of modern nihilism which claimed absolute freedom as a right and principle of philosophy in protest to given reality. As a consequence, it claimed to be bound by nothing. The person was autonomous and self-sufficient in a manner contrary to any meaning Aristotle might have given to these expressions.

Camus recognized that this claim to unlimited freedom and to absolute autonomy was the remote cause of the tyrannies of the twentieth century, which were not accidents but long-term products of philosophy. Modern tyrannies were thoughts projected into action not arbitrarily but as a result of an unrooted metaphysics that no longer had any limit in theory for action. The twentieth century has seen its politicians claim to be philosophers, and its philosophers claim to be motivated by compassion, by the autonomous "rights" of all people. This claim would involve the rejection of any limit on human thought or action. The incipient rejection of communism in the last decade of this century has reaffirmed the limits.

[33]Ibid.
[34]Ibid., 237.

Camus' analysis of modern decadence situated him on the side neither of the believer nor of the ideologue, neither Yogi nor Commissar, as he entitled one of his books. Like Plato and Aristotle, Camus understood that "the Caesarian revolutionary" somehow followed logically from philosophic thought.[35] The "moderation" Camus finally proposed, which in practice was not unlike that proposed by Aristotle in *The Ethics* and *The Politics* or by St. Thomas in his "Treatise on Law," differed from them in principle because Camus' only solid intellectual basis was the rejection of any absolute. He understood the modern claim to absolute truth in this world to be exclusively ideological. In itself it was based on the rejection of the claims of religion and philosophy. Camus, as it were, rejected the rejection and thereby found his way back to a limited reality. "To ensure the adoration of a theorem for any length of time," he reflected, "faith is not enough; a police force is needed as well."[36] The absolute nature of totalitarian police forces led Camus to examine the ideas from which they arose.

Modern thought was nihilistic in its premises. It began with a refusal to accept a God who created a world in which suffering and evil existed. It likewise rejected any redemption in which the Creator-God now incarnate also suffered. God could not be like the one described in the religious tradition. Redemptive suffering or love could not, within the terms of this world, explain or justify the evils found in it. "The struggle between truth and justice began here for the first time (Dostoevsky); and it will never end."[37] That truth and justice for Camus had to be seen in opposition was the result of the premise that no transcendent solution was permitted. A good God could not have created a world in which evil, even by accident or human freedom, could have existed. God was to be hated and rejected symbolically and practically by the human construction of a world not dependent upon him. Man in this "new world" inhabited by a "new Adam," a "new man,"

[35]Ibid., 298.
[36]Ibid., 122.
[37]Ibid., 55.

would show his independence by specifically rejecting the most important elements of original creation and nature.

The Rebel is divided into four parts. The first describes metaphysical rebellion among the philosophers, which is concerned with efforts to account for what is wrong with the world and to discover theoretic alternatives to *what is*. The second is poetic rebellion, which fashions these alternate worlds by human art in some detail. The third is historical rebellion which seeks to put these now purged ''myths'' into political reality. The final section contains Camus' rejection of the horror involved in these latter efforts and his attempt to rediscover ''limits'' without at the same time lapsing into either religion or ideology.

Camus was right in seeing that both poetry and metaphysics in the modern era have become ''politics.'' Though this was to happen after his time, he might also have foreseen that politicization would be the fate of any religion that sought to explain itself in ideological terms. Aristotle had understood that if humans were the highest beings, then politics would be the highest science. But Aristotle also saw that to protect the human as its limited self, the first principles of being and action could not be subject to the artistic side of the human intellect.[38] Rather they had to be discovered by a finite intellect as constituent aspects of *what is* already, of what is not subject to human making.

''A nihilist is not one who believes in nothing, but one who does not believe in what exists,'' Camus wrote.[39] The issue could not be stated any better. Camus wanted to condemn what was admittedly wrong in the actual world, even to condemn God, if necessary. Likewise Camus wanted to affirm with the rebel that something was good. This desire explains his attention to art and beauty which could not totally remove themselves from reality even though they sought to improve on it, create it anew. But for Camus this ''transcendent'' good could be found only in the world. There was no reality beyond the finite reality. ''It is not sufficient to live, there must be a

[38]See Charles N. R. McCoy, *The Structure of Political Thought* (New York: McGraw-Hill, 1963) 29–72.

[39]Camus, *The Rebel*, 69.

destiny that does not have to wait for death. It is therefore justifiable to say that man has an idea of a better world than this."[40]

It was Machiavelli who allowed the politician to become an artist independent of the prudence to which the classical politician was to be bound because of unchanging human nature, which he did not form. Beauty, while it does connect us with reality, as Camus said, also leads us, in the case of an artist who creates it, to a human source. By contrast the Beauty of which St. Augustine spoke, that "Beauty ever ancient, ever new," led through nature to a metaphysical source not subject to human freedom, except in so far as that freedom could, and should, accept *what is*.

In his concern to "find a better world than this," Camus no doubt was thinking within the scope of what Aquinas called second nature or secondary causality. Could God create free but finite beings who could actually cause other things, including themselves, to exist in a different manner, in either a worse or a better way? And if this were possible, would there be such a thing as real risk in *what is* so that evil and suffering might appear as a result of the nature of such finite beings? The real alternative might be either free beings who had the possibility of suffering and committing evil or nothing at all. Modern ideology claims that the human intellect can change this alternative. The modern rebellious mentality essentially prefers nothing to the reality *that is* and to God its cause.

The nihilist, as Camus said, does not believe in what exists. Chesterton, in almost the identical intellectual situation, wrote at the end of *Heretics:* "We shall be left defending, not only the incredible virtues and sanities of human life, but something more incredible still, this huge impossible universe which stares us in the face. We shall fight for visible prodigies as if they were invisible. We shall look on the impossible grass and the skies with a strange courage. We shall be of those who have seen and yet have believed."[41] Camus wanted to account for what existed without the necessity of first believing in its good-

[40]Ibid., 262.
[41]Chesterton, *Heretics*, in *Collected Works*, vol. 1, 207.

ness. Chesterton better understood the nihilist's challenge. For orthodox belief holds the primacy of the world in which we find ourselves, with its evil and suffering. To accept the existing world requires the greater faith and the greater reason.

Camus, to reject the ideologies, had to rediscover nature. "When nature ceases to be an object of contemplation and admiration, it can be nothing more than material for an action that aims at transforming it. . . . In the common condition of misery, the eternal demand is heard again; nature once more takes up the fight against history."[42] In history evil and suffering of the innocent—and of the guilty—do happen. The problem, as Camus saw, is not so much that evil and suffering are found but that they need to be explained. "In the eyes of the rebel, what is missing from the misery of the world, as well as from its moments of happiness, is some principle by which they can be explained. The insurrection against evil is, above all, a demand for unity."[43]

In his famous question about the existence of God (*ST* I, 2, 1), Aquinas saw the necessity of accounting for evil and suffering before a good God. Aquinas cited Augustine who had remarked that a good God "provides well even about evil." To this Aquinas added that he "permitted evil and elicited good from it." Neither Augustine nor Aquinas fell into the intellectual trap of modernity which demands a complete human rational explanation of the divine ways. Psalm 92 says, "How great are thy deeds, O Lord! How fathomless thy thoughts!" The charge against God from modern thought on the basis of existing evil has arisen from the claim of finite intellect to know the divine ways, particularly on the matter of suffering and evil.

The rejection of the redemption given in Christ for Camus set the stage for a human alternative. "How to live without grace—that is the question that dominates the nineteenth century."[44] This living without grace meant implicitly the rejection of grace in that very manner it was originally presented

[42]Camus, *The Rebel*, 299-300.
[43]Ibid., 101.
[44]Ibid., 225.

to humanity: "The cross is Christ's punishment. . . . He intercedes, he submits to the most extreme injustice so that rebellion shall not divide the world in two, so that suffering will also light the way to heaven and preserve it from the curses of mankind."[45] The systematic rejection of the Cross is directly related for Camus to the curses of humanity about the kind of world we are given, even with its beauty.

People thus insist that the way of Christ as it pertains to their own existence and the transcendent destiny of each person cannot be justified if it involves the possibility of our freely choosing evil and of our suffering because we are finite and do evil. God, not the person, created the world in which these things happened. So God, not the person, was at fault. What is at issue here, of course, is the question of whether we ourselves as particular beings who can and do choose evil, who can and do suffer, ought to exist.

In Christian doctrine, each human being is created freely. Neither the individual nor the universe itself needs exist. The existence of both the individual person and the universe as a whole needs to be explained. Neither explains itself. God did not "have" to create because of some lack in his own being. Nor can we hold that the world exists because God was somehow lonely.[46] The cause of the existence of what is not God must be found not in creation but in the nature and freedom of the First Being or God. However, each free being can choose itself over God. Human persons need not but can choose against God by preferring themselves. This dangerous freedom is intrinsic to human nature. To propose anything else would be to propose some other kind of being; that is, it would be to deny the possibility or goodness of what does in fact exist.

Evil is the lack of a good in what does exist, which is why suffering is so easy to substitute for it. To eliminate in principle the very possibility of evil would at the same time eliminate the possibility of any free being other than God. Suffering is connected with finiteness.[47] Were suffering evil

[45]Ibid., 110.

[46]See James V. Schall, *Redeeming the Time* (New York: Sheed & Ward, 1968) 65–120.

[47]See C. S. Lewis, *The Problem of Pain* (New York: Macmillan, 1962).

as such, it could not be redemptive or even tolerable. Yet the ''suffering servant,'' anyone who suffers, is not on that account evil. This is not to deny, however, that suffering of its nature directly points to what ought not to exist.

The orthodox answer to evil and suffering rejects the ideological protest against their existence, which proposes their total elimination by organizing a perfect society in this world. Rather it locates their final resolution beyond the political life, beyond the ''complete'' life of a person in this world. The alternative to immortality and resurrection is, in modern thought, ''the future.'' Camus again put the matter in proper perspective: ''The future is the only transcendental value for a man without God.''[48] However, Camus also understood that the future involves something that does not now exist. ''He who loves his friend loves him in the present, and the revolution wants to love only a man who has not yet appeared. To love is, in a certain way, to kill the perfect man who is going to be born of the revolution.''[49] This observation protected Camus from a modern ideology that could not save the individual as such but had to concern itself with the whole, the species, the collectivity.

This species-being is in effect a logical abstraction in which distinct human individuals are absorbed into some presumably future being.[50] ''Man, who hated death and the god of death, who despaired personal survival, wanted to free himself in the immortality of the species. But as long as the species does not dominate the world, as long as the species does not reign, it is still necessary to die.''[51] The species evidently need not die, particularly if it can subsume into itself both space, so that it includes all people in its artistic-political system, and time, so that the end of history is reached.

Human beings exist in reality as individual persons with names. There is a finite number of them, each has an intellect, each is called to happiness, to the highest things, to perma-

[48]Ibid., 166.

[49]Ibid., 239.

[50]See Schall, *Reason, Revelation, and the Foundations of Political Philosophy*, 163–81.

[51]Camus, *The Rebel*, 247.

nence. This permanence is defined by the Greeks as immortality and by the Christians as resurrection or everlasting life. When this transcendent destiny is denied, in the name of a world in which evil and suffering should not exist, the only "being" that remains is "species-being." But this sort of being has existence only in the mind, as the idea of all humanity in time and space. The effort to bring it forth from the mind into reality destroys the kind of actual being found there because the latter is not the product of human making.

The alternative to individual redemption is necessarily the salvation for all in this world. "The species must be deified, as Nietzsche attempted to do, and his ideal of superman must be adopted to assure salvation for all. . . ."[52] The attempt to place this now deified species into the world as a substitute for the transcendent destiny of each person in resurrection must logically leave no one out. "Total revolution ends by demanding . . . the control of the world."[53] This demand, Camus understood, is not in the twentieth century a product of mere greed or ambition but of philosophic necessity. Indeed, it is the result of philosophic choice, once the classical philosophic and revelational alternatives of contemplation and resurrection are put aside. Even totalitarianism is "spiritual" and, as Camus knew, must be met at that level.

Camus concluded that his only alternative was a kind of compassion. He called for a more gentle Mediterranean world as opposed to the colder winds from the north of Europe, though even he, at the end of his life, was aware of the resurgence of Islam from his south.[54] "Those who find no rest in God or in history are condemned to live for those who, like themselves, cannot live: in fact, for the humiliated."[55] Camus wanted no salvation "if it must be paid for by injustice and oppression." Rather it was in the present, not in the future or in the transcendent, that any real worth must lie. "Real generosity toward the future lies in giving all to the present."[56]

[52]Ibid., 107.

[53]Ibid.

[54]Ibid., 300. See "The New Mediterranean Culture," *Lyrical and Critical Essays*, 189–98.

[55]Camus, *The Rebel*, 304.

[56]Ibid.

Those ''deprived of grace,'' to recall his words, must practice this ''generosity'' among themselves in some limited but blind way.

The intelligence of Europe, the universal civilization, has been ''impatient'' with limits and has plunged into ''human excesses'' that have bloodied the twentieth century. Recalling Plato, Camus wrote, ''the men of Europe, abandoned to the shadows, have turned their backs upon the fixed and radiant point of the present.''[57] They have in fact ''deified themselves and their misfortunes began.'' The alternative is not a faith which accepts both the limits and the transcendence. ''The only original rule of life today [is] to learn to live and to die, and, in order to be a man, to refuse to be a god.''[58]

The refusal of people to be gods, no doubt, is the human side of the first commandment. Indeed, in Genesis the essence of the temptation of Adam was exactly ''to be like God,'' with man himself not God causing the final distinction of ''good and evil.'' But what it is to be a person is related to the fact that in the incarnation, God became man. People did not become gods. They remained themselves, human beings. The great doctrine of redemption claims nothing other than that even before the divinity people ought to remain finite, limited beings. The doctrine of the resurrection of the body suggests that God knows what we want better than we do. The great spiritual problem of each person is whether he or she will accept this gift. Camus, like Chesterton, did rediscover hints of a faith that already existed.

Camus' alternative, however, at first sight appears to be full of pride. ''But if man were capable of introducing unity into the world entirely on his own, if he could establish the reign, by his own decree, of sincerity, innocence, and justice, he would be God himself.''[59] St. Augustine could not have stated our fundamental temptation better. Yet Camus' theory of limits, his awareness of the worldly alternatives to divinity which drove him back to moderation, retained that element of refusal of the something more, of the ''superabundance''

[57]Ibid., 305.
[58]Ibid., 306.
[59]Ibid., 285.

which Aquinas found in creation. Camus wanted to love human beings without loving God. He wanted the second commandment deliberately separated from the first.

Recall that Camus had asked, "But if those believers I see do believe, what is the object of their faith?" In the end the object of his own faith was everything that God wanted of us except God. Unlike Chesterton, Camus remained the "heretic" who did not choose the only "heresy" capable of justifying and rejoicing in limits—orthodoxy itself. He wrote, "Heretics . . . are men who want to go faster than God." He concluded that "method does not try to convince people immediately. That is the task of grace." In wanting to go "faster than God," in wanting "immediately" to know the ultimate things about suffering, about good and evil, Camus understood himself to be "deprived of grace." No doubt he was right. We do end up with the "only Christ we deserve" because we have in our theories no place for the actual Christ who dwelt among us during the reign of Augustus Caesar when the whole world was at peace, who died during the time of Tiberius Caesar, when Pontius Pilate was governor in Palestine. Ultimately, we are not deprived of grace. We are indeed given a Christ we do not deserve. This is what God is like.

Chapter VI

"He Will Listen as Thou Walkest": Random Thoughts on Praying

If the Christ we have is not the Christ we "deserve," we must attend to the fact that Christ asked us to pray. Christ taught us how to pray, even what to pray. The fact that we are asked and taught to pray should indicate a curious aspect of our wondering what this God whom we know exists must be like. The accusation of not caring for creation or human beings is often made against Aristotle's First Mover or God. Plato was most concerned that we do not bribe the gods by sacrifices and petitions for that would make us want God for our own paltry reasons. Yet the God *who is* in the incarnation asked us to pray, to "pray always," as St. Paul remarked. "Why?" we might ask ourselves. This question requires us to know the most intimate mystery about the relation of God to ourselves, that God is love. God expects our love. Prayer is the expression and reality of the mutual freedom that this love demands.

To comprehend what this relation of prayer and love might mean, let me begin with some considerations of St. Augustine (to whom I shall return in chapter 11) and Nietzsche. Whenever I have compared my reading of Augustine and Nietzsche, I have had the impression that I was discovering in both men the same kind of personal, elevated form of discourse. When we listen to Augustine, to his confessions addressed to God, we feel that we are allowed to exist within a friendship, inside a soul who stands in openness to receive what he does not always want to accept. Even in his *Soliloquies*, we feel that Augustine is not just talking to himself.

Augustine's speech is directed to a Hearer, though he does not mind if we listen in. He insists on explaining himself. He acknowledges his errors. He is not content until the "reasons why" of his questions are articulated. He does not remain silent before the truth. "We were at another time moved to do well, after our hearts had conceived of thy Spirit; but in the former time, forsaking Thee, we were moved to do evil; but Thou, the One, the Good God, hast never ceased to do good. And we also have certain good works, of Thy gift, but not eternal; after these we hope to rest in Thy great hallowing" (*Confessions*, XIII, 38). Augustine praises without embarrassment. What is true, what is beautiful receives his commendation.

Nietzsche, no doubt, had quite a different outlook on the world. Nonetheless, what seem to us to be his blasphemies appear to be addressed to the same Being whom Augustine had been praising. Indeed, we suspect that Augustine would have quite understood what Nietzsche was talking about. We can be fairly certain that Nietzsche knew of Augustine, who, at one time or another in his life, had pretty much the same sort of problems as Nietzsche, perhaps even more perplexing ones.

Let me cite something from Nietzsche to illustrate what I am talking about. The following passage occurs in *The Anti-Christ*: "That we find no God—either in history or in nature or behind nature—is not what differentiates *us*, but that we experience what has been revered as God, not as 'godlike' but as miserable, as absurd, as harmful, not merely as an error but as a *crime against life*."[1] What is to be noticed about this passage is the most curious "anti-atheism," if it can be put that way, contained in it, even despite its professed godlessness. Nietzsche is not concerned so much to deny God. He wants to differentiate himself from mere un-believers. He lets God know what bothers him. He wants us, his readers, to know too, but we seem rather unimportant. We are not his main audience. Nietzsche is not a silent atheist but a disappointed one.

[1]Nietzsche, *The Anti-Christ*, no. 47, in *The Portable Nietzsche*, ed. Walter Kaufmann (Harmondsworth: Penguin, 1968) 627.

Nietzsche's famous "God is dead," moreover, always seemed addressed to the neighbors, not to the fact. The rhetoric of upgrading an "error" into a "crime" betrays the need to justify oneself before some unacknowledged judge. At times Nietzsche himself seems to be this very judge, yet he is not concerned with philosophic proof—"no God in history, in nature, or behind nature"—but to let us know how he sees what has been considered godlike, almost as if he protesteth too much.

The point of this consideration of St. Augustine and Nietzsche, however, is to emphasize that prayer does assume an object, or, better, a someone who hears our protestations and appeals, be it for our needs, for our daily bread, or for enlightenment about what is truth. Whatever we might say about the person as a social being, as a being in family, polity, Church, or general society, prayer is based on the notion that there is also a direct, personal connection between finite, individual people, with a name, and God. However social our being is, each of us has our own capacity to reach directly beyond ourselves, beyond society, to *what is*, without in any way denying what is due to the reality of ourselves, of our society, or of our world.

C. S. Lewis collected a series of brief passages on spiritual topics from the Scottish writer George MacDonald, including several remarks on prayer. The following passage touches the heart of what I want to say about prayer and the Deity: "Never wait for a fitter time or place to talk to Him. To wait till thou go to church or to thy closet is to make Him wait. *He will listen as thou walkest*."[2] We ought, no doubt, to pray in church. Scripture in fact tells to shut the door of our closet and pray. MacDonald, however, had something else in mind, and it reveals much about what God is like. Briefly, God likes to hear from us. Does this presuppose some deficiency in God? If it does, it means that God is not God. Actually, what it assumes is proper personhood in God. Indeed, the human notion of personhood is derived ultimately from the Trinitarian discussion about the diversity in God in the Three Persons.

[2]*George MacDonald: An Anthology*, ed. C. S. Lewis (New York: Macmillan, 1974) no. 237, 101. Italics added.

Our personhood emphasizes that nothing in us that is specifically our own can be caused by God directly except insofar as he already gives us being and continues us in existence and grace. We must know, act, and choose. Waiting and patience seem to exist in God, even when, like Nietzsche, we complain in the face of the Divinity that everything about creation is all wrong. What I like about this passage from MacDonald is its randomness, its awareness that prayer, which can and should be structured at times, flows within the ordinary rhythms of our daily lives, our very walking about.[3] We do not need some formula to begin or to continue to pray. What we need is some awareness, some insight into our metaphysical incompleteness, or, if that is too exalted, into our finiteness and sinfulness. We need to know that things exist we did not cause. Situations exist we cannot resolve by ourselves. The truth that inspires prayer is the truth of who and what we are. We are finite, fallible beings, our particular selves, who have been given names.

At the beginning of Lent one year, friends from Tulsa gave me a collection of John Henry Newman's *Meditations and Devotions*. The first entry, contained in a section called "Meditation on Christian Doctrine," was called "Hope in God—Creator." Newman gave this meditation in the form of two short conferences on March 7-8, 1848. His consideration is only about four pages long. I like his notion of prayer here because he united piety, a good, robust, Latin word, with intelligence. We do not, I think, pray well unless we think well. And we must pray to think well. "Prayer is the first defence of the mind," Caryll Houselander remarked.[4] Psalm 94:10 reads, "Yahweh, the teacher of mankind, knows exactly how men think, how their thoughts are a puff of wind." We can hope that these "puffs of wind" are only our vain thoughts. However, St. Paul told the Colossians pretty much the same thing: "Make sure no one traps you and deprives you of your freedom by some secondhand, empty rational philosophy based

[3]See James V. Schall, "Spiritual and Physical Exercise," *The Distinctiveness of Christianity* (San Francisco: Ignatius Press, 1982) 256–70.

[4]Caryll Houselander, *The Comforting of Christ* (New York: Sheed & Ward, 1947) 96.

on principles of the world instead of Christ'' (2:8). Prayer does need to be defended against empty thoughts.

The history of Christian prayer shows that this relatively simple practice we call prayer can become too formalized and organized. This complexity or difficulty of devotion and meditation can be used also as an excuse not to pray at all. Such an excuse, I hope, will not be made of what follows, of these random thoughts on prayer, these thoughts that, like St. Augustine and perhaps Nietzsche, implicitly assume that there is someone to pray to, to whom we may explain ourselves even as we walk along.

The need of someone to pray to can be made clear in another way. In an essay in the *New York Times*, Phyllis Lee Levin wrote about a tour she had made in Scotland from an inn called Ardsheal House to the famous Island of Iona, just off Mull: ''There (on Iona) St. Columba and his companions established a lonely and moving place to contemplate what has gone before and what is left: the ruins of a nunnery, the boldly conceived, intricately carved crosses, the 20th Century restoration of the 12th Century St. Oran's Chapel, and Ben Nevis, Scotland's highest mountain, on the horizon.''[5] St. Columba and his companions did *not* ''establish a lonely and moving place to contemplate what has gone before and what is left.'' They rather established a monastery in such a place to address themselves to God, not to our passing condition.

I received a postcard from a student who had been spending the semester at a southern English university. She wrote: ''It is Spring . . . and everything is *green*. Purple, yellow and white flowers have sprouted up everywhere. It is fantastic sitting in the field outside my front door and watching the sun shift, the shadows of the trees change, and the herd of cows move during the course of an afternoon. Things could not be much better.'' One cannot but be touched by this vivid awareness that can fill an English spring. There are grounds for prayer here. But my young correspondent may not yet have realized that life must be sustained also when things are not

[5]Phyllis Lee Levin, ''A Scottish Inn: Ardsheal House,'' *New York Times*, June 5, 1988, Sec. XX, 39.

better. Still, life is, as I have suggested, most poignant when we are happy.

I bring this rural scene up here, because Newman, who must have seen some of these same English scenes as my young friend, was particularly attentive to such personal experience. ''God has created all things for good; all things for their greatest good; everything for its own good,'' he reflected in this ''Meditation on the Creator.''

> God knows what is my greatest happiness, but I do not. There is no rule about what is happy and good; what suits one would not suit another. And the ways by which perfection is reached vary very much. . . . Thus God leads us by strange ways; we know He wills our happiness, but we neither know what our happiness is, nor the way.
>
> Let us put ourselves into His hands, and not be startled though He leads us by a strange way. . . . Let us be sure He will lead us right, that He will bring us to that which is, not indeed what *we* think best, nor what *is* best for another, but what is best for us.[6]

Newman stressed the very unique way that leads each person to God. Everything is ruled for its own good. In an era of equality this will sound odd. But our diverse ways are something Newman, with the whole Christian tradition, insisted on. He refused to admit that we are wholly alike or that God leads us by identical paths. We are not treated the same. We are treated as we need to be treated. We are treated with a superabundance of gift and grace. Our treatment will never be the same as that of someone else.

God might have done everything by ''Himself,'' Newman wrote, in a contrary-to-fact illustration, ''but it has been His will to bring about His purposes by the beings He has created. We are all created to His glory—we are created to do His will. I am created to do something for which no one else is created.''[7] This notion of the unique creation of each human person for some specific purpose, which first will be his own

[6]John Henry Newman, *Meditations and Devotions* (Harrison, N.Y.: Roman Catholic Books, n.d.) 5.

[7]Ibid., 6.

salvation, must lie at the center of any notion of prayer. Individual creation establishes the intimate link existing between each person and God, a link that cannot repeat itself in any life other than ours. Prayer is a recognition on our part that our particular creation is understood fully only in our own unique situation. This understanding awaits acceptance by our own wills.

Caryll Houselander, in her lovely book, *The Reed of God*, wrote in a similar fashion: "Sometimes it may seem to us that there is no purpose in our lives, that going day after day for years to this office or that school or factory is nothing else but waste and weariness. But it may be that God has sent us there because but for us Christ would not be there. If our being there means that Christ is there, that alone makes it worthwhile."[8] Lest we be overly impressed by what this statement might mean, we must likewise admit, in St. Paul's terms (Rom 5:16), that even our sins can cause this presence of God to come about. God can repair our disorders by expanding the good in which any evil, even our own, was begun and carried out. Evil always stands in some good. Because it has no substance of its own, evil can happen only by choosing some good thing in the wrong way. We are beings who really do choose good things, even when we choose wrongly. Repentance is our coming to see this good with clarity and attributing it to its proper source, not to ourselves.

For whatever else we may be created, we remain created for God Himself, as St. Augustine affirmed (*Confessions*, I, 1). Newman added that God "preferred to regain me rather than to create new worlds."[9] This remark is addressed to the problem of what happens when we reject God's will for us by our choices. The drama of redemption is of more significance than the drama of original creation. The drama of how God redeemed us, at what cost, subsumes into itself the wonder of creation. The cost, the story of Christ's actual life on earth, must become the primary object of our prayer. To see how God deals with us in the particular providence that each of us has

[8]Caryll Houselander, *The Reed of God* (Westminster, Md.: Christian Classics, 1985) 32.

[9]Newman, *Meditations and Devotions*, 8.

from our beginning, indeed, as St. Paul wrote (Eph 1:4-7), from all eternity, we must make Christ's Passion the heart of our prayer.

The "Evening Prayers" for Sunday in the Divine Office contain this Pauline petition: "In this life we fill up in our own flesh what is still lacking in the sufferings of Christ." Prayer must address itself to this somber admonition. We recognize that the innocent suffer. Some would use this fact to doubt God. In response the incarnation simply says that God suffered. Sometimes, not always, we ourselves suffer innocently. Christ associated others, beginning with his own Mother, with himself in his suffering. When we look at this question of what is lacking, we realize that Christ's own sufferings have taught others to pray, to endure what life has given to them. No suffering in this life is without a salvific potential. This ultimate truth means that in this world there are those who suffer for others just as Christ did. They cannot do this by themselves. The discourse of God with each of us is related to similar discourse with every other person in the whole range of human life, especially in human sufferings.

We find that when we have erred, we are within the sufferings of others. We cause, in part at least, the suffering and anguish of others. We ought not to be blind to this potential. God does not will our deaths or our punishments, both will come by the normal working out of our lives, but He does, so to speak, will our will. Even if we do our own will, God insists that we affirm not our own will but his. Through the sufferings of the innocent and indeed of the guilty, we face the most disquieting questions about ourselves. The prayers and sufferings of others are not useless or wholly inexplicable. Rather they are the context of God's providence confronting our wills in the process of saving our souls, redeeming each one of us, body and soul, the whole of what we are.

In the *Book of Common Prayer* we read, "Almighty God, unto whom all hearts be open, all desires known, and from whom no secrets are hid, cleanse the thoughts of my heart by the inspiration of thy Holy Spirit, that I may perfectly love thee and worthily magnify thy Holy Name. Amen." Again we note that God is addressed and identified in the prayer itself. Just as Nietzsche's address was ostensibly designed to denigrate

God, so the address in the *Book of Common Prayer* was designed to ''magnify thy Holy Name.'' Both recognize that the presence of God requires our response, which ought not to be neutral. Ever since the contrast between Plato's philosopher-king and his worst tyrant we have known that the worst and the best are very close together in our hearts. Although lethargy often describes the story of our unique lives, in the higher things we are not to be lukewarm and blind to the dramatic movement that is equally part of our lives. Yet the ordinary and the normal also magnify and reject. No life escapes what it is ultimately about.

What is God like? God can be magnified or rejected. Either action lies within the power of each rational creature. God treats every creature after the manner in which the creature exists. God calls us as we would be called. The philosopher Eric Voegelin, in his *Conversations,* wrote the following somewhat abstract but still pertinent lines about what we need to understand about a Being to whom we pray.

> In classic philosophy and Christianity, the solution to the sorrows of man—death and life . . . are answered through turning toward God. . . . Deformations occur if you refuse to turn around and persist in the state of alienation. Explicit persistence in the state of alienation . . . is possible only after Christianity has differentiated the problem of existence—a relation of man to the unknown God who is not intra-cosmic . . . but extra-cosmic. Then only . . . can there arise the conception of an extra-cosmic existence of man in revolt.[10]

This man in revolt we have seen in Nietzsche, though the sorrows of man remain. But Voegelin is correct. The character of this ultimate revolt requires us to acknowledge some transcendent being. We find the solution to our sorrows in a turning to God.[11]

''Pray all the time,'' Paul told the Ephesians, ''asking for what you will, praying in the spirit on every possible occa-

[10] *Conversations with Eric Voegelin,* ed. R. Eric O'Connor (Montreal: Thomas More Institute, 1980) 80.

[11] See Marion Montgomery, ''Deconstructionism and Eric Voegelin,'' *Crisis* 6 (June, 1988) 42–44.

sion'' (6:18). What sort of a God would ask us to pray all the time? Are we not supposed to use ''every possible occasion'' for more useful items, even things commanded by this same Lord? What sort of a being are we dealing with here? We do not easily picture ourselves constantly on our knees or in whatever position our tradition teaches us to pray. Perhaps we can pray less formally, for example in our strolling. But would we ever get anything done if we prayed always? If whenever someone asked of us, ''what are you doing?'' we answered, ''praying,'' would we not seem somewhat odd? Did St. Paul perhaps have another kind of prayer in mind? Can we, by some conscious act directing ourselves in an habitual way, make everything we do into a prayer but still leave ourselves free to concentrate on whatever else it is that we are supposed to be doing? Ignatius of Loyola, among other saints, thought we could do something like this: At the beginning of each day we could say, ''Grant, O Lord, that I be not deaf to your calling, but prompt and diligent to fulfill Your holy will.''

A friend wrote: ''The whole day can be an extension of the Mass, if we have the right intention and if we make that intention an habitual thing. In whatever we are doing, working, walking, writing, visiting, whatever, we are trying to allow what is not divine in us and in our work to become divine through union with Christ.'' This is the same point, isn't it? Nothing is divine in us until we allow it to be. The union of the will of God and our wills is the whole drama of redemption in every life.

Woody Allen decided once that he should give an address to graduating seniors at a local university. Allen spoke most wittily of a serious subject:

> More than any other time in history, mankind faces a crossroads. One path leads to despair and utter hopelessness. The other, to total extinction. Let us pray we have the wisdom to choose correctly. I speak, by the way, not with any sense of futility, but with a panicky conviction of the absolute meaninglessness of existence which could easily be misinterpreted as pessimism. It is not. It is merely a healthy concern for the predicament of modern man. (Modern man is here defined as any person born after Nietzsche's edict that

> "God is dead," but before the hit recording "I Wanna Hold Your Hand.")[12]

I cite this passage for its gentle chiding of modern man. Does Allen hint that the desire to hold someone's hand could undermine the theories of the "death of God"?

But I also cite this excerpt because it touches on one of the biggest difficulties with prayer that we encounter. Perhaps we could call it "collectivist" prayer, prayer for the "large" issues. We pray for eternal peace, for the total elimination of human hunger and suffering, for the complete fraternity of humanity. The smaller issues, like how to save our souls, we pay little attention to. We are justified, in this view, by the big picture, not by the ordinary course of our lives. In the "collectivist" mentality we are "responsible" not for ourselves but for abstract humanity down through the ages.

In fact, however, we ourselves are the ones who have the responsibility for which we are finally accountable. We read in the First Letter of Peter, "And you are sure of the end to which your faith looks forward, that is, the salvation of your souls?" (1:9). It is not that the inner-worldly goals ought not to be attended to in our prayers, though even here we ought to pray that we do specifically what we can do. But we must recognize that these vast and abstract goals can easily be substitutes for God. Christianity is a faith based on the incarnation. In it transcendence is not abstract. Hopkins' poem put it accurately: "Man's spirit will be flesh-bound when found at best, / But uncumbered. . . ."[13] The notion that we can be "flesh-bound," but "uncumbered" is exactly the point of the prayer of the Christian. Ours is not a gnostic salvation dependent on our own resources or our own construction. Our salvation is only really ours because it is not ours in the giving. The "flesh-bound" faith, the incarnational faith, remains the great scandal to the philosophers.

There are many questions about prayer—how much prayer? when? where? in what form? The famous "Jesus

[12]Woody Allen, *Side Effects* (New York: Ballantine, 1980) 81.

[13]Gerard Manley Hopkins, "The Caged Skylark," *The Poems of Gerard Manley Hopkins*, fourth edition, ed. W. H. Gardner and N. H. MacKenzie (London: Oxford, 1967) 71.

Prayer,'' so much evident in the novels of the great Slavic writers, is simply, ''Lord Jesus Christ, be merciful to me, a sinner.'' The central prayer is, however, and will ever remain, the Mass. This prayer, this liturgy, is something we did not formulate wholly by ourselves. It is a rite we witness; we are there. Should we say Mass every day? Go to Mass every day? If we can we should, I think.

A good friend wrote with regard to the Mass, in a reflection that means much to me: ''Our life is an ever growing toward God. This growth happens over time. It takes Mass after Mass after Mass. One Christmas Eve or one Easter Vigil won't do it, but time after time, season after season, the slow extension of the Incarnation through time.'' The presence of the Lord among us makes us realize our time-boundedness. To students graduating, to young couples just getting married, to the old, the growing, the busy, the best advice about prayer is simply, as I now think, go to Mass. Just be there. ''What do you have that you have not received?'' St. Paul asked the Corinthians (1 Cor 4:7). What this might be, this inventory of what we have not received, we take at the beginning of Mass. We then follow the Mass. We recall that it too, like our own lives, was simply given to us. This improbable rite is the central prayer of our faith. ''Do this in memory of me.'' ''As often as you eat this bread and drink this cup. . . .''

C. S. Lewis said something in one of his letters about the Christian sacrifice that is worth recalling in this context of prayer and Mass.

> The advantage of a fixed form of service is that we know what is coming. *Ex tempore* public prayer has this difficulty; we don't know whether we can mentally join in it until we've heard it—it might be phoney or heretical. We are therefore called upon to carry on a *critical* and a *devotional* activity at the same moment: two things hardly compatible. In a fixed form we ought to have ''gone through the motions'' before in our private prayers; the rigid form really sets our devotions *free*. I also find the more rigid it is, the easier it is to keep one's thoughts from straying. Also it prevents getting too completely eaten up by whatever happens to be the preoccupation of the moment (i.e. war, an election, or what

> not). The *permanent* shape of Christianity shows through. I don't see how the *ex tempore* method can help becoming provincial, and I think it has a great tendency to direct attention to the minister rather than to God.[14]

Much of what Lewis said here will go against current enthusiasms, but he was on target. He understood the prevalence of ideology among us. Devotions should indeed be free of current fads and provincialisms, free of the mind directed to the minister and not to God. The permanent rhythms of the rite of the Mass and of the sacraments best serve our prayer. Devotion and criticism can both be necessary aspects of faith, but not, as Lewis said, at the same time. When we doubt the orthodoxy of what is being said or celebrated, we cannot properly pray. The very structure of our being demands that to pray well we need to believe well.

Why is it we do not pray well? After a very good homily on prayer at her parish in Denver, my cousin asked me, ''What do you think of prayer?'' I replied, ''Anymore, I mostly say the Rosary myself.'' And I do. It is a fixed prayer that allows us the freedom to pray, to remember the outlines and details of Our Lord's life in the context of the very particular things we pray for. Joseph Ratzinger remarked that in recent years there is a certain over-concentration on the Eucharist to the ignoring of other forms of prayer. ''The Eucharist is the heart and center of our worshipping life,'' Ratzinger said,

> but in order to be this center it must have a multi-layered whole in which to live. The Eucharist presupposes baptism; it presupposes continual recourse to the sacrament of penance. . . . It presupposes personal prayer, family prayer, and para-liturgical prayer of the parish community. I would just like to mention two of the richest and deepest prayers of Christendom . . . the Stations of the Cross and the Rosary. One of the reasons why, nowadays, we are so discountenanced by the appeal of Asiatic or apparently Asiatic religious practices is that we have forgotten these forms of prayer. The Rosary does not call for intense conscious ef-

[14]C. S. Lewis, Letter of April 1, 1952, in *C. S. Lewis: A Mind Awake*, ed. Clyde S. Kilby (New York: Harcourt, 1968) 147.

> forts which would render it impossible but invites us to enter into the rhythm of quiet, peaceably bringing us peace and giving a name to this quietness of Jesus, the blessed fruit of the womb of Mary.[15]

The Mass ought to lead us to pray and our prayer lead to the Mass; they are intimately related.

Within the tradition of the Church, in so many differing ways, we are taught how to pray. It is well if we are taught the Rosary from our youth, as I was taught by my grandmother and my father, with much agony to both in the teaching. We will discover its value mostly when we need it, long after we have already learned it.

Again, what if we do not pray well? On April 6, 1964, the year she died, when she was quite ill with lupus, Flannery O'Connor wrote to Janet McKane: "I do pray for you, but in my fashion, which is not a very good one. I am not a good pray*er*. I don't have a gift for it. My type of spirituality is almost entirely shut-mouth. . . . This book of C. S. Lewis on prayer is a good one but I don't like to pray any better for reading it."[16] Not only is there something charmingly honest about O'Connor's reflections, but they contain much wisdom about prayer. She reminds us that prayer is never easy, even with the best of guides such as C. S. Lewis. But O'Connor prayed, albeit "shut-mouth," as she put it. The New Testament warned us of those who prayed too ostentatiously. It is better to be the miserable publican, who could only say from the back of the Temple, "Lord, be merciful to me, a sinner" (Luke 18:9-14). The one who prayed poorly prayed the best.

The word of our age is "sincerity" or, more recently, "compassion."[17] These words, by virtue of their intense subjectivism, lead us to abandon an objective criterion of good and evil. One way to save everyone, of course, is to hold that every-

[15]Joseph Ratzinger, *Feast of Faith*, trans. Graham Harrison (San Francisco: Ignatius Press, 1986) 152-53.

[16]Flannery O'Connor, *The Habit of Being*, ed. Sally Fitzgerald (New York: Vintage, 1979) 572.

[17]See James V. Schall, "The Most Dangerous Virtue," *The Praise of "Sons of Bitches": On the Worship of God by Fallen Men* (Slough, England: St. Paul Publications, 1978) 53–62.

one is ''sincere,'' or that God is so ''compassionate'' that nothing really makes any difference. We develop a theory in which it is impossible for anyone actually to reject God. Yahweh said to Job, ''Do you really want to reverse my judgment and put me in the wrong to put yourself in the right?'' (Job 40:8). The tendency of sincerity and compassion is to substitute our judgment for God's. Because we remove any responsible act from our power, we eliminate our need for God's forgiveness.

Caryll Houselander again put it well:

> Sentimentalists are continually saying that God is love and so could not allow anyone to perish in hell, that God is love and so could not allow evil to triumph on earth. Might it not be as logical to say that God, who is love indeed, will turn away from and abandon men who burn down, suffocate and torture each other? Who do these things, not only in cold blood, but after years of deliberate preparation, who use every resource of nature and science and all the might of the human intellect to wreck the lives and break the hearts of one another? Is it so unreasonable, to ask, could a God who is all love take these people to his heart?
>
> This is the answer: in men God sees His only Son. He does not see us so much wicked as lost; it is not so much our sins He sees as the wounds sin has made on the Body of Christ.[18]

This seeing that our worst evils have results in the actual life of Christ shows us what God is like in the face of our sins. God does not have the sort of compassion that would permit us to change the structure of reality so that whatever we do is good. But by seeing what we do and its effect, we may learn. This ''seeing'' is what grounds our turning around, our ability to act as spiritual beings even in the light of our own spiritual choices. The closer we get to spiritual things, the more important it is for us to have our ideas of God correct, doctrinally correct. It makes all the difference what we think about God, for it makes a difference what we think at all.

Sincerity will not save us. Compassion will not save us. Prayer and truth are connected. We have separated our prayer institutions from our truth institutions to the detriment of both.

[18]Houselander, *The Comforting of Christ,* 118.

The separation has been fateful in many ways. We have come to picture piety as possible without truth; for this reason we can think that sincerity or compassion will substitute for truth. This is why the great figure of Aquinas remains so central, for it is Aquinas who, in a very Augustinian passage, stands for the unity of piety and truth. "The human mind can view the whole range of things, and therefore instinctively craves to know their cause, which, ultimately, is God alone. Happiness is not attained until this natural appetite is at rest. Not any sort of understanding will do: only divine understanding will satisfy; only knowing God will produce the state where restlessness is stilled" (*CG* III, 25). Aquinas is not rejected by modern thought because he did not see the whole. He is rejected because he did see the whole with the conditions of piety and faith required to comprehend it. Aquinas was the first to realize that everything was, as he said near his death, but "straw" compared to everything that was yet to be revealed to us.

What is God like? We know that we are capable of solving many important problems by ourselves. We can put this in an extreme formulation to claim that we can do all things by ourselves. Prayer is only possible in a world in which, knowing that we want to know and love all things, we recognize our own insufficiencies. But the insufficiencies that count for us are those which have to do with our ultimate destiny, with the salvation of our own souls. Does this mean that the activities of this world are nothing with regard to our souls? Clearly not. Aquinas remarked that there is an order in our relation to the world. The lower is for the higher, which does not deny that the lower is valid and worthy of attention.

John Paul II in Poland in 1987 said to the sick, "Dear Brothers and Sisters! Complete in your sufferings what is lacking in the People of God throughout the land of Poland! Complete it! This is your vocation in Christ crucified and risen."[19] This teaching is not for the Poles alone but is directly from St. Paul for everyone. Prayer and suffering, like prayer and truth, join together. We should ask the sick to pray for us. This no-

[19]John Paul II, Address of June 14, 1987, in *L'Osservatore Romano*, English edition, August 10, 1987.

tion of making up what is lacking is among the most mysterious of Christian teachings. We know that Christ suffered and died for the sins of everyone. We also know that Christ's agonies did not remove all suffering from the world. The question remains, then, of what "use" is this suffering that remains? Surely it is not for God's good. God by definition lacks nothing.

This particular creation is one in which what is not God has something to do with what is directed to the end of creation itself. What is this end? Fundamentally, it is to bring what is not God into the life of God insofar as this is possible. The possibility depends on the nature of the being that is not God. The being that clearly knows that it is not God is, of course, the human being. This being, paradoxically, is the creature tempted to be God. But the person who seeks to substitute himself or the world for God will not pray to himself. Prayer exists in a world of those who specifically realize that they are not themselves the fullness of the good.

Tertullian wrote: "Prayer is the one thing that can conquer God. But Christ has willed that it should work no evil, and has given it all power over good. . . . Prayer cleanses from sin. . . . All the angels pray. Every creature prays. . . . What more need be said on the duty of prayer? Even the Lord Himself prayed."[20] What is God like? Someone who can be "conquered" by prayer? What can this mean about God? It can only mean that God responds to spiritual creatures after their own manner, as enfleshed beings, but beings who know their acts. If prayer is a "duty," it can only be another way of saying what we are, creatures capable of not doing our duty and knowing that we do not do it. Prayer means that nothing we do, not even our sins and evils, is left unresponded to by God. And God's response, as a friend once said to me, is always in the line of the good in which any evil initially existed.

Prayer is intended to develop our love for God and our love for others, especially those who have been given to us. St. Thomas taught that our knowledge was ordered to our love.

[20]Found in the Divine Office, Thursday, Third Week of Lent, Second Reading.

We need to love to know certain fundamental things. I wish to conclude this chapter about prayer not with some things that I have necessarily figured out myself but which friends have taught me. It is all right to meet a truth which we did not arrive at first by ourselves. We should rejoice in those who love us enough to give us truth. This is why pride and truth are so opposite to one another, yet so close. They are opposite because in pride we will allow only what we have discovered or made by ourselves, yet they are close because truth is meant for us.

The first point about prayer leading to love is that this normally happens through our own families, especially through our mothers. It is not an accident that Mary is such a central figure in the prayer life of the Church. I have often pondered the following remarks:

> Mothers really have what no one else has, and what so many ultimately seek as they vainly sacrifice all for that which will result in ultimate power. Mothers come closer to identifying with God than any other creature in any other state. Even angels are beneath them in this role. The obvious difference is that we co-create from something not solely created from nothing. This must be considered as given. I still feel, however, we are uniquely one with the Divine Presence. Not only do we bring forth, we are *there* from the beginning. There is no thought associated with life that is not in absolute association with one's mother. She is—I am. For the formative first years, mothers are the center of the universe. We give a totally dependent being his first definition of "is," and we identify that which is good and that which is evil in an ordered environment, the structure of which ultimately allows the child freedom of choice.
>
> Mothers allow their children to see themselves as good and loveable through their loving them for no other reason than that *they are* and they are good. If children see mothers as all good, all knowing, all present, all powerful (and they do by virtue of their helplessness), as well as all loving, the transition to knowledge of God's love and His role in the child's life as he matures and separates from the "known" center of the universe to the "Real" center of the universe will simply be a natural process.

This is a remarkably true statement of what is central in our life of prayer. It is ordered to the reality that begins in us and ends in our love of God. We cannot and do not ever do anything to relate to God all by ourselves. Particular people in our lives guide us within God's providence.

Once we have been born of such a mother, we can still reject the love of God for the love of ourselves. We can build our own cities, not the City of God. This possibility of missing the ''real'' center of the universe is an abiding one, and we should not doubt it. That we find our true end requires that the love we receive be made a part of our lives. We begin by seeing that however important or sincere we are, we are not the origin of the distinctions of good and evil, of being and not being.

Our inmost thoughts are open to God. This openness does not mean that we are determined or that it is impossible for us to change. The very fact that God knows our deeds means that we can turn away from them if we want or need to. We are not constrained by what we have done or even by what we know. Life is a self-revelation. It reveals us to ourselves. But we are not our own. What we can do is to seek to find ourselves before God, to keep our inner selves open to God and to discipline ourselves to do so. We do not want a world in which we allow only ourselves. Yet we really exist. We are to direct ourselves to the highest things because we learn in our own self-reflective experience that nothing else satisfies us. Our prayer begins from an accurate understanding of what we are, an understanding that realizes that God loves us and that we have an inner life that we can order, but again not totally by ourselves.

Friends of mine made a weekend recollection at a retreat house in Georgia. After the days of reflection, again on this same topic of our love of God and our prayer, this was the summation:

> In retrospect, the contrast between Newman and Mother Teresa, whom I was reading during the retreat, illustrated nicely how it is that both the intellect and the heart lead to God. I was struck perhaps more by Mother Teresa's placid heart, so full of love for the Lord that she truly does lose

> herself in love. By her example she explains better than any scholastic argument that the virtue of charity does not consist in mere acts of kindness, rather in a total love of God so compelling that it simply wells over into our relations with His creatures. As the retreat master mentioned in one of his talks, when you exercise love you are exercising your highest faculty: the power to love is higher than intellect alone.

The love of God does not militate against the knowledge of him, but rather guides and influences it. Both will and intellect are essential to our being. Prayer, which includes our understanding and our will, ought to well over into our relations with our friends and those who reach into our lives. The total love of one another is the only possible response to the total love of God.

What is God like? Remember, we have been asked to "pray always." This is stated as a command and a duty, if only to draw our attention to the seriousness of what we are asked to do. What this turns out to be, on examination, is to love God above all things, and to love those who have been given to us. This love, however, is not something we make up by ourselves. It is a response to what God is, to what anyone whom he has created is. The very possibility that we love God depends on what is inside of us, what kind of a being we are. We are capable of attending to what we know, and what it is we are to know and love is not merely ourselves. When we arrive at this point, prayer is a kind of walking and talking with the personal source of all things. This source hears us and orders the world that we may achieve, even in our sufferings and sins, that for which we exist, to love God and those he has given to us, and this to eternal life.

Chapter VII

The Inexpressible Value of Existence

The reality of God, what God is like, must account not merely for what can be said against God by rational creatures, but what can be said for laughter and prayer, which are paradoxically perhaps more difficult to account for than evil and disorder. The great mystery is not why does God exist but why does anything other than God exist. Among the things that are not God which do exist are, astonishingly, ourselves. We may or may not be surprised that God exists but we only have half a heart if we are not surprised that we ourselves exist. And it is not merely that we exist but that we exist in a universe both large and small. This is a universe so diverse and so vast that we can hardly begin to take notice of what is not ourselves, yet one so small that all reality seems to lie within our own narrow world.

Both in our spirituality and in our normal relationships with our friends, we must take account of what is before us that is not ourselves. No one has explained this contingent reality, its wonder and its importance to us, a reality that includes ourselves, better than Thomas Aquinas or G. K. Chesterton. I cite them together not merely because Chesterton wrote a famous biography of St. Thomas but because both are near to the heart of the wonder in which all laughter and prayer exist. Nor is it strange that both Aquinas and Chesterton were careful to state the arguments against God and his creation correctly. They would have admired, even while not agreeing with Camus' careful effort to state how he understood the world (see above, chapter 5). They taught that our intellects are given to us not merely to redeem ourselves but to redeem the world and what goes on within it, even its evil, even our own evil.

In one of his characteristic passages, Chesterton wrote: "And if any of us or all of us are truly optimists, and believe as Browning did, that *existence has a value wholly inexpressible,* we are most truly compelled to that sentiment, not by any argument or triumphant justification of the cosmos, but by a few of these momentary and immortal sights and sounds, a gesture, an old song, a portrait, a piano, an old door."[1] Chesterton understood that the ultimate things are found most often not in abstract argument, however valuable it might be, or in some overarching system but in common experiences as simple as that of looking at a photo or hearing a piano played by our sister or seeing an old door through which we once passed. He remarked that for a very small child a door was much more fascinating than a toy. The marvel of existence is as much present in the least of things as in the greatest. Nowhere perhaps can we come closer to what God is like than by considering the *what is,* the inexpressible value of the existence of small and apparently insignificant things. We might discover some theoretic reason why God created a rational being. But we are utterly perplexed that he created the myriad of curious and tiny things strewn about everywhere in the universe.

I once assigned for an undergraduate seminar, besides some rather heavy books by Voegelin, Strauss, MacIntyre, Nietzsche, Plato, and Augustine, a volume containing *Heretics* and *Orthodoxy*.[2] I explained to the students, few of whom, I think, had ever heard of Chesterton, that his books were designed to take the place of Aquinas, even though I did not actually assign Chesterton's own *St. Thomas Aquinas*.[3] They looked at me oddly and wondered why I did not just assign Aquinas himself. One surprised student told me later that he kept looking at this Chesterton book in his room, reading snippets from here and there in it. He could not believe how good,

[1]G. K. Chesterton, *Robert Browning,* 1914, pp. 50-51, in *The Quotable Chesterton* (San Francisco: Ignatius Press, 1986) 114-15.

[2]*The Collected Works of G. K. Chesterton,* Vol. 1 (San Francisco: Ignatius Press, 1986).

[3]Ibid., vol. 2.

how provocative, it was, no matter where he picked it up and read. "Who is this Chesterton anyhow?" he asked me, rather helplessly, even suspiciously. "Why have I never heard of him?" I was tempted to reply, too cynically, "You have never heard of Chesterton because you are in a university." But I decided just to say, "Well, you've heard of him now; consider yourself fortunate."

At the end of his 1970 book, *Shaw and Chesterton: The Metaphysical Jesters*, William B. Furlong gave an estimate of Chesterton's lasting influence: "It seems idle to speculate too long on the mere direction from which the Chesterton revival will spring. The truth is that any one of the G. K. C.'s—the probing literary critic, the artist of the fantastic novels, the poet in soaring Gothic come most quickly to mind—could be the first one to come back in popular favor. The Chesterton revival will certainly come."[4] Gertrude White, in 1988, wrote similarly, "There are clear signs now, more than fifty years since his death, that a re-appraisal and re-evaluation of Chesterton is at hand."[5]

For many of us, Chesterton has been an infinite secret of sanity whom we possessed in a kind of forbidden society of common admiration, whose members we met in odd places when we chanced to discover someone else who also loved Chesterton. We selfishly hoped that no one but ourselves would know of this wonderful man but we found ourselves constantly citing him, so some suspected. We are at first envious that we did not think of the felicitous wording that he did but in the end we are glad that we didn't. If Chesterton teaches us anything, it is that it is all right for someone else, even God, to have discovered something first.

I hope, on learning of new attention to Chesterton, we do not "re-appraise" or "re-value" him too much but simply read him again. No book or article on Chesterton, and I have written a few myself, is nearly as good as the original Chesterton. He is like Scripture; he ought to be taken straight. We need

[4]William B. Furlong, *Shaw and Chesterton: The Metaphysical Jesters* (University Park: The Pennsylvania State University Press, 1970) 187.

[5]Gertrude White, "The Gospel according to G. K. Chesterton," *The Chesterton Review* 14 (May, 1988) 212.

to apply to Chesterton what he advised us to do with Christ: "To begin with, we must protest against a habit of quoting and paraphrasing at the same time. When a man is discussing what Jesus meant, let him state first of all what He said, not what the man thinks He would have said if he had expressed Himself more clearly."[6] To do this with Chesterton, to say what he meant, would involve, I think, simply reading him out loud, a practice I heartily recommend. With great delight I have read to my classes Chesterton's marvelous short essay, "Why I Am Not a Socialist," one of the real gems of social philosophy.[7] In this essay he developed the great theme of liberty and property, of liberality and gift, the idea that creation need not exist, and that is the best part of it. Henry Veatch remarked that we should read Aristotle as if here were a recent modern writer that no one ever heard of before. This same approach is most valid for Chesterton. If we didn't tell anyone, no one would know that his books, except for a quaint reference now and then, were not written yesterday afternoon.

Earlier generations of students, like mine, were told specifically *not* to read Chesterton. This admonition caused some of us to go right out and read him for, we darkly suspected, something was there that we were not being told. At first I thought the neglect of Chesterton was due to the supposed embarrassment of second-rate academics at his lack of what was called erudite scholarship. But now I realize that the real opposition to Chesterton came from those who did not hold the fundamentals of sanity, orthodoxy, and philosophical first principles that he did. They have long since shown their true colors. They knew that Chesterton made impossible the pretense that there were no problems with their own intellectual presuppositions. When we read him now, some ninety years after he began to write, Chesterton seems to have foreseen the direction the spirit of this century was to take.

[6](*)G. K. Chesterton, *Varied Types* (New York: Dodd, Mead, 1908) 141. Notes prefixed with an (*) indicate they are also found in *The Quotable Chesterton*, ed. George Marlin, Richard Rabatin, and John L. Swan (San Francisco: Ignatius Press, 1986).

[7]G. K. Chesterton, "Why I Am Not a Socialist" (originally in *The New Age*, January 4, 1908) *The Chesterton Review* 7 (August, 1981) 189–95.

Lately I have come to realize how central Nietzsche has been to the intellectual structure of modernity. I have been even more surprised that I did not previously notice how often Chesterton treated Nietzsche. He says in *The Common Man*, for example:

> Nietzsche . . . preached a doctrine which he and his followers regard apparently as very revolutionary; he held that ordinary altruistic morality had been the invention of a slave class to prevent the emergence of superior types to fight and rule them. . . . It is calmly and persistently supposed that the great writers of the past, say, Shakespeare for instance, did not hold this view, because they had never imagined it; because it had never come into their heads. Turn up the last act of Shakespeare's *Richard III* and you will find not only all that Nietzsche had to say put into two lines, but you will find it put in the very words of Nietzsche. Richard Crookback says to his nobles: "Conscience is but a word that cowards use, / Devised at first to keep the strong in awe."[8]

Chesterton understood the truth and made it possible to see it in a way almost no one else ever did. We might even say that no one ever put the truth more unforgettably, more uniquely, or, indeed, more happily. Yet Chesterton never claimed that this truth was exclusively his, almost as if to suggest that truth is both utterly unique in itself and utterly meant for everyone. He put Aquinas' concern for revelation on this basis. In order for everyone to have a chance to know the highest things, God has to make them known because time, passion, or the trouble of daily living would not allow most ordinary people in most ages the opportunity to know what God was like and what he wanted of them.

If we love reality, we do not articulate the cosmos in a general formula but rather talk about doors and songs and old trees. For Chesterton the great mystery was not the existence of God but the existence of anything else. The "strangeness" of things that "is the light in all poetry and indeed in all art, is really connected with their otherness; or what is called their

[8](*)G.K. Chesterton, *The Common Man* (New York: Sheed & Ward, 1950) 24.

objectivity."[9] What these things are cannot be found by "staring inwards at the mind."[10] We humans as beings with real bodies have to go out to meet what exists. What existing things are is supposed to become a "part of the mind; nay, according to Aquinas, the mind actually becomes the object."[11] These objects are there even if we do not think about them. But they are also to be thought about because they are not us. The spirituality of Chesterton was delightfully and solidly grounded in matter. He defended the Christian sense of mortification and asceticism but only if that sense did not imply that the physical world was evil. Evil was located in no material thing, only in will.

I sometimes think, however, the most dangerous book Chesterton ever wrote, and it sits like a time bomb over our era of eugenics, genetic engineering, divorce, birth control, working wives, and confused families, is his *What's Wrong with the World*. This is his book on the woman, the child, the man, and the home. Nowhere is Chesterton more right and our age more wrong than on these very topics.[12] The modern feminist ideology has followed nearly exactly the path Chesterton predicted for it. It is almost eerie to read him, which is perhaps why we don't. He noted that feminist ideology would utterly conform to prevailing intellectual egalitarian theory and would neglect real women, their children, and their loves.

James Boswell once described a mutual friend as "a very universal man, quite a man of the world." Johnson replied, "Yes, Sir; but one may be so much a man of the world as to be nothing in the world. I remember a passage in Goldsmith's *Vicar of Wakefield*, which he was afterwards fool enough to expunge: 'I do not love a man who is zealous for nothing.' "[13] What I want to take up is Chesterton's attack, in *St. Thomas*

[9]Chesterton, *St. Thomas Aquinas*, in *Collected Works*, Vol. 2, 541.

[10]Ibid.

[11]Ibid.

[12]See James V. Schall, "On Things Worth Doing Badly," Introduction, *What's Wrong with the World, The Collected Works of G. K. Chesterton*, vol. 4, 1987, 11–30; "The Rarest of All Revolutions: G. K. Chesterton on the Relation of Human Life and Christian Doctrine," *The American Benedictine Review*, 32 (December, 1981) 304–27.

[13]*Boswell's Life of Johnson* (London: Oxford, 1931) II, 283.

Aquinas, on nothingness. This book is the great defense of variety and fruitfulness in things, of the connection of *what is* to its cause in *I Am*.[14] Chesterton understood our mind's capacity to arrive at newness and difference by its capacity to know, a capacity grounded not on internal self-reflection but on its connection with sense and with the stunning reality of doors and rocks, of "eggs is eggs."[15]

St. Thomas, Chesterton observed, was not an Eastern philosopher who really wanted precisely "nothing."

> [St. Thomas] was not a person who wanted nothing; and he was a person who was enormously interested in everything. . . . As compared with many other saints, and many other philosophers, he was avid in his acceptance of Things. . . . It was his special spiritual thesis that there really are things; and not only the Thing; that the Many existed as well as the One. I do not mean things to eat or drink or wear, though he never denied to these their place in the noble hierarchy of Being; but rather things to think about, and especially things to prove, to experience and to know.[16]

Chesterton was conscious of modernity, that is, of the philosophies that were based on doubt. He wrote more than a half century ago, "Most modern philosophies are not philosophy but philosophic doubt; that is, doubt about whether there can be any philosophy."[17] Like St. Thomas, he addressed himself to the original minds of student and teacher to confront them directly with reality, with the shock of what they had been failing to see and how to think about what was there.[18]

Throughout his reflections on Aquinas, Chesterton seems to have had as his target St. Augustine, or better the Augustinians, and through them the moderns who came after and the Platonists who went before. Chesterton saw in Augus-

[14]Chesterton, *St. Thomas Aquinas*, in *Collected Works*, Vol. 2, 494.
[15]Ibid., 515.
[16]Ibid., 505.
[17]Ibid., 543.
[18]See Frederick D. Wilhelmsen, "The Great Books: Enemies of Wisdom," *Modern Age* 31 (Summer/Fall, 1987) 323–31.

tine and the Platonic mind the attempt to bypass the world, to think that reality can be generated from thought. "St. Thomas, for all his love of Greek philosophy, saved us from being Platonists . . . [certain] theologians had somewhat stiffened into a sort of Platonic pride in possession of intangible and untranslatable truths within; as if no part of their wisdom had any root anywhere in the real world."[19] Chesterton put it succinctly. We are to study "facts, not truth."[20] What is in the mind does not come from the mind. There is an avenue into ourselves from what is not ourselves. Aristotle became important not as someone who paganized Christianity but as someone who reinforced Christianity's radical bent to realism. Some critics "vaguely imagine that anybody who is humanising divinity must be paganising divinity; without seeing that the humanising of divinity is actually the strongest and starkest and most incredible dogma in the Creed. . . . St. Thomas was becoming more of an Aristotelian, when he insisted that God and the image of God had come in contact through matter with a material world."[21] Chesterton understood that the defense of matter involved the defense of incarnation, that philosophy was the legitimate enterprise also of the theologian and the common person, not exclusively of the philosopher.

For Chesterton, the great doctrine of creation was what made the difference.

> Granted all the grandeur of Augustine's contributions to Christianity, there was in a sense a more subtle danger in Augustine the Platonist than even in Augustine the Manichee. There came from it a mood which unconsciously committed the heresy of dividing the substance of the Trinity. It thought of God too exclusively as a Spirit who purifies or a Saviour who redeems; and too little as a Creator who creates. That is why men like Aquinas thought it right to correct Plato by an appeal to Aristotle; Aristotle who took things as he found them, just as Aquinas accepted things as God created them.[22]

[19]Chesterton, *St. Thomas Aquinas,* in *Collected Works,* Vol. 2, 428–29.
[20]Ibid., 492.
[21]Ibid., 433.
[22]Ibid., 468.

The defense of ordinary things, begun in revelation by the doctrine of the incarnation, required the earlier doctrine of creation, the doctrine that things are things, "eggs is eggs."

Chesterton understood the central teaching of St. Thomas, his doctrine of *ens* or being.[23] In *St. Thomas Aquinas* he elaborated the argument for being in perhaps the clearest way anyone has ever formulated it, taking pains to talk both to the philosophers and above their heads to ordinary folks. Human action is endowed with such seriousness that whatever one's metaphysics, a person must believe in something that transcends this life. This position presupposes the question of existence and essence, why there is something and not nothing, why this thing is not that thing, the stability of things, Chesterton's "eggs is eggs." "Action follows being," as St. Thomas frequently stated, in Chesterton's translation of *actio sequitur esse*.

I want to continue not with Chesterton's analysis of the existence of God, of essence and existence, but with his treatment of evil. Evil is the principal objection, as St. Thomas indicated, to God's existence. Chesterton affirmed that "the work of *hell* is entirely spiritual."[24] This position about the spiritual nature of evil or hell follows from the basic idea that all *things* are good, even if they are limited, that is, even if this thing is not that thing and will not "become" that thing no matter how long we wait. Not even the most rabid evolutionist, Chesterton pointed out, waits until something good becomes evil.[25] Yet the goodness of things makes our actions full of drama and adventure, because we really can disorder the world with our choices. "Nothing seems more quaint, for instance, than the speculations about what would have happened to every vegetable or animal or angel, if Eve had chosen *not* to eat the fruit of the tree. But this was originally full of the thrill of choice; and the feeling that she might have chosen otherwise."[26]

[23]Ibid., 529.
[24]Ibid., 485.
[25]Ibid., 536.
[26]Ibid., 546.

The question of what divides the human being from God no doubt is a fundamental one. Chesterton insisted on keeping at least one division, that which keeps finite beings finite. This division requires Infinite Being to be precisely infinite. Chesterton wanted to keep people from "being" gods by enabling them to remain themselves. The great doctrine of free will lies ever at the heart both of finiteness and of dignity.

> Nobody would say that [St. Thomas] wanted to divide Man from God; but he did want to distinguish Man from God. In this strong sense of human dignity and liberty there is much that can be and is appreciated now as a noble humanistic liberality. But let us not forget that its upshot was that very Free Will, or moral responsibility of Man, which so many modern liberals would deny. Upon this sublime and perilous liberty hang heaven and hell, and all the myterious drama of the soul. It is distinction and not division; but a man *can* divide himself from God, which, in a certain aspect, is the greatest distinction of all.[27]

For all his worry about St. Augustine, Chesterton in this came down on the side of the Two Cities which are ultimately divided by what we choose.

Chesterton was careful to emphasize that mortification and penance are to be directed to the consequences of the Fall. "[Asceticism] is never a doubt about the good of Creation."[28] Though he is particularly hard on St. Augustine and the Augustinian tradition in his discussion of the Manichean temptation to make matter the cause of evil, Chesterton, as far as I can see, agrees substantially with St. Augustine about the negative reality of evil. Evil is not a thing but something lacking in a spiritual power, in the order of its will.

> That "God looked on all things and saw that they were good" contains a subtlety which the popular pessimist cannot follow, or is too hasty to notice. It is the thesis that there are no bad things, but only bad uses of things. If you will, there are no bad things but only bad thoughts; and especially bad intentions. Only Calvinists can really believe that

[27]Ibid., 435.
[28]Ibid., 484.

> hell is paved with good intentions. That is exactly the one thing it cannot be paved with. But it is possible to have bad intentions about good things; and good things, like the world and the flesh, have been twisted by a bad intention called the devil. But he cannot make *things* bad; they remain as on the first day of creation.[29]

On the first day of creation things were, as Genesis tells us, good.

Chesterton took a surprising amount of time with the idea that no being as such is evil. He saw the fundamental clarification that must be made about the location of evil in an act of the will if we are to proceed with the more important arguments: Why is there something rather than nothing? Why is this thing not that thing? Clearly if a being which is not God is by that fact alone evil, then the only alternative we have is to escape from what is said to cause the evil, namely matter, and to become not ourselves, but God. This conclusion results in the great heretical doctrine that there is nothing but God. Chesterton saw that Aquinas and Aristotle defended God by defending the worthiness of ordinary things. A doubt about the reality of things, even if they are not God, is what Chesterton called the "first treason," the denial of the "first truth." "[St. Thomas] will not deny what he has seen, though it be a secondary and diverse reality."[30]

Like Voegelin and Strauss, Chesterton was quite certain that there was a significant break in philosophy with modernity.[31] He placed the break more or less where they did, with Machiavelli or Descartes, with the immediate reaction to St. Thomas among the nominalists and spiritual Augustinians. "In so far as there was ever a bad break in philosophical history," Chesterton wrote, "it was not before St. Thomas, or at the beginning of medieval history; it was after St. Thomas and at

[29]Ibid., 485.

[30]Ibid., 537.

[31]See Eric Voegelin, *The New Science of Politics* (Chicago: University of Chicago Press, 1953); Leo Strauss, *Natural Right and History* (Chicago: University of Chicago Press, 1952); *City and Man* (Chicago: University of Chicago Press, 1964). See also James V. Schall, *Reason, Revelation and the Foundations of Political Philosophy* (Baton Rouge: Louisiana State University Press, 1987).

the beginning of modern history.''[32] Again with intimations of Nietzsche, Chesterton saw that for the first time in history the modern mind began to doubt the value of life itself. ''Never until modern thought began, did they [Christians] have to fight with men who desired to die. That horror had threatened them in Asiatic Albigensianism, but it never became normal to them—until now.''[33] He wrote, ''Now nobody will begin to understand the Thomist philosophy, or indeed the Catholic philosophy, who does not realise that the primary and fundamental part of it is entirely the praise of Life, the praise of Being, the praise of God as the Creator of the World.''[34]

Unlike Voegelin, who conceived of the transcendent experience as militating against doctrine or dogma, Chesterton argued that the mind was made to know, to discriminate between this position and that. The human mind is not doing what it was made to do if it does not discriminate and make definitions and dogmas. This capacity to define accurately is what saved Christianity from mere religion. ''A real knowledge of mankind will tell anybody that religion is a very terrible thing; that it is truly a raging fire and that authority is often quite as much needed to restrain it as to impose it.''[35] It was dogma not religious enthusiasm that saved the goodness of the body against the Manichees in the beginning. ''It was precisely the creed and dogma that saved the sanity of the world.''[36]

Chesterton thought that the mind is to be used to do what it is supposed to do, that is, to learn from things, to draw conclusions from what it can perceive. This knowledge was based on the nature of the mind itself and of the things it encounters through its senses in the world. ''St. Thomas bothered his head with every hair-splitting distinction and deduction, about the Absolute or the Accident, merely to prevent them [the philosophers and the Muslims] from misunderstanding Aristotle.''[37] For St. Thomas, ''the mind was not lit solely from

[32]Chesterton, *St. Thomas Aquinas*, in *Collected Works*, Vol. 2, 465.
[33]Ibid., 489.
[34]Ibid., 483.
[35]Ibid., 483.
[36]Ibid., 487.
[37]Ibid., 422.

within."[38] Chesterton began with one observation that he recalled even as a child: Grass exists, that is, something exists. A child is already aware of *ens*. "There *is* an Is." This is where we begin. He added, very characteristically, "very few unbelievers start by asking us to believe so little."

What followed from this beginning intuition was the principle of contradiction, that a thing cannot be and not be at the same time. This principle is based not in the mind but in things. It is the great "fact of being." It is implicit in knowing the existence even of one thing not ourselves, even the grass. Truth is a thing of the mind but it refers the mind to *what is*. We have a capacity to know; this is our level of being. We put our mind into act by thinking, by affirming or denying whether what we have in our mind is what is out there. This affirmation or denial, Chesterton said in a remarkably cryptic statement, is the origin of the ultimate "war of the world."[39]

The second principle of facts, of things, is that they change. The lesser forms of being are not nothing but neither are they the "fullness of being." Most thinkers forgot being and took mutability. St. Thomas, however, maintained "that the ordinary thing at any moment is something; but it is not everything it could be."[40] This fact leads to the question of a being that is "everything that it can be." Even when we have found out many things, we are still left with things that change and those, like ideas, that do not. And what changes, changes into something. "Things change because they are not complete; but their reality can only be explained as part of something that is complete. That is God."[41] Things that do not explain themselves lead to that which is itself.

Chesterton saw that the whole modern world, to avoid this conclusion, wrestled with the doctrine that something can come from nothing. This was a position which he simply called "unthinkable." Amusingly, he put it this way: "The world does not explain itself, and cannot do so merely by continu-

[38]Ibid., 525.
[39]Ibid., 529.
[40]Ibid., 531.
[41]Ibid.

ing to expand. But anyhow, it is absurd for the Evolutionist to complain that it is unthinkable for an admittedly unthinkable God to make everything out of nothing, and then pretend that it is *more* thinkable that nothing should turn itself into everything."[42] The whole of the argument both with the Arab Aristotelians and with modern cosmology and science is contained within this brief statement about what it is we can and cannot think.

Chesterton saw the essential problem with all modern philosophy to be, "the notion that because what we can see does not satisfy us or explain itself, it is not even what we see." But we see what we see, "eggs is eggs." St. Thomas rather argued that "the defect we see, in what is, is simply that it is not all that is."[43] God *is*. Here Chesterton saw the significance of the classic Aristotelian-Greek-Arabic argument about the eternity of the world, about the philosophic fact, as St. Thomas saw, that we could not disprove this eternity of the world from reason.

To defend creation, St. Thomas defended Aristotle who did not hold the creation of the world. The eternity of the world may be theoretically possible. But that did not prove it needed no Creator, whom we know about from revelation and can see to be at least possible from reason.

> For what St. Thomas means is not a medieval picture of an old king; but this second step in the great argument about *Ens* or Being. . . . That is why I have introduced it here in the particular form of the argument that there must be a Creator even if there is no Day of Creation. Looking at Being as it is now, as the baby looks at the grass, we see a second thing about it; in quite popular language, it *looks* secondary and dependent. Existence exists; but it is not sufficiently self-existent; and would never become so merely by going on existing. The same primary sense which tells us it is Being, tells us that it is not perfect Being; not merely imperfect in the popular controversial sense of containing sin or sorrow; but imperfect as Being; less actual than the actuality it implies.[44]

[42]Ibid., 534.
[43]Ibid., 531.
[44]Ibid., 533.

The first step is that changeable things really are there, in the way they are, changeable, but there, outside of our minds. The second step is that even if things continue to be themselves, they do not explain themselves. They do not explain why they have particular essences which are not something else. Their changeable condition is a reality whether or not there is evil or sorrow. Something cannot come from nothing, certainly not the "some" things we actually see and know.

This brings us to the third step in Chesterton's presentation, namely, that this change of changeable beings implies a change to something. What is to guarantee that this change is not toward something evil? In effect, what is the inner nature of this Being which simply is and contains the explanation of why something not itself also is? "It is not enough," Chesterton observed, of those who argue that change is the only reality,

> that there is always a beyond; because it might be beyond bearing. Indeed, the only defense of this view is that sheer boredom is such an agony, that any movement is a relief. But the truth is that they have never read St. Thomas, or they would find, with no little terror, that they really agree with him. What they really mean is that change is not mere change; but is the unfolding of something; and if it is thus unfolded, though the unfolding takes twelve million years, it must be there already. In other words, they agree with Aquinas that there is everywhere potentiality that has not reached its end in act. But if it is a definite potentiality, and if it can only end in a definite act, why then there is a Great Being in whom all changes already exist as a plan of action.[45]

The very existence of change, he thought, clear to common sense, was indicative of purpose, indeed of person.

Chesterton noted that Aquinas had been accused of being too "anthropomorphic," while others said he was "too much of an agnostic." Chesterton himself at this very juncture, to prove his own point, remarked, "but we do not need even St. Thomas, we do not need anything but our own common sense, to tell us that if there has been from the beginning

[45]Ibid., 535–36.

anything that can possibly be called a Purpose, it must reside in something that has the essential elements of a Person."[46] And as if he could not resist the vivid, amusing example, he added, "there cannot be an intention hovering in the air all by itself, any more than a memory that nobody remembers or a joke that nobody has made." He argued with modern philosophy, as did St. Thomas, on its own grounds.

Like St. Thomas, Chesterton was willing to grant that an argument should last however long it is necessary to complete it. Also like St. Thomas, he realized that most men and women do not have all the time that philosophers do. He thought, however, that the world, when it was confused, needed not so much a saint as a philosopher.[47] Philosophy itself had been disordered in the modern era. Common folks began to see that "as the eighteenth century thought itself the age of reason, and the nineteenth century thought itself the age of common sense, the twentieth century cannot as yet even manage to think itself anything but the age of uncommon nonsense."[48] That Chesterton would have thought he had to reconsider the remarks he made at the beginning for the end of the twentieth century is philosophically doubtful. This is why he is an abiding presence in our era. He put his finger on the real issue, that of the philosophic disorders of the modern mind. He even understood, as Stanley Jaki has noted, the disorders in science.[49]

Chesterton, with St. Thomas, did not believe that the truths of science and the truths of revelation arrive at different conclusions.[50] But having arrived at the truth of things by two different ways, the fact remains that God did not need particular things, neither individually nor collectively. This truth, when not understood in its glory, often scandalizes because it seems to suggest that there is no purpose for the world or for people in it. In an ultimate sense, this is true, for the

[46]Ibid., 536.

[47]Ibid., 425.

[48]Ibid.

[49]Stanley L. Jaki, *Chesterton: A Seer of Science* (Urbana: University of Illinois Press, 1986).

[50]Chesterton, *St. Thomas Aquinas*, in *Collected Works*, Vol. 2, 474.

purpose of the world is the human being, and the purpose of the human being is God. However, having arrived by the strictest common sense observation and logic at the reality of God, Chesterton added one final truth about what this God might be like, again couched in the difficulties of the theorists of his time, but with a truth that could be followed by anyone:

> Dean Inge, who had been lecturing the orthodox for years on the stern duty of accepting all scientific discoveries, positively wailed aloud over this truly tactless scientific discovery [that the world might have an end]; and practically implored the scientific discoverers to go away and discover something different. It seems almost incredible; but it is a fact that he asked what God would have to amuse Him, if the universe ceased. That is a measure of how much the modern mind needs Thomas Aquinas. But even without Aquinas, I can hardly conceive any educated man, let alone such a learned man, believing in God at all without assuming that God contains in Himself every perfection including eternal joy; and does not require the solar system to entertain him like a circus.[51]

The very fact that God does not "require" anything but his own inner life means that what is not God exists freely, exists because of some reason that is not a determined necessity, not a lack in God (see below, chapter 9). Chesterton saw this truth and that what proceeded out of God would, therefore, be rooted in "eternal joy."

The real "war of the world" which Chesterton saw was in the recognition of real being. Modern social and political ideology has been the result of the removal from being of any order or law not humanly made.[52] In this ideological sense human freedom is dependent on one's freeing oneself from being as such, not in knowing what being is. The liberation of humanity from *what is* has opened the way for the most rigid and dangerous of social forms because nothing in their structure, no natural order, prevents any ideas from being put into place in practical life. Chesterton had already sensed this even-

[51]Ibid., 532.

[52]See James V. Schall, "Human Rights as an Ideological Project," *The American Journal of Jurisprudence* 32 (1987) 47–61.

tuality. "I remember when Mr. H. G. Wells had an alarming fit of Nominalist philosophy," he wrote,

> and poured forth book after book to argue that everything is unique and untypical; as that a man is so much an individual that he is not even a man. It is a quaint and almost comic fact, that this chaotic negation especially attracts those who are always complaining of social chaos, and who propose to replace it by the most sweeping social regulations. It is the very men who say that nothing can be classified, who say that everything must be codified. Thus Mr. Bernard Shaw said that the only golden rule is that there is no golden rule. He prefers an iron rule; as in Russia.[53]

More than half a century after Chesterton wrote these lines practically nothing needs to be changed, except that perhaps for the first time even Russia wonders about its own "golden rule."

Chesterton, in conclusion, saw in St. Thomas the truth that existence is inexpressible. It is simply there, "eggs is eggs." We need to express accurately what it is we know of what we encounter in the world. "Seeing truth must mean the appreciation of being by some mind capable of appreciating it."[54] We must begin and end, Chesterton thought, with "gravel and grass," with very ordinary things. They are classified together as being but classified differently because they are not the same. "All things are; but among the things that are is the thing called difference, quite as much as the thing called similarity. And here again we begin to be bound again to the Lord, not only by the universality of grass, but by the incompatibility of grass and gravel."[55] The world of the Creator lies in the questions of why there is something rather than nothing and of why the grass is not the gravel.

St. Thomas seemed "fairly certain that the difference between chalk and cheese, or pigs and pelicans, is not a mere illusion, or dazzle of our bewildered mind blinded by a single light; but is pretty much what we all feel it to be."[56] The ges-

[53]Chesterton, *St. Thomas Aquinas*, in *Collected Works*, Vol. 2, 535.
[54]Ibid., 529.
[55]Ibid., 538.

ture, the old song, the portrait, the piano, the old door, the grass, the eggs, the pigs, the chalk, the pelicans, and the cheese, these are the things that exist and from which we begin to know the delight of existence. From these ordinary things, we wonder about the nature of that fullness of being which explains why "eggs is eggs" and pelicans are not pigs, why something, any particular thing, is so much more interesting than nothing. We wonder why the fact of something, of the gravel and the grass, the chalk and the cheese, requires us to argue to the reason why they are at all, to why gravel is not grass and why chalk is not cheese.

This argument about the cause and nature of the wonderful things we find about in our world, this argument which, if it be a good one, may indeed take forever, as Chesterton suspected, leads not to nothing but to *what is*, to *I Am*, to the God who "contains in Himself every perfection including eternal joy." This God does not need the creatures who know and choose to "entertain Him like a circus." But God does want human creatures to know and to love also what is not themselves, the grass and the gravel, the old doors and the gestures, and, yes, even the very Godhead in its full Trinitarian reality.

[56]Ibid., 436.

Chapter VIII

Unknown to the Ancients: God and Friendship

The love of God is the end of our prayer, just as the delight of God stands at the origins of our own joy. God does not lack anything. Yet from ancient philosophy we have received the suspicion that something was given to us which is lacking in God, namely friendship. We shall see more of this topic of the fullness of God in the following chapter. First let us take a look at this perplexing question of whether the relationship of man and God can be designated, as in the Gospel of John, as a friendship. Is this where the "inexpressible value of existence" finds the words and the Word by which all things come forth and return to the cause of our existence, to God?

Three passages, one from Boethius, one from Cicero, and one from Dante, serve to introduce this topic. Each passage reveals something about the relation of human to divine existence, which is what we want, above all, to designate as friendship. (This effort assumes that friendship does exist among human beings and can be understood in its essence.) Aristotle had argued that there could be no friendship between God and the human being because the distance between them in the order of being was too great. If there is any objection to Aristotle, it cannot be that he was wrong on his own principle.

The following are the particular considerations with which I want to begin:

1) "Let us examine, so far as we lawfully may, the character of the divine nature. . . . The common opinion . . . is that God is eternal. Let us, therefore, consider what is eternity. . . . Eternity is the simultaneous and complete possession of infinite life." (Boethius [d. 525 A.D.], *De Consolatione Philosophiae*, V, 115.)

2) "Friendship may be defined as a complete identity of feeling about all things in heaven and earth: an identity which is strengthened by mutual good will and affection. With the single exception of wisdom, I am inclined to regard it as the greatest of all the gifts the gods have bestowed on mankind." (Cicero [d. 43 B.C.], *De Amicitia*, V, 19.)

3) "The proper work of the human race, taken as a whole, is to actualize at all times the entire potentiality of the possible intellect, primarily for speculation, and secondarily—by extension and for the sake of the other—for action." (Dante [d. 1321 A.D.], *De Monarchia*, I, 4.)

The first passage, from Boethius, suggests that the possession of infinite life ought to be eternal. What we want of the deepest things is for them not to end. Such eternity seems impossible for mortals, so that we have often been tempted to look on the very desire as erroneous or even dangerous. From this viewpoint, all theories of brotherhood or comradeship or love which postulate a finite alternative to eternity are less than what human beings actually want.

The second observation from Cicero identifies the centrality of friendship as the greatest of the gifts of the gods to humankind. Wisdom and friendship are seen to be related in that the exchange of truth and wisdom is what friendship is about.

In the third selection Dante affirmed that all the potentialities are already in each human being. He recognized that our inner life is to result in a world reflective of that very life, both as understood and as lived in private and public life. Without identifying the divine with the human world, without denying any presence of God in the world, Dante postulated an inner-worldly history that is to be reflective of the divine order.

1. *The Unanswered Questions Posed by Friendship*

Friendship leads us to the highest things, to the question of what God is like in dealing with us. To discuss this question, no doubt, is one of the fundamental purposes of civilization, of the city itself, as Aristotle taught us (1324b24–1338a12). Reflective converse about the highest things can only safely take place among friends, among those who can with Plato be ''always in love with that learning which discloses to them something of the being that *is* always'' (485b). Ever since Socrates we know that there is a fundamental problem about the safety of the philosopher in the city, as there is a problem about the well-being of the city against the wandering philosopher. The ''private life'' which Socrates as a philosopher chose to lead in Athens could not ultimately keep philosophy merely as a private topic among friends (29e–32a). The public began to take notice of what he taught and how it effected the city. But what friends have to discuss with one another is not exhausted by the city and its life. Even for the good of the polity the institutions of friendship cannot be themselves solely tools of the polity.

The question of friendship leads us both to transcendence, to what God is like, and to civilization, to what we are like, to the life that surpasses the city as well as to the life of the city. Friendship leads to the contemplation and action that mirror in the city itself our conception of what is higher than the city. It leads to our belief that all things are bound together somehow, so that friendship becomes likewise the focus of *what is*. But friendship can do this because it is one of the highest things, even though it is also, as Aristotle taught, one of the things that we must seemingly deny to God (1159a5-6). Friendship describes at its heart a mutual relationship, a delight, though it includes all of life, even its sadness. This all-inclusiveness is possible because friends themselves are rightly ordered to being, to *what is*. Friends do not ''create'' themselves or the world they live in but rather choose to live in the one that exists. Ultimately friendships depend on whether our philosophies permit us to reach a reality which is not merely ourselves. Friendship presumes rather than deplores the variety and multiplicity of *what is*, particularly the human reality.

The exclusivity of friendship does imply the "all things in common" of Plato but in a very different manner from that proposed in *The Republic* (449c).

Paradoxically friendship rejoices in the fact that our friends must be few in order that in any meaningful sense we have them at all. This particularity means that it is all right for us to be ourselves and not someone else. Yet our infinite variety and mysteriousness are redeemed because we can know and delight in the order of reality we did not ourselves make and know that we did not make. The order of friendship is an order we suspect to be directed, as our friends are, to our own particular and ultimate good. Dante's concern that all our potentiality be actualized is, at its deepest levels, dependent on the quality of our friendships. Our friends are, as Cicero said, "other selves." But they absolutely are not ourselves. This radical otherness constitutes the wonderment of friendship in its essential understanding, an understanding that takes us to the highest things, to the suspicion that friendship, despite Aristotle's reservation, lies somehow at the heart of the divinity itself.[1]

We often talk of "making new friends." This is precisely what we do not do. We discover others already "there," already "made," as it were, not products of our own fashioning, even though we influence our friends and they us. But this "influence" or "love" we bear to our friends ought to make them more what they are, not more what we are or want them to be. Friends are in the nature of gifts, not artifacts. Friends are the highest realization of the notion that to us all things are gifts. The concept of gift, the *donum*, stands close to the essence of the highest things.

In an essay he wrote in 1910, called "What's Right With the World?", G. K. Chesterton remarked:

> There has crept into our thought . . . the idea that unity is itself a good thing; that there is something high and spiritual about things being blended and absorbed into each other. . . . Now, union in itself is not a noble thing. Love

[1]See James V. Schall, *Redeeming the Time* (New York: Sheed & Ward, 1968), 216–24.

> is a noble thing; but love is not union. Nay, it is rather a vivid sense of separation and identity. When Dante meets Beatrice, he feels his distance from her, not her proximity. . . . And what is true of these grave and heroic matters . . . is equally true of all the lighter and less essential forces of appreciation, of surprise. Division and variety are what is right about the world.[2]

Without this sensitivity to and surprise at the grounded, irreducible otherness of things, neither friendship, God, nor polity would have any real meaning among us.

What is at stake in the metaphysics of gift and surprise is the validity of our individual uniqueness and its interiority. In the ontology of knowledge and friendship, this absolute otherness we experience need not remain alien to us, even though it remains in its origins *not* us. We are potentially richer than we actually are, but only if we grant the reality of what is not ourselves. How we stand to what is not ourselves depends upon our interiority and that of others. And in the case of other human beings, knowing or loving them depends also on their freedom. Even though the world is given to us, we still must choose it. In this choice we reveal to our friends whether we are ultimately loveable or not.

By our knowledge, we know about the realities which are not ourselves. We do not know ourselves directly. Our knowledge of ourselves results from a gift, from what is not ourselves. We know ourselves in first knowing something else. What we can know, as Aquinas pointed out, following Aristotle, is any existing thing other than ourselves (*ST* I, 85, 1). Even God's existence we know only if we begin here, with knowing some particular thing which exists but which is not itself God.

We human beings must begin our knowledge with something containing matter, even though we do not necessarily know only things in this state. For we can know about *anything that is,* at least whether it is, as Aquinas said, even in the case of Being itself (*ST* I, 2, 1–8). The fact that we ourselves

[2]G. K. Chesterton, "What's Right With the World?", *A Chesterton Anthology,* selected and with an introduction by P. J. Kavanagh (San Francisco: Ignatius Press, 1985) 346.

are particular and limited in our being does not prevent us from being open to all that is not ourselves, even perhaps to transcendent being. We experience both particularity and universality in our very structure. The soul through intelligence is thus *capax omnium* (capable of all things), capable of knowing *all that is* (429a19). But what is the purpose of this contrasting sense of limitlessness and limitedness that we seem to find present in our very being, not only in our willed evils, but, even more mysteriously, in the highest reaches of our experiences of the good and the beautiful, as Plato called them (505a)? Why is joy so much more mysterious than sadness?

Let us pay some further attention to the question of friendship, that extraordinary topic which Aristotle in his *Ethics* felt worthy of spending more time on than any other topic except, perhaps, as Cicero put it, "wisdom" itself, the contemplation of *that which is*. After many years of teaching the classical authors to generations of students here and abroad, I am always struck by the power which these passages on friendship from Aristotle carry, by the always unexpected impact they continue to make in the twentieth century on those who would be free enough to confront them. Friendship for Aristotle turned out to be the highest bond of the polity, of civilization, far more important than justice, the highest of the moral virtues (1159b25–1160a30).

Friendship, as the classical writers saw, touches upon all ultimate issues. As St. Augustine remarked, "friendship" applies even to the naked strength of that "band of thieves" that composed the governing classes of most existing states in history, without which they could not retain their power (*De Civitate Dei*, IV, 4). Friendship, however many its corruptions, betrayals, varieties, and paradoxes, remains the most fascinating subject of our own reflection and experience. So much attention do we pay to friendship that we wonder if it is more than "natural," if indeed friendship is not somehow like God himself.

The most beautiful tract on friendship in our literature, alongside those of Aristotle and Cicero, is that from the Last Supper, wherein Christ said to the apostles, "I no longer call you servants, but I have called you friends" (John 13:20; 15:15).

What is remarkable about this incident, from our point of view, is the reason Jesus gave for this new denomination, namely, "because I have made known to you everything I have learned from my Father." Such a passage is uncannily related to the observation in Aristotle that such a communication of a human being with God was impossible. Yet, there is the claim of Jesus.

Such a passage in Scripture intellectually forces us back to Aristotle and reinforces Cicero's contention that friendship at its most exalted levels consists in the free, mutual exchange of the highest things. Friendship cannot be apart from truth and the order of *what is*. Nonetheless, this conversation on friendship took place on the eve of Christ's subsequent execution at the hands of the state. The very context of the discourse raises the question of the permanence of friendship. Also it indicates that friendship exists in part in conversation.

With this reminder of the death of Christ, we cannot but recall the scene in the *Phaedo* when Xantippe, hearing that the ship from Delos determining Socrates' day of death had been sighted returning to Athens, spoke eloquently. Plato put it this way: "So we went in, and found Socrates just released, and Xantippe, with his little boy, sitting beside him. Then when Xantippe saw us, she cried out in lamentation and said, as women do, 'Oh, Socrates. Here is the last time your friends will speak to you and you to them.'"

We can wonder if Xantippe, his wife, considered herself also to be Socrates' friend, or whether the mere fact she was sitting quietly beside her husband with their little boy revealed yet another sort of friendship. Was this a reminder that friendship varies not merely on its basis of utility, pleasure, or the good, but also on the relationship of the kind of persons involved.[3] Christian marriage took up and deepened this implied theme, which Aristotle also hinted at, that marriage involves a friendship between the partners and with God. The very result of the sacrament was to be a friendship in the unique relationships of a family, but likewise a relationship in the highest things, in the things of truth and of God.

[3]See James V. Schall, "The Totality of Society: From Justice to Friendship," *The Thomist*, 20 (January, 1967) 1–26.

Aristotle remarked that husband and wife, if they were of great virtue, could be friends in the exchange of the highest things (1162a15–28). Marriage is thus a school for the virtues. Probably it is with reference to this passage in Aristotle that Raissa Maritain called her book, as we have seen (chapter 3), *We Have Been Friends Together*.[4] Xantippe, for her part, saw more clearly than the others that the philosopher's last day should be spent discoursing with his friends about ultimate things, in this case, about the immortality of the soul (61b ff.). For it was this astonishing argument which enabled Socrates to face his own death calmly.

Socrates had said in *The Apology* that philosophy was nothing else but a preparation for death, which was itself by no means to be considered the worst kind of evil (27d ff.). Death was not worse than choosing to stay alive at any cost. The converse doctrine subsequently served in Hobbes to ground modern political philosophy in its characteristic principle that the continuation of life at any cost is the highest good.[5]

Discourse on the highest things, on death and immortality, on friendship and truth, stands at the heart of our intellectual tradition.This is what we do when we have done all else. The poignancy of our friendships is linked to this discourse; our civil polity, at its best, is designed to record in human time what we conclude about these experiences. In the *Crito,* Socrates did not escape from prison because of the plea that he would be more useful to his friends and family if he stayed alive (45d ff.). He taught thereby that friendship follows virtue, and that what virtue is, though we have to put it into our own reality, is discovered, not made, by us.

In the tenth book of *The Republic,* Socrates observed that "none of the human things are worthy of great seriousness" (604a ff.). This remark set the stage for a long controversy between philosophy and civilization. This controversy erupted again in modern times when Machiavelli insisted that we

[4]Raissa Maritain, *We Have Been Friends Together,* trans. J. Kernan (New York: Longmans, 1942).

[5]See Leo Strauss, *The Political Philosophy of Hobbes,* trans. E. M. Sinclair (Chicago: University of Chicago Press, 1962).

should not consider those same higher concerns to be the most serious realities. He urged us rather to "lower our sights," so that we would not be distracted by transcendental questions from the political life. Since Machiavelli had already rejected philosophy, he wanted us to consider only political life, not the things that could not be otherwise (*Prince,* ch. 15).

But Plato could not take human civility that seriously either. Because Socrates, the philosopher, was killed by the best of existing cities, the only city wherein he seemed safe to discourse about the highest things without interruption or risk was in that city to be built in speech (592a-b). And even in this best city, the philosopher arrived at the same issue of immortality which the real Socrates met on his last day—as if to say that this question does not arise only in the face of death and tragedy but lies in the very core of the experience of contemplation and joy, in the communication to one another of the highest things, which is the proper act of friendship (608d).

Aristotle told us, in almost the very words Machiavelli later intended to reject, that we should not listen to those who "advise us, being men, to think of human things, and being mortal, of mortal things, but [we] must, so far as we can, make ourselves immortal, and strain every nerve to live in accordance with the best thing in us; for even if small in bulk, much more does it in power surpass everything" (1177b32–1178a2). Such a passage, so familiar to those who love Aristotle, has had in the history of thought an unexpected consequence. For many thinkers have chosen to look upon it as anti-human, as if somehow the higher realities in their very existence might imply a kind of reduction of the person's intrinsic worth. But Aristotle had said that politics would be the highest science only if we were the highest being, which we are not (1141b1–2). Friendship based on a view that accepts our given reality, in which we are not the highest being, is considerably different from friendship based on the view that we are the highest being and thus that there is no transcendental opposition to us. The stake of God in this controversy seems clear.

In the sixth book of *The Republic* we find this passage:

> For pretty speech is . . . most opposite to a soul that is always going to reach out for the whole and for everything

> divine and human. . . . To an understanding endowed with magnificence and contemplation of all time and all being, do you think it possible that human life seem anything great? "Impossible," he [Glaucon] said (496a).

Again we have both Plato and Aristotle, the classical representatives of the philosophic tradition, telling us that human life as such, the life of the mortal as mortal, the life Aristotle defined as the properly political life, cannot be all that great (1178a8–b8).

This view clarifies for us how to perceive the greatness we have. Ours is a limited greatness. It is a greatness the revelational tradition will paradoxically ground in humility.[6] For we are not the beings who constitute reality as such but the beings who, being already constituted human from nature, as Aristotle noted, receive what exists as good, though not made by ourselves (1258a21–23). We can receive freely and properly what we can also reject. We must not only understand what we are but also choose to be that (1152a32–35). Choice follows understanding. The true drama of history and civilization consists in seeing how men and women choose for or against their status in reality. In the revelational tradition, this choice will be the very foundation of their being offered an end higher than that anticipated by the philosophers.

If we see the history of modern philosophy as developing from Occam to Descartes to Nietzsche under an effort to make us great because we are the sole cause of ourselves—the mortal thinking only mortal things—our greatness becomes much less than the one the classics had in mind. When Plato suggested that human life lacked greatness, he intended to imply not that human life was unworthy in itself, but that something else actually was more worthy. The dignity or glory of human beings was to be grounded in their very "unseriousness," in their openness to the higher realities. This is why in *The Laws* we find the human being described again as something not serious, as the "puppet" or the "plaything" of God. We simply exist, but God is not dependent upon our existence

[6]See Ernest Cassirer, "The Crisis of Man's Knowledge of Himself," *An Essay on Man* (Garden City, N.Y.: Doubleday Anchor, 1944) 15–40.

(644d; 803c–e).[7] Human dependency will be the basis, furthermore, of Aquinas' revolutionary doctrine that the world is created not in justice, the political virtue, but in mercy (*ST* I, 21, 4; 65, 2).

Already here we have a hint of what will be the fullness of the revelational tradition, a hint of what will make writers like St. Augustine, as we shall see, look more deeply into Plato's theme that our relation to God and God's to us on both sides is rooted in freedom, not necessity (*De Civitate Dei*, VIII, 11). Since we need not be, in no other possible universe could our existence be more dubious and precarious. Yet in no other universe could our existence, at the same time and for the same reason, be more exalted. Even though we need not be, we nonetheless exist as we are. We are the mortal, the finite, the intelligent being in the physical universe, the being that gives the universe its final inner meaning because we can first receive, know, and then articulate meaning—"grace upon grace," as it says in the Prologue to John (1:16).[8] All of the metaphysics for a theory of real transcendence and hence real friendship lies here. Civilizations are distinguished ultimately by whether they structure themselves to allow such a view of the world to be operative in their midst.[9] Philosophy and civilization depend on each other and both depend on political philosophy, on whether something other than "man for himself" is allowed to enter our ken.[10]

2. *Intellectuals and Unanswered Questions*

In a letter dated June 1, 1956, Flannery O'Connor, speaking of her friends Robert and Sally Fitzgerald, wrote: "Mrs.

[7]See James V. Schall, *Far Too Easily Pleased: A Theology of Contemplation, Play, and Festivity* (Los Angeles: Benziger-Macmillan, 1976).

[8]See John H. Wright, "The Bible and the Hermeneutical Horizon," *Theological Studies* 43 (December, 1982) 651–72; Stanley Jaki, *Cosmos and Creator* (Edinburgh: Scottish Academic Press, 1980).

[9]See, in this connection, the discussion of Lord Bauer on the differing modes of civilization resulting from their ideas about reality with regard to development, P. T. Bauer, *Reality and Rhetoric: Studies in the Economics of Development* (Cambridge: Harvard, 1984).

[10]See Leo Strauss, *City and Man* (Chicago: University of Chicago Press, 1964).

Fitzgerald is 5 feet 2 inches tall and weighs almost 92 pounds except when she is pregnant, which is most of the time. They have been married nine years and expect their seventh child next week. She says she is gliding around as usual 'like Moby Dick.' Her face is extremely angular . . . though attractive, and she does have the pulled back hair and bun. Robert was brought up a Catholic but left the Catholic Church when he was about eighteen to become an intellectual.''[11] O'Connor saw that reason and faith are for many people, especially intellectuals, incompatible. Apparently, if someone wants to belong to this elite group we call the intelligentsia, he must opt for philosophy against faith. This alternative is not the classic view of Thomas Aquinas, which would rather argue that faith perfects reason in its own order. Reason and faith cannot be contradictory in theory and are not contradictory in any particular instance. ''*Jus autem divinum, quod est gratia,*'' St. Thomas held, ''*non tolit jus humanum, quod est ex naturali ratione.*'' (''Divine right order, which is grace, does not take away human right order which is from natural reason'' [*ST* II–II, 10, 10].) On the philosophic basis of openness to any reality, from whatever source, the positions and arguments of revelation should be factors in reasoning. They should be considered as possible responses to questions arising from experience and reason.[12] Are we not unsettled by the unanswered questions legitimately arising from philosophy, especially friendship?

In these considerations on God and friendship something more about philosophically unanswered questions can be said, if said carefully. I do not think the evidence which lies in the order of both practice and contemplation yields mere insolvability. Rather, in Newman's sense, something more persuasive, more curious, yes, more mysterious, seems to be involved. Transcendence is not by our own powers wholly open

[11]Flannery O'Connor, *The Habit of Being,* ed. Sally Fitzgerald (New York: Viking, 1979) 171.

[12]See Ralph McInerny, *St. Thomas Aquinas* (Notre Dame: University of Notre Dame Press, 1977); Etienne Gilson, *Reason and Revelation in the Middle Ages* (New York: Charles Scribner's, 1938); James V. Schall, *Reason, Revelation, and the Foundations of Political Philosophy* (Baton Rouge: Louisiana State University Press, 1987).

to our reason. Let us return to Aristotle's discussion on friendship in *The Ethics*. Friendship requires of its essence agreement on the truth of the highest things. We cannot get at the core of friendship unless we recall that friendship itself, what Aristotle called true friendship, must be first based on a right order of each of the friends to *what is*. "Perfect friendship is the friendship of men who are good, and alike in virtue; for these wish well alike to each other *qua* good, and they are good in themselves" (1156b7–9). Friendship is destroyed if it does not seek to live in the world itself, a world which is received, not made, by the friends. The mutual standing of friends to one another presupposes and fosters their orientation to transcendence, to God.

I want to approach Aristotle through one of my favorite cartoons, Mel Lazarus' *Miss Peach*. In one series, Francine says, rather haughtily, to Arthur in their kindergarten class, "A person has to have at least one friend." Arthur replies philosophically, "Naturally. You need someone to confide in." Francine continues, "Arthur, you're good friends with Walter, aren't you?" Arthur answers proudly, "Oh, yes, we're the best of friends in the world." "How long have you known him?" "Ever since we were born we've been very, very extremely close," Arthur informs her. Francine adds curiously, "I've always wondered—has he any brothers or sisters?" At this question, however, Arthur becomes extremely agitated and snaps, "How should I know?" Francine objects, "But you're best friends." Arthur then yells, "So what? That doesn't give me the right to pry into his personal life!" Francine persists, "Well, do his parents ever mention any?" Arthur self-righteously responds, "I don't speak to adults unless spoken to—and they have never spoken to me." Francine, perplexed at this turn of the argument, inquires, "But you've been in his house a jillion times—have you ever seen any?" Arthur screams at her, "I don't go sneaking around opening doors! You know, being a person's friend doesn't give one the right to unlock his secret heart, you know!" And finally, to a thoroughly deflated Francine, who only wanted to know of Walter's brothers and sisters, Arthur solemnly walks away, reflecting out loud,

"Even if *you* don't, I believe in the sanctity of the human soul."[13]

In this amusing account are many of the elements that lead us to re-propose those inquiries and ironies that arise naturally and necessarily from our experience of friendship. The operative principle is that the positions of revelation will not, by themselves, seem like anything more than pious talk unless they are directed to our active intelligence. We already should have formulated certain basic questions because of the experience of human living, questions to which we have found no fully proper and satisfactory response. Aquinas, for his part, realized that the human intelligence, even at its best, would be prone to go off in a thousand different directions on any topic, especially on the highest issues (*ST* I–II, 91, 4). To any possible question many plausible answers might be proposed, together with an infinite number of implausible ones. The time we have been given to pursue them all seems very brief. If we are to know something about the most essential questions, a case can be made at least that we need some direction. But the direction must arise within our freedom.

Our natural tendency to find an infinite plurality of solutions to the highest questions is why our public and university orders are, in appearance, congeries of tentative and alternative views of humanity and the world. I would not totally exclude modern universities from the contemplative order wherein truth is sought for its own sake. Yet I do not think that they are the main centers of the search for transcendence and meaning. The surprising persistence of religion—surprising in terms of the Enlightenment theory that progress causes its eventual demise—is surely related to this abiding confusion in the order of philosophy, a confusion or perplexity, as I mentioned, that Aquinas emphasized in his arguments about the need for revelation (*ST* I–II, 91, 4; II–II, 22, 1, ad 1). I think this higher pursuit can go on, will go on, is going on, even in the most dire circumstances. But in a relatively free or open society the institutions of friendship, as well as those of worship, will be the ultimate guarantees of our concern for God.

[13]Mel Lazarus, *Miss Peach*, (New York: Grosset & Dunlop, 1972).

Aristotle, in his devastating analysis of the successful tyrant, perceived that even in the political order friendships are a threat to tyranny. The tyrant must do everything possible to assure the general equality of everyone. He must be sure everything is absolutely open to him. He must abolish all institutions in which something which the tyrant does not know can occur.

> [The tyrant] must put to death men of spirit; he must not allow common meals, clubs, education, and the like; he must be upon his guard against anything which is likely to inspire either courage or confidence among his subjects; he must prohibit literary assemblies or other meetings for discussion and he must take every means to prevent people from knowing one another (for acquaintance begets mutual confidence).
>
> Further, he must compel all persons staying in the city to appear in public and live at his gates. . . . A tyrant should also endeavor to know what each of his subjects says or does. . . . Another art of the tyrant is to sow quarrels among the citizens; friends should be embroiled with friends. . . . And whereas the power of a king is preserved by his friends, the characteristic of a tyrant is to distrust his friends, because he knows that all men want to overthrow him, and they above all have the power (1313b1–30).

We see that the humor of Arthur and Francine's discourse on friendship and privacy has philosophical overtones.

Friendship is not friendship if it knows nothing of the friend's particular life, how many brothers or sisters one has. It is likewise, as Rousseau seems to have realized, a personal, private thing in need of protection from the tyrannical state or prying opinion which would corrupt it (*Social Contract* I, 6; II, 7). Friendship relates to polity both as a threat to it, whether for good or evil, and as a question of order and priority. Polities are designed to outlive the individuals composing them, but polities and civilizations do not themselves fall into the order of substance or being.[14] Strictly speaking, we can only

[14]See J. M. Bochenski, *Philosophy—An Introduction* (New York: Harper Torchbooks, 1972) 93–101; James V. Schall, "The Reality of Society according to St. Thomas," *The Politics of Heaven and Hell: Christian Themes from Classical,*

be friends with one another, with beings in the order of rational substance. We cannot be friends with a polity. Issues of friendship and intelligence thus transcend any civil order.

What are these issues? In Dostoevsky's novel, *The Idiot*, dedicated to the Pauline theme of wisdom and foolishness (1 Cor 1:18), to the possibility of any true Christian being able to live in the actual world and remain uncorrupted, the question is asked, "Why is it that we can never know everything about another person?"[15] It is a perplexing question. The Christian answer would hold that our incomplete knowledge prevents our full domination of another. Finite limits can restrict power and preserve some range of freedom. Any effort to know another person can be corrupted by original sin into efforts to own that person. Sidney Hook, in almost the opposite sense, remarked that some things about another person we would just as soon not know—if he or she betrayed friends or country, for example.[16] The fact that we cannot know everything about another person testifies to our finiteness, itself a good, and to the possibility of our being what we are. Yet the essence of the love of friendship seems to be that we want to know everything about another person, even the faults if the world be constructed in mercy. Our incapacity to know all about our friends seems to imply an ultimate irrationality in the world.

This conclusion leads us either to a kind of despair about the highest things or to the suspicion that each person is made for something more than what is constituted by human communication of whatever kind, however noble it may be. This latter view implies a certain grounding of each person's existence in a higher transcendence. Existential incompleteness argues not to nothingness but to an actual completeness, which has caused what is naturally incomplete (*ST* I, 2, 3, ad 3). This tension between the incomplete and its transcendent origin is

Medieval, and Modern Political Philosophy (Lanham, Md.: University Press of America, 1984) 235–52; Henry Veatch, *Human Rights: Fact or Fancy?* (Baton Rouge: Louisiana State University Press, 1985) 124–30.

[15]Fyodor Dostoevsky, *The Idiot* (Baltimore: Penguin, 1955) 627.

[16]Sidney Hook, "On Western Freedom," in *Solzhenitsyn at Harvard* (Washington: Ethics and Public Policy Center, 1980) 97.

what in principle guarantees human dignity and, ultimately, the non-manipulative nature or status of our unique personhood.

But although the great Russian novelist may legitimately wonder why it is that we can never know everything about another person, the revelational tradition, addressing itself curiously to this same problem, has held that we are known in our fullness but only by God. This knowing is not a threat to us but a completion of what we are. What is surprising, even startling, about Dostoevsky's question is not its apparent hopelessness but its manifestation of an unsuspected truth about ourselves, namely, that at some level we do want to be fully known. The splendid isolation of knowing only ourselves becomes an ultimate rejection of reality. Indeed, the classical definitions of hell have to do with the possibility of doing exactly and completely our own will.[17]

In the beautiful Psalm 139 we read (vv. 1–3):

> Lord, thou has examined me and knowest me.
> Thou knowest all, whether I sit down or rise up;
> And hast discerned my thoughts from afar.
> Thou hast traced my journey and my resting places,
> and art familiar with all my paths. (New English Bible)

This passage, when addressed to the philosophic tradition, should incite our wonder about what kind of a being might fully know us, who would obviate the justifiable fears we might have for our privacy and our autonomy.

Such words from the psalmist, I think, should be read with a vivid appreciation of the poignancy latent in Dostoevsky's question. For it implies that we are wholly known to another person, a transcendent one. This line of thought allows us to return to the world of human friendships with a new perspective. The most perplexing thing about our friendships is their impermanence when their very essence requires

[17]See James V. Schall, "On the Neglect of Hell in Political Theory," *The Politics of Heaven and Hell*, 83–106; "On the Evil and the Responsibility for Suffering," *Another Sort of Learning* (San Francisco: Ignatius Press, 1988) 112–25.

lastingness. The failure to be wholly known by another finite person, because of limitations of both time and fidelity, which are reflections of actual experience, cannot be understood without at the same time at least wondering about our desire to be fully known. This desire includes the realization that if we are to be fully known, even by a divine person, we have to choose to be known, just as we choose to let our human friends know us.

Yet this question of Dostoevsky has its darker side. For it was he too, in *The Brothers Karamazov,* who remarked that if God does not exist, all things are possible. St. Paul had said that to those who love God, all things work together unto the good—even sin, St. Augustine added (Rom 8:28). But, as Dostoevsky may have been prophetically aware, the credibility of God would, for many, be most challenged by the "possible" things that in fact came to exist among us. These dire things came to be on a much more drastic scale than even Aristotle pictured in his worst tyrant, even though this same tyrant claimed the need to know everything about his subjects. Friendship, our desire to be fully known by someone else who loves us, can, in the order of a perverse polity, lead with ironic logic to a tyranny in which we are fully known only by those who hate us. We cannot escape the reaches of good and evil that would define, in St. Augustine's terms, which city we finally choose to be our own.

That there are things about ourselves or others that we do not want to know suggests the need of some way to account for our chosen evils—there are, strictly speaking, no other kinds but chosen ones. But it also requires some realization that the laws of existing polities, as Plato saw in book ten of *The Republic,* do not punish or reward adequately all that goes on among actual human beings, either their evil or their good deeds. Actual justice, which reveals justice to be a terrible virtue, forces us to insist that a final resolution of actual justices with rewards and injustices with punishment must take place, if not in the city, then at least in what transcends it. This incompleteness in the history of actual justice and injustice was the political reason, as Hannah Arendt pointed out, that the doctrines of immortality and hell were posited in the first place, why they continue to have a political function.[18] We can argue that the doctrine of hell in our century and civilization has been replaced by a pseudo-political doctrine of a substitute hell—the Gulags, terrorists, abortion clinics, concentration camps. The concentration camps were theoretically justifiable because they purported to remove and punish the causes of injustice in a world wherein no transcendence over history limited what was possible, what could be done. What is perhaps the distinguishing mark of the twentieth century, in which perhaps one hundred million people, not counting the pre-born, have been eliminated for ideological purposes, has been the utter logic of our political substitutes for an eternal hell.[19] The political-ideological systems which compiled this record in the twentieth century were, ultimately, the premises of intellectuals.[20] The executors who perpetrated these things were not madmen, but thinkers and doers, out to improve the world by destroying what they could define as evil and therefore as punishable. The ultimate wars remain and are fought in the obscure cells of our minds.

In the modern projects which took upon themselves the responsibility for all reality and placed it exclusively under human control, evil had to be relocated in the world.[21] Determined ideologues were sure justice was somehow violated and its cause easily located. They were right in this assumption that much evil existed. But they forgot St. Augustine's admonition that evil is to be located in the will, not in ontological being. They were sure that retribution was a moral demand. They decided, finally, that they were the only ones left to correct what had gone wrong. Hence, modern ideology testifies to the power and the temptation to reorder the world, to humanity's inability to rest content with what appears to be disordered. A new human inner-worldly order is conceived to replace a

[18]Hannah Arendt, *Between Past and Future* (New York: Viking, 1968) 133-34.

[19]See Schall, "On the Neglect of Hell in Political Theory," *The Politics of Heaven and Hell*, 83–106.

[20]Paul Johnson, *Modern Times* (New York: Harper Colophon, 1985) 729-30. See also Paul Johnson, *The Intellectuals* (New York: Harper & Row, 1988).

[21]See Eric Voegelin, *Science, Politics, and Gnosticism* (Chicago: Regnery, 1968).

transcendental order that does not yield its full intelligibility or rationale in this world, or at least does not yield it in strictly human terms. Eric Voegelin was perceptively right to locate the real source of this modern disorder in the loss of faith of believers themselves. This loss of faith allowed intellectuals to seek the solution to transcendental problems in the political movements of this world rather than in that faith wherein ultimate questions are properly located.[22]

The elimination of large classes or groups of humanity had its intellectual origins not so much in Aristotle's self-centered tyrant as in the desire to create a perfect world. This effort led, as a positive, political project, to the need to identify and eliminate what was conceived to be the cause of the evils which admittedly abound. This is why, almost invariably, the greatest killers of our time have been intellectuals, not mere autocrats or tyrants. This is also why the simple identification of tyrants or autocrats with totalitarian rulers is so dangerous, as it confuses the lesser error of tyrants with the much greater one of totalitarian rulers. In a kind of grizzly manner, however, this extreme solution of the ideological pursuit of justice attests to the abiding power of justice as an ideology and to the human impulse to reflect justice in that reality closest to humanity, namely, in an orderly polity or civilization. The question becomes, consequently, is there anything which, while not denying justice, can also transcend justice?

The solution to Dostoevsky's question is not to reject any desire fully to know another person, which desire is somehow healthy in its essence. It is to wonder how such a question might be resolved without the attraction of modern ideology which, to give it credit, is rooted in the desire of all to share in all, to humanize the world, to eliminate evils and barriers. Ironically, the worst consequences are often the obverse sides of something quite noble and worthy. The vivid paradox of the classic definition of evil remains. Evil is conceived not as "nothing," but as the lack of something which ought to be there. If the Aristotelian treatise on friendship is related to the treatise on justice, it is not merely because both treatises deal

[22]Ibid., 109.

with the same subject matter, that is, our relations with others. It is also because the treatise on friendship, on the basis of human reason and experience, poses more profoundly than the treatise on justice what needs to be resolved if the questions implicit in friendship are not to destroy, in the name of justice, either the civil or the metaphysical orders (1159b25–29).

Our very existence involves risk. One way to get rid of any unpleasant thought of a hell or ultimate reckoning for violations of right—a way even the totalitarians reject—is to rid ourselves of any philosophic seriousness about human life or enterprise. We could make the human being an insignificant metaphysical entity with his actions of no real import in their meaning or extent. We need to understand how we can protect intellectually the freedom and worth of a finite being, whose actions can have ultimate significance, and at the same time acknowledge to ourselves our incapacity to resolve all the intended and unintended consequences of our actions in the order of polity and civilization.

Our situation is like that encountered by little Sally, dressed in pajamas, ready for bed, who comes up to Charlie Brown who is reading in a chair. "When we die, will we go to heaven?" she asks him. "I like to think so," Charlie replies, somewhat confusedly. Sally continues, "When we get there, will we meet all those bugs we've stepped on?" Charlie, looking over the arm of the chair, says "Will we what?" "Will we meet all the spiders and bugs and things we've stepped on all our lives?" She now has Charlie's attention. She repeats, "I'm wondering if we'll see all of them in heaven and if we'll have to apologize to them. . . ." Still getting no answer, she asks Charlie, "What do you think?" He replies, "I don't have the slightest idea." She returns to her bedroom and in silence stands transfixed. She hurries back to Charlie to tell him, "There's a spider on the ceiling of my bedroom." Charlie is now thoroughly perplexed as Sally asks pleadingly, "Why don't you pound it for me? You can apologize to it later."[23] Our demands for justice have metaphysical limits.

[23]Charles Schultz, *Peanuts*, United Features, January 26, 1986.

3. *Reason and Revelation: Possible Answers to Real Questions*

From the Oratory in Birmingham, England, John Henry Newman on December 21, 1867, wrote a letter to his lawyer friend, Mr. Edward Badeley, to whom he wished to dedicate one of his books of poetry in appreciation for all the help he had received during the days of the Oxford Movement. "In poetry, as in metaphysics, a book is of necessity a venture," Newman wrote. "I wish [this dedication] to be the poor expression, long-delayed, of my gratitude, never intermitted, for the great services you rendered to me years ago, by your legal skill and affectionate zeal. . . . We are both of us, in the decline of life: may that warm attachment which has lasted between us inviolate for so many years, be continued, by the mercy of God, to the end of our earthly course, and beyond it!"[24] Newman provides the setting for our final considerations on how friendship teaches what God is like.

The problems of evil, freedom, and transcendence pose for us concerns of the greatest urgency. These same problems exist at a more poignant level when they involve our highest activity, especially the activity, or the mutual activity, that Aristotle called the friendship of good people. When he realized that friendship dealt with what is deepest in human life, Aristotle wondered fleetingly why it was necessary to deny friendship to God. If we could not see friendship in God, wasn't there some kind of defect in God? I consider this one of the most surprising and profound passages in all of classical literature, the fact that Aristotle sensed the problem. We are asked if a genuine spiritual reality like friendship must be denied to the highest transcendent reality.

The situation is like that described by Plato in his famous Seventh Letter: "Dionysius, who had gathered the whole of Sicily into a single city, and was so clever that he trusted no one, only secured his own safety with great difficulty. For he was badly off for trustworthy friends; and there is no surer criterion of virtue and vice than this, whether a man is or is not destitute of such friends" (332c). The implication is that

[24]John Henry Newman, *Newman: Prose and Poetry*, selected by Geoffrey Tillotson (Cambridge: Harvard University Press, 1970) 801-02.

a successful tyrant will end up lacking that which is most necessary and desirable for a human being to have. To achieve these very desirable things was why he became a tyrant in the first place. Aristotle posed the same dilemma at a higher level when he asked whether we could be friends with God. He answered negatively, since he thought the distance between us and God too great. Since God has no equal, he is solitary, moving all else by love and desire (1075b5). The proper object of divine thought is thinking itself (1074b34). What is to be concluded from this solitariness of God? It is, I think, that there is an uneasiness with this position, lofty as it is. Something seems wrong. Friendship ought to exist in God. We ought to be friends with him. But Aristotle gives us no hint, other than the remarkable fact that he brought the issue up at all, that he is not content with the reality and truth of his position as it stands. We hardly see any alternative.

The force of Aristotle's argument should not be underestimated. Essentially, it is this: 1) The highest things in human life exist in friendship; 2) God must be deficient because he lacks a friend; 3) No friendship between the human being and God is possible because there is no basis for communication between them. Aristotle seems merely to be recording the evidence available to us. And he is quite right: this is the evidence. But he is also right to note a certain perplexity about such observations. Somehow it seems to hint at a perfection in us that does not exist in God. God appears on the basis of human reflection to be deficient. "For without friends, no one would choose to live, though he had all other goods," Aristotle had shrewdly observed (1155a5–6). Without anticipating revelation, it seems clear that one possible answer to Aristotle's dilemma would be that we could posit friendship in God and then some corresponding way in which God could appear in the human form in which friendship normally happens among us (1099b11–16). The difference between Aquinas and Aristotle results from the impact on philosophy when these latter positions involving friendship in God, that is, the doctrine of the Trinity, and friendship between God and humanity, the incarnation, are considered in the light of Aristotle's legitimate observations.[25]

[25]See Schall, *Redeeming the Time*, 65–97; *The Dictinctiveness of Christianity* (San Francisco: Ignatius Press, 1982) 114–25.

A second issue arising from Aristotle's treatment of friendship concerns his remark about our wishing the best for our friends. This wishing good for a friend should not be taken to deny that "it is for himself most of all that each man wishes what is good" (1159a13). Aristotle did not subscribe to any thought of self-annihilation or any notion that somehow the happiness of the universe is not intended for each human being. He knew that we do want happiness for ourselves. Indeed, he even inquired whether we would wish the best for our friend if the friend would be so changed that we would no longer have the same basis for friendship, say, if he were to become a king, or a philosopher, or a god. This twofold concern, that we wish our friends to remain what they are, that we also wish the best for them, again serves as the basis of the realistic metaphysics on which Aquinas built his understanding of reason and revelation.

We should not like to be given happiness on the condition that we ourselves become someone else.

> When one party is removed to a great distance, as God is, the possibility of friendship ceases. This is in fact the origin of the question of whether friends really wish for their friends the greatest goods, e.g., that of being gods; since in that case their friends will no longer be friends to them, and therefore will not be good things for them (for friends are good things). The answer is that if we were right in saying that friend wishes good to friend for his sake, his friend must remain the sort of being he is, whatever that may be; therefore, it is for him only so long as he remains a man that he will wish the greatest goods (1159a5–11).

Aristotle must at least have suspected some higher possible end—"but perhaps not all the greatest goods; for it is for himself most of all that each man wishes what is good" (1159a11–12). The doggedness with which Aristotle held to this idea of our own individual being and happiness is remarkable. But he was not an individualist in the negative sense. He refused to solve the problem of the good by proposing either annihilation or loss of our being through absorption into some higher entity. He could reject such defective solutions because of his theory of knowledge, in which all things become ours, and his theory of friendship, in which we rejoice in the good which is not merely a repetition of ourselves.

A final perplexity that is graphically illustrated in Aristotle arises from his realization that we would not want to be happy merely by ourselves. "Surely, it is strange, too, to make the supremely happy man a solitary; for no one would choose the whole world on condition of being alone, since man is a political creature and one whose nature is to live with others" (1169b17–19). This passage must be read in the light of the fact that Aristotle held man's highest act to be contemplative and self-sufficient, after the life of the First Mover, which apparently is solitary. "The activity of God, which surpasses all others in blessedness, must be contemplative; and of human activities, therefore, that which is most akin to this must be most of the nature of happiness" (1178b21–23). Again the dilemma: there is an insistence that happiness be precisely ours, that it be contemplative, that it be the consideration of the highest things. But also Aristotle knew that we cannot be fully happy by ourselves and, in fact, that we can "contemplate our neighbors better than ourselves and their actions better than our own" (1169b34). He understood that the highest things can be communicated by rational beings to one another.

Aristotle at this point asked what is perhaps the most intriguing question of all—how many friends can we have? One or two at most over a complete lifetime was his general answer. His reasons for holding this proposition are of great significance. They relate both to the nature of the highest virtue itself and to the full and complete life in which it must be expressed. In the case of friendship between husband and wife, for example, the clearest case of one-to-one friendship, besides all the other relationships they might have with regards to the children, Aristotle held that it may be possible for this relationship to be based on virtue "if the partners are good; for each has its own virtue and they will delight in the fact" (1162a26–27). He then asks, "as regards good friends, should we have as many as possible or is there a limit to the number of our friends?" (1170b29–30)

Aristotle had already observed, however, that a city is held together mostly by friendship in which the citizens are in agreement about what sorts of things they will act upon together (1155a21–22). It would seem at first sight that all people should ultimately be our friends. If they are not, something is wrong with the universe. Is it not an injustice that we be deprived of the friendships of the many good men and women whom we do not now know, or who have lived before or will live after our times? And Newman was quite right to hope that death did not finally destroy our present friendships.

Aristotle insisted that a human life normally passes through a "complete life," that is, all the stages from birth to old age. Not much time is available for doing all things or conversing with many friends (1100a5). Since friendship takes a long time and requires much association and exchange of life, reality prevents us from knowing many friends. The very desire to have many friends may be, in Aristotle's view, one of those signs of a human tendency to rebel against the structure of reality, the refusal to accept the "bondage" our being gives us, which prevents us for our own good from making our own world (982b29).

Unless we follow the view that he was speaking ironically, so that he meant the same things as Aristotle, Plato, in book five of *The Republic,* seems to have eliminated the exclusivity of friendship. Indeed, it is characteristic of universalist utopias, which have followed this extreme Platonic model, to propose as their goal a sort of universal friendship of the highest order. What prevents its achievement is usually defined as family or property or rule. The removal or modification of these impediments, it is hoped, will eliminate the barriers between people.[26] Aristotle did not follow this line of thought. He realized, in a biting quip, "how much better it is to be the real cousin of somebody than to be a son after Plato's fashion" (1262a13–14).

But even more, anticipating so much political theory in our century, Aristotle remarked, against Plato's literal proposals in *The Republic,* that the root of the problem lies in the proper conception of friendship—what it is we have when we choose it. "For friendship we believe to be the greatest good

[26]See Schall, "Christian Guardians," *The Politics of Heaven and Hell,* 67–82.

of states and the preservation of them against revolutions; neither is there anything which Socrtes so greatly lauds as the unity of the state which he and all the world declare to be created in friendship. But the unity which he commends would be like that of the lovers in the *Symposium* who, as Aristophanes says, desire to grow together in the excess of their affection and from being two to become one, in which case one or both would certainly perish'' (1262b8–15). Not only did Aristotle insist that our friendships be ours, but that their objects remain what they are.

The desire to build a public world in which friendship is a factor ought not to be seen as the contradictory position to having in reality but a few good friends. The latter, the few friends, imply a better world and friends are, indeed, the source of all true action in the world. Aristotle was surely right there. Yet he underscored a famous dilemma, the one based on our perishability and on the time we have been given in this world to make any friends at all, which takes in itself a lifetime. He said, for example, speaking of the nature of deliberation and choice, ''Choice cannot relate to impossibles, and if anyone is said to choose them, he would be thought silly; but there may be a wish even for impossibles, e.g., immortality'' (1111b21–23). Does this not mean that in desiring immortality we are simply, to use Aristotle's remark, ''silly?'' ''Love is ideally a sort of excess of friendship and that can only be felt toward one person; therefore great friendship too can only be felt towards few people'' (1171a11–12). Is this too but another sign of nature's vanity?

The classical treatise on friendship stands by itself. If we are at all alert and open to the sort of reflection on ourselves to which a true classical treatment will always lead us, we will find that the same questions and perplexities that struck Aristotle still strike us. The perennial quality of these questions is something of a comfort, a reassurance about our common heritage and lot. We too find that the most friends, good friends, we can ever have in our own single lifetime are few. We understand that friendship is a good in itself, that it consists in the exchange of life, truth, and action in one lifetime. Yet this life ends in a death which contradicts what we most want. Friendship concerns not merely truth but the truth we hold and the reality to which we conform in an existing world that we did not make. We recognize that friendship extends beyond ourselves. We do not want to be solitary in the highest things. It is unsettling that what seems so permanent also seems to end.

We should be known in our most private lives by a friend who loves us fully. We do not need any revelation to tell us any of this. In fact, if we have not already experienced somehow these wonderments in the depths of our lives, no particular revelation will really be possible for us. In a world that, as friendship often attests, is suffused with joy, such questions, we think, ought not to end in despair or resignation, ought not to end in our having to construct solutions.

We are left in the ancient treatises somewhat with the dilemma of the folks in the Mudville of Casey fame. Let me recall the famous last stanzas, after, much to the Mudville fans dismay, strike two had been called against mighty Casey (E. Thayer, 1888):

> The sneer is gone from Casey's lips, his teeth are clinched in hate,
> He pounds with cruel vengeance his bat upon the plate;
> And now the pitcher holds the ball, and now he lets it go,
> And now the air is shattered by the force of Casey's blow.
> Oh, somewhere in this favored land, the sun is shining bright,
> The band is playing somewhere, and somewhere hearts are light;
> And somewhere men are laughing, and somewhere children shout,
> But their is no joy in Mudville—mighty Casey has struck out.

This is the point where Aristotle would leave us, with hopes of a world in which his questions, our questions, would be answered differently. But for what concerns us, our permanence, our friends, our relation to God, Aristotle has left us answers that provide us with no joy. I will not say, to be sure, "mighty Aristotle has struck out." He established the very framework in which the game might be played. He made it possible for more profound answers to be proposed and taken seriously.

To understand what God is like, what I wish to consider finally are those answers from revelation, from transcendence, that are directed to the perplexities we find in our friendships. Only when this higher order of revelation and transcendence is rightly understood can the order of polity and civilization be what it is. It is not a substitute for God or transcendence, nor a replacement for friendship, but a genuine, limited human creation reflective of the whole of *what is*. The English historian Christopher Dawson wrote in 1931: "True civilization is essentially a spiritual order, and its criterion is not material wealth, but spiritual vision. It seeks a *theoria*—an intuition of reality which is expressed in metaphysical thought and bears fruit in artistic creation and moral action."[27] Both spiritual and material expressions of a culture burst forth to the visible eye, but the roots of any new creation are in the soul.

Civilization is first dependent on the friendships and, through them, on the willingness of people to accept in themselves and love in others the ultimate questions and the answers given to them. Eric Voegelin was right in maintaining that civilizational crises are not matters of "inevitable fate." For "no one is obliged to take part in the spiritual crisis of society; on the contrary, everyone is obliged to avoid this folly and live his life in order."[28] The hypothesis of this argument is that the openness to truth that ought to define all human beings will include a consideration of the revelational answers to the philosophical questions. In considering what God is like, the content that revelation offers will not be neglected. This position does not imply the rationalist premise that, therefore, reason will fully understand revelation by the mind's own powers. But it will serve both to eliminate certain alternatives to legitimate questions arising in friendship and suggest that the highest things do not leave the human intellect completely stranded in its own dilemma.

Aquinas, when he came to define what was meant by charity in revelation, did nothing more than return to Aristotle's discussion of friendship. "*Caritas amicitia quaedam est*

[27]Christopher Dawson, *Christianity and the New Age* (Manchester, N.H.: Sophia Institute Press, [1931] 1985) 98.

[28]Voegelin, *Science*, 22-23.

hominis ad Deum" ("Charity is a certain friendship of man with God" [*ST* II–II, 23, 1]). For anyone familiar with the philosophic tradition, this clearly was an answer to the position of Aristotle that God and the human being could not be friends. Aquinas did not suggest that Aristotle had been wrong in his argument on the basis of the evidence he had in philosophy. What remained beyond Aristotle's powers of analysis was how the issue could be resolved. Aquinas agreed with the point of Aristotle's suspicion that the difference could not be resolved on the basis of reason alone. The credibility of revelation was, however, related to the peculiar questions that did arise in the philosophical experience. The doctrines of a Trinity within the Godhead, the incarnation of one of the Persons of this Trinity, the resurrection of the body, the definition of the life of God as a friendship—each of these positions is directly consequent to Aristotle's own dilemmas about friendship and its limitations.

Aquinas wrote: "Charity signifies not only love of God, but also a certain friendship with him. This adds to love a mutual relationship in a mutual communication, as it says in the Eighth Book of *The Ethics*" (*ST* I–II, 65, 5). The reason I find these words of Aquinas especially powerful is because they so clearly are rooted in the thought of Aristotle about the essence of friendship. Aristotle's reflections correspond directly, it seems to me, with what we experience when we actually have friends. The poignancies we encounter, the lifetime it takes, death and the desire for permanence, the communication of the highest things, pleasure, the love of actual human beings, not abstractions—these are found in Aristotle. The revelational tradition at its best addresses our curious worry and suspicion that nature has something within it which is truly "in vain," namely, that what we human beings experience at our highest moments of joy and wisdom has no grounded resolution in *what is*.

The question of whether the revelational answers to the deepest philosophic perplexities remain in vain, as the whole of the modern world seems to testify, on evidence that always seems inadequate and contradictory, I will leave open. Let me again recall, finally, a sermon preached by John Donne at St.

Paul's in London, on the evening of Christmas Day, 1624. It bears an imagery, I think, of particular beauty: "One of the most convenient Hieroglyphicks of God, is a Circle; and a Circle is endlesse; whom God loves, hee loves to the end: and not onely to their own end, to their death, but to his end, and his end is, that he might love them still." All transcendence, friendship, and civilization come together in this imagery. It is the essential imagery of what God is like as we see God reflected through our highest human experiences of love and friendship. Love and friendship are the very analogies by which God ultimately explains the divine life to us.

Chapter IX

The Trinity: "So Aweful a Subject in Mixed Company"

In a conversation on May 7, 1773, Samuel Johnson was asked whether a distinction existed between practical and speculative. His unnamed questioner worried whether it would be "wrong for a magistrate to tolerate those who preach against the doctrine of the Trinity."[1] Johnson replied that no one of piety should introduce such a query "in mixed company," meaning into a group in which there were present those without sufficient intellectual acumen to follow the subtleties of the argument. The very discussion in their eyes would raise many doubts and make Johnson himself appear to question this central doctrine. We must distinguish between what is "right" and what is "politick." If the tenor of the question at issue were "what is right," then the topic ought not to be allowed. Johnson implied that if the question were "is it politick," the discussion could go on since there would be risk of greater damage in forbidding it.

Boswell went on to explain Johnson's position on the principal topic itself, that is, the Trinity: "Though he [Johnson] did not think it fit that so *aweful* a subject be introduced in a mixed company, and therefore at this time waved the theological question; yet his own orthodox belief in the sacred mystery of the Trinity is evinced beyond doubt, by the following passage in his private devotions:—'O Lord, hear my prayer,

[1]*Boswell's Life of Johnson* I (London: Oxford, 1931) 515.

for Jesus Christ's sake, to whom with thee and the Holy Ghost, three persons and one God, be all honour and glory, world without end, Amen.' "[2] The word that Johnson used to describe the Trinity, be it noted, was "awe-ful," that is, full of awe. The word "awe" signifies our overwhelming reaction to that which causes reverence, or wonder, sometimes fear. It especially describes our proper response to the presence of the divinity. Though it can be a word of fright, it means "being struck," being taken or overtaken by something beyond us, yet by something now in our ken, though not under our control.

This word "awe-ful" is replete with meaning for any discussion of Trinity. Johnson was right to use it. But in its recent form, "awful," the word has lost much of its force. Fowler, in his *Modern English Usage,* described how such words as "terrible" or "awful" have come to mean almost the opposite of their original content. They have often become substitutes for "very." Fowler cited, as an example, the following passage from James Thurber: "The other day (said I) I read a love scene in a story that went like this: 'Am I beautiful?' she asked him. 'Terribly,' he said. And then he asked her, 'Do you love me?' 'Horribly,' she said. Why (I was then asked) don't you go home and write something humorous, don't you want to? 'Frightfully,' I replied." Fowler commented on the oddity of this amusing passage: the process of decline, he thought, began with the word "awfully," as in the expression he is "awfully funny."[3] Johnson's use of the word "aweful" suggested how we react to the proper understanding of the doctrine of the Trinity and more especially to what it stands for. The word means something that causes us to be full of awe when we begin to grasp the full import of what it is we confront in the fullness of God, or even in the barest glimmer of him.

The question of what God is like comes back to the central doctrine of God in the New Testament. God is Trinity, even though Trinity is not itself a biblical term but one probably first

[2]Ibid., I, 516.

[3]H. W. Fowler, *A Dictionary of Modern English Usage* (New York: Oxford, 1965) 618.

coined by Tertullian in the third century A.D. So great an authority as St. Thomas advised us to think circumspectly about the Trinity. "When we speak of the Trinity," he wrote, "we should proceed with caution and modesty, because, as Augustine said [*De Trinitate* I, 3] 'nowhere is error more dangerous, nor investigation more difficult, nor discovery more fruitful' " (*ST* I, 31, 2). While not doubting the danger or the difficulty, the fruitfulness of this doctrine is what is most striking here.

The term Trinity seems fitting because of the way Jesus and his mission in the world are presented to us in Scripture, wherein his being and action are described through Father, Son, and Holy Spirit. Whatever term we choose to use, it is the perfection of the intellect to seek the best way to find and use accurately the expression that most closely fits reality, without ever identifying word and being except as the Apostle John in his Prologue describes Jesus himself.

Elio Guerriero wrote in this regard, "The Word operates in life, and life in its turn is illuminated by the Word. For the Christian this fundamental experience is founded on the very life of the Trinity."[4] We can say of the world and all that is in it, that it is *not* God. We can likewise say of the world and all that is in it that it is something *like* God. God revealed himself not primarily in the context of explaining what God is like but in explaining what we are like. And all else seems to exist because of what we are like. Our present knowledge of what God is like is as through a glass darkly, as St. Paul put it. "We all experience our own existence as not existing out of itself but as coming from somewhere even if we don't know from where," Eric Voegelin remarked.[5] This situation, Voegelin held, suggests that we do want to know, at least insofar as we can, why our lives are in some sort of "tension" which constantly draws us to know and love that out of which we came.

"We are made in the image and likeness of God," Frank Sheed wrote, "and God is Trinity. Ignorance of the Trinity,

[4]Elio Guerriero, "Introduction," *Catholica: The World Catholic Yearbook, 1987* (San Francisco: Ignatius Press, 1988) xiii.

[5]*Conversations with Eric Voegelin*, ed. R. Eric O'Connor (Montreal: Thomas More Institute, 1980) 9.

then, has as a by-product ignorance of ourselves, both ignorances are widespread, the second rooted in the first.''[6] ''To know'' ourselves, the classical philosophical goal, we need to know God, the revelational goal. The introspection by which we know ourselves will turn out to be, as St. Augustine recognized, one path by which we catch glimpses of the inner life of God. To know ourselves it is not sufficient to know only ourselves. We know ourselves first by knowing something, not ourselves, a most glorious example of our dignity and our dependency. This truth is the formal foundation of our hope of ultimate joy, for we know that joy is not something that we can finally give ourselves. Even if we despair, even if we seek to give what we conceive might be an alternative explanation, this truth remains for us obvious and clear. Joy is given to us, not made by us. The structure of the world must in the end arrive at a reality in which such joy can find its intelligible origin. Christian thought argues that only the Trinity can fulfill this necessity both in thought and in reality.

''Jesus not only announces the Gospel, the Good News, but he himself is the Gospel,'' John Paul II remarked. ''In fact, in the whole of his mission, by means of all that he does and teaches, and finally by his Cross and Resurrection, he 'reveals man to man' (*Gaudium et Spes*, #22), and opens up to him the perspectives of that happiness to which God has called and destined him from the beginning. . . . Christ's mission consists above all in the revelation of the Good News *addressed to mankind*. It is aimed at the human person. . . .''[7] We do not so much search for God but God searches for us in order to address us, to inform us of what we are really like in ourselves, of what we are concretely destined for in this universe.

But in the process of God revealing our own condition to us, we have certain hints and shadowings of what God might be like in the inner self of the divine life, hints and shadowings contained necessarily in the very statement of our

[6]Frank Sheed, *God and the Human Condition* (New York: Sheed and Ward, 1966) Vol. 1, *God and the Human Mind*, 272. This discussion of the Trinity by Frank Sheed, 212–94, remains one of the very best.

[7]John Paul II, Address of April 27, 1988, #1 and #2, *L'Osservatore Romano*, English edition, May 2, 1988.

individual purpose and destiny. We are so thoroughly made for a serious yet joyful purpose that our lack of knowledge of what God is like derives not just from the immensity of God but also from the limited nature of our own intelligence and will. Even though we are limited, we are open to *all that is*. In the end we do not want to know ourselves so much as to know the Good that brought from nothing the particular being that we know ourselves to be.

Traditional spirituality insisted on the importance of not setting our hearts on this transitory world. We in our turn have attempted to exalt God by exalting humanity. In one sense it is legitimate enough to exalt the human being. The dignity of the Creator is indeed enhanced when humanity, however limited it might be, realizes that it exists at all and appears in a certain definite way.[8] But when the human being opposes God because of some perceived imperfection in humanity or the world that God, presumably, has caused, this exaltation becomes dangerous. The fact that we can reject God, a truth lying at the root both of human and divine freedom, intimates that the alternatives to God will turn out to be something similar, some imitation of God's inner-life. Most often this imitation will be some worldly or ideological simulation of the societal life of God, now claimed to be constructed by humanity for itself.

In the only other passage in *The Life of Johnson* that mentions the Trinity, Johnson and Boswell were discussing sermons, especially the *Sermons* of the Rev. Dr. Samuel Clarke (1675–1729). Johnson thought that Clarke had a rather good style. "I should recommend Dr. Clarke's *Sermons* were he orthodox. However, it is very well known *where* he was not orthodox, which was upon the doctrine of the Trinity, so as to which he is a condemned heretick; so one is aware of it."[9] Clarke was a follower of Newton. He sought to prove the existence of God mathematically and was said to be, as a result of his labors, the cause of David Hume's doubts. Clarke's treatise on the Trinity was more Arian than Christian in expres-

[8]See Stanley L. Jaki, *Science and Creation* (Edinburgh: Scottish Academic Press, 1974).

[9]*Boswell*, II, 189.

sion. He allowed three complete substances in God, which touched on heretical versions of the Trinity; and for him the Son was less than the Father.

Battista Mondin has pointed out that many of the recent theological discussions of Christ in particular are neo-Arian. They attempt to make Christ a representative of humanity under one or another man-for-others form. He is exalted but not the specifically divine Man of the Creeds.[10] "The definition [of Nicaea that Christ is true God] *does not cease to be relevant today* in the face of tendencies, both old and new, to see Christ merely as a man, however extraordinary, but not as God," John Paul II remarked on this same point.

> To admit or support them would destroy the Christological dogma and, at the same time, it would imply the annulment of the entire Christian soteriology. If Christ is not true God, he does not transmit divine life to humanity. Therefore he is not the Saviour of mankind in the sense set out by *Revelation* and *Tradition*. If this truth of the Church's faith is denied, the entire edifice of Christian dogma collapses, the integral logic of the faith and Christian life is nullified, because the keystone of the whole construction is eliminated.[11]

The divinization of humanity in modern philosophy requires the de-divinization of Christ and his place in the Trinity. The "logic of the faith," as the Holy Father calls it, remains a protection of what we are told God is like, of what we are like.

We do not much like to hear anyone described as a "heretick," as Johnson correctly described Clarke. We want to believe that what we hold in these apparently obscure matters does not mean much. Yet right-thinking in these issues may indeed be what upholds civilization. Wrong-thinking may be what tears it down. With Johnson, I hold that it does make a difference that we think rightly about what God is like, about what Trinity is like in its wholeness and in each of its members. Frank Sheed again put the matter well:

[10]Battista Mondin, *L'Eresia del Nostro Secolo* (Torino: Borla, 1971).

[11]John Paul II, Address of March 9, 1988, in *L'Osservatore Romano*, English edition, March 14, 1988.

> Intellect is one of the great twin powers of the soul. In so far as it remains unnourished, our personality lacks full development. The food of the intellect is truth, and the Trinity is the supreme truth about the Supreme Being. Merely because it is truth, there would be a defect of human dignity in ignoring it. Thinking that there is only one Person in God is incomparably worse than thinking the world is flat. People would find the latter piece of ignorance intolerable, quite apart from any practical difference that the earth's sphericality makes to us—it would be shameful not to know. But ignorance about the Supreme Being is more abject poverty than ignorance about any of the lesser beings he has created out of nothing. If there were no other profit, that would be sufficient.[12]

The world we act in is the world that exists. For that reason, the understanding we have of the ultimate reality, however confused, will affect both our spiritual lives and our relationship to others. Our understanding of the world is a function of our ideas about God or whatever we might designate as the ultimate truth or reality.

Regarding this very issue, G. K. Chesterton on July 1, 1909, wrote the following letter to *The Nation* in London:

> Sir.—Mr. Sidney Low's statement that creeds do not greatly affect conduct is a very common one at the present time. To me it seems not only obviously untrue, but obscurantist and oppressive in the worst degree. Priests are accused of despising human reason, but no priest ever despised it so utterly as to assert that its highest conclusions about the cosmos make no difference whatever. . . . This is the worst obscurantism: to say that even if we find the truth it will make no difference; that a man in a triangular world will behave just like a man in a square world; and a man in a good universe exactly like a man in a bad one. It really amounts to saying that a man's head is a useless appendage to his automatically cheerful body.[13]

To think correctly about the Trinity is an especially graphic example of Chesterton's point, for the Trinity is not merely

[12]Sheed, *God and the Human Condition*, 294.

[13]G. K. Chesterton, "Do Religious Beliefs Affect Conduct?" *The Chesterton Review*, 14 (May, 1988) 181.

Aristotle's "thought thinking on itself," though it is at least that, but it is the most important information we have about what God is like. To attend to its meaning is to attend to what we most want to know. To explain the Trinity wrongly puts everyone in a kind of strained mixed company, makes our head merely to be a useless appendage. The Pope, Chesterton, and Johnson understood quite clearly that it does make a considerable difference what we believe about God.

The revelational answer to the question of what God is like has to do directly with the teaching that God is triune. Johnson's prayer was orthodox, and the fact that his prayer was to the Trinity made a difference in everything else. "O Lord, hear my prayer, for Jesus Christ's sake, to whom with thee and the Holy Ghost, three persons and one God, be all honour and glory, world without end. Amen." Christians begin and end their confessions and prayers with this very expression, in one of its many forms, "In the Name of the Father, and of the Son, and of the Holy Spirit." Not merely is the Trinity a precise doctrine, it is also the object of prayer and the source of action about the highest things. The Trinity implies not merely that we want God but that God searches for us in our particularity. The inner life of the triune God is not something static or closed but something offered to our own capacity and to our own choice, offered to us as that which we most want to know and possess.

But why ought we to attend to this doctrine of the Trinity? Contrary to theories of tolerance or ecumenism or openness that would imply that ideas, especially ideas of God, do not make too much difference, I think that it is important to make every effort to think about the inner life of a God. God is revealed to us as begetting a Word from all eternity, as Spirit. To be straightforward about it, I hold that we think better, live better, and pray better if we think correctly about what God is like. I do not, like Plato, think that all of our evil is due to our ignorance or to our lack of orthodoxy. Such is the attractiveness of "all those lovely things" of which St. Augustine spoke that there can be and are perfectly orthodox sinners. St. Ignatius included ourselves in the subject matter of his meditations on sin, along with the sin of the angels and that of our first parents.

Flannery O'Connor put the matter clearly in a letter of December 9, 1958, to Cecil Dawkins:

> All your dissatisfaction with the Church seems to me to come from an incomplete understanding of sin. This will perhaps surprise you because you are very conscious of the sins of Catholics; however what you seem actually to demand is that the Church put the kingdom of heaven on earth right here and now, that the Holy Ghost be translated at once into all flesh. . . .
>
> Christ was crucified on earth and the Church is crucified by all of us, by her members because most primarily she is a Church of sinners. Christ never said that the Church would be operated in a sinless or intelligent way, but that it would not teach error. . . . To have the Church be what you want it to be would require the continuous miraculous meddling of God in human affairs, whereas it is our dignity that we are allowed more or less to get on with those graces that come through faith and the sacraments and which work through our human nature. God has chosen to operate in this manner.[14]

Like St. Ignatius in his contemplation, O'Connor understood that what God was most concerned about in his relation with human beings was the relation of his life to each of theirs in the very finite and sinful condition in which they exist.

Revelation, directed as it is to everyone, is directed especially to believers who know themselves and who know how God has acted to reveal himself in the world. This fact is why we are not surprised to see that Mark's Gospel begins with the words baptism and repentance. To claim that "here we have the complete explanation of the Trinity in a few brief words," would be silly. But this sort of boastfulness is probably much more pleasing to God than the more skeptical notion that it makes no difference what our ideas of God are like. To doubt our intellectual capacity to know anything for sure destroys our very intellectual power. This power was given to us that we could understand—and understand ever more deeply—whenever something intelligible was addressed to us.

[14]Flannery O'Connor, *The Habit of Being*, ed. Sally Fitzgerald (New York: Vintage, 1979) 307.

If we are unexpectedly challenged by revelation, as we should be, it is because we are supposed to think about what is directed to us. What it is that is revealed to us is, substantially, how we can, while remaining ourselves, go about living within this inner life of God—we who are created, fallen, and redeemed, as we are described in revelation, as we know ourselves to be.

In retrospect, it is astonishing that the very first controversies that at Nicaea and Chalcedon caused the Church to use her teaching authority in a general, formal way were those which concerned the understanding of the Trinity and the incarnation of one member of this Trinity into this world. Following Aristotle's dictum that a small error in the beginning would, if not corrected, yield a great disorder in the end, the Church was constrained to employ non-biblical philosophic terms like nature, person, relation, and substance to explain accurately what was being said in Scripture about God. Often this effort has been criticized as contrary to the intention of revelation. Almost the opposite is the case. The Church instinctively seemed to understand from the beginning that the Scriptural account was also designed for our comprehension. It was all right if we had to work at understanding the Trinity with our own most acute powers of precise reasoning. The point of faith, ultimately, is to know.

This very necessity to think about what God was like in revelation brought up the further question of how human thought related to what was being presented in this same revelation. Was the human being a whole so that whatever intelligible object presented itself to him he could grasp in some sense? Or was God so separate and mysterious that nothing of him could possibly be known even to clarify our minimum intellectual needs? The intellectual and spiritual engagement of God with the human being, not to mention the incarnation which was "Word made flesh," could not but involve human understanding. Human experience had already contained long discussions of what the gods were like—that there were many, that they acted rather like people, that there was a god of good and one of evil, that we were parts of god, that the gods could be bought off, that the gods had no concern for us, that the gods were spirits, even that perhaps there were not gods. In the Old Testament no god is said to be like Israel's God; something quite new is claimed for this Yahweh. And though denying nothing of the God of Abraham, Isaac, and Jacob, something even newer is claimed for God in the New Testament.

In his treatise *On The Trinity*, St. Augustine included a chapter appropriately entitled "The Infirmity of the Human Mind." It is difficult not to be amused by his earnestness here, his concern that we do not let the difficulty we have about knowing God prevent us from grasping what we indeed can learn about the Trinity. By an analogy with our own being which thinks and wills, St. Augustine's great treatise had sought to explain the unity and diversity in God. He held that we could have some appreciation of God's inner life from our own inner being if we would just attend to the analogy he tried to make. His account is, no doubt, one of the greatest discussions of the Trinity that we possess. He rejected the idea that because the Trinity is difficult to understand, because our minds are "infirm," we do not have to worry about using them. Recalling St. Paul's terminology (1 Cor 13:12), St. Augustine explained:

> They, then, who see their own mind, in whatever way that is possible, and in it that Trinity (being, mind, will) of which I have treated as I could in many ways, and yet do not believe or understand it to be an image of God, see indeed a glass, but do not so far see through the glass Him who is now to be seen through the glass, that they do not even know the glass itself which they see to be a glass, i.e., an image. And if they knew this, perhaps they would feel that He too whose glass this is, should by it be sought, and somehow provisionally be seen, an unfeigned faith purging their hearts, that He who is now seen through a glass may be able to be seen face to face.[15]

Not unlike Aristotle who remarked in the last book of *The Ethics* (1177b25–1178a8) that we should seek to know all we can of the First Mover even if it be ever so little, for that little is worth

[15]St. Augustine, "On the Trinity," XV, 24, *The Basic Works of St. Augustine*, vol. 2, ed. Whitney J. Oates (New York: Random House, 1948) 869.

more than all other knowledge, St. Augustine insisted that we learn what we could of the triune God. He was convinced that we have an avenue through our own being, however dark, to what God might be like and to the full knowledge of the God we seek, face to face.

In a sermon he preached the Sunday after Trinity Sunday at Lincoln's Inn in 1612, John Donne curiously wrote:

> To save this man, body and soule together, from the punishments due to his former sinnes, and to save him from falling into future sinnes by the assistance of his Word preached, and his Sacraments administered in the Church, which he purchased by his bloud, is this person, The *Lord*, the *Christ*, become this *Jesus*, this Saviour. To save so, All wayes, In soule, in body, in both; And also to save all men. For, to exclude others from that Kingdome, is a tyrannie, an usurpation; and to exclude thy selfe, is a sinfull, and rebellious melancholy. But as melancholy in the body is the hardest humour to be purged, so is the melancholy in the soule, the distrust of thy salvation too.[16]

Salvation reaches individuals through preaching and sacraments. The presence of Christ become man, even in the midst of our sinfulness, is the context of the discovery of what God is like. We ought not to have that "melancholy of soule" that would distrust our own salvation.

The Church, in its teaching history, has sought to state ever more clearly what it holds to be true about God. It seeks to have those who define themselves as Christians declare that they are so. It has not hesitated to ask us to make a human act, an announcement in speech, before the divine. Christianity is incorrigibly incarnational in its very faith. Each person is to recite the same Creed affirming the Father, the Son, and the Spirit. The Church has insisted that everyone who can reason at all recite the Creeds aloud. This recitation implies that we need to be heard. The Church has also understood that those who teach or who have intellectual pretensions are more in need of this profession than anyone else. This recitation at Mass

[16]*The Complete Poetry and Selected Prose of John Donne,* ed. Charles M. Coffin (New York: The Modern Library, 1952), 480.

and on other occasions is the one time we are asked before God to state what we believe him to be like in words, however theoretical, words which have been hammered out on the basis of the evidence we have. We are not requested to state just what "we" believe, as if we were giving some kind of pious opinion or conformist assent to a collective statement, but to state what it is that "I" believe. I am to speak the words and mean them so that the hearer will know this Creed is the frame of my life and action.

At the council of Florence (1438–45), for example, a group known as the Jacobites were invited to make a definite profession of faith to show that they understood Catholic teaching on the Trinity. The remarkable profession they were required to make, because they wanted to believe intelligibly, went like this:

> The Holy Roman Church founded by the call of Our Lord and Savior, firmly believes, professes, and preaches, that there is one true, omnipotent God, who is unchanging and eternal, Father, and Son, and Holy Spirit, one in essence, three in persons: the Father is unbegotten, the Son is begotten of the Father, the Holy Spirit proceeds from the Father and the Son. The Father is not the Son nor the Holy Spirit; the Son is not the Father or the Holy Spirit; the Holy Spirit is not the Father or the Son; but the Father is only the Father, the Son is only the Son, and the Holy Spirit is only the Holy Spirit.
>
> Only the Father of his substance generated the Son, only the Son is generated of the Father alone, only the Holy Spirit proceeds simultaneously from the Father and the Son. These three persons are one God, not three gods, because of the three, there is one substance, one essence, one nature, one divinity, one immensity, one eternity, and all are one where the opposition of relation does not prevent it (*Denziger* 703).

I cite this passage—and there are a number of other similar ones in official Church statements—not so much to explain each article but to note the majesty with which the Church insists on the uniqueness of each Person, yet each one's belonging together in one substance. The Father is not the Son nor the Holy Spirit. The Church must insist on this distinction because this is the evidence. This distinction of persons is there to tell us what God is like. The otherness within the Godhead is before and beyond creation. The inner life of God is complete in itself. What is not God, especially we ourselves, does not exist because God somehow needs us for something lacking in him. Rather we exist because God is free.

When we ask what is God like, we ask for a specific purpose. It makes a difference to us if we exist because something was lacking in God or because of the fullness of God. I have always had a great fondness for Johan Huizinga's *Homo Ludens*. This remarkable book suggests why our relation to God is not deterministic in the slightest but is rooted rather in freedom and abundance. Except faintly from our experience with play we have no prior awareness of the possibilities open to God in dealing with us. Yet this serious play, in a way, turns out to be the spirit of revelation itself.

Huizinga begins to get at what I mean about the relation of the human being and the Trinity:

> You can deny, if you like, nearly all abstractions: justice, beauty, truth, goodness, mind, God. You can deny seriousness, but not play. But in acknowledging play you acknowledge mind, for whatever else play is, it is not matter. . . . From the point of view of a world wholly determined by the operation of blind forces, play would be altogether superfluous. Play only becomes possible, thinkable and understandable when an influx of *mind* breaks down the absolute determinism of the cosmos. The very existence of play continually confirms the supra-logical nature of the human situation.[17]

The import of Huizinga's observation is that the cosmos seems to have intrinsically within it something more than a deterministic order. Within the rational human world a kind of play seems simultaneously to be going on. And this apparently goes on not in opposition to reason but beside it, beyond it, within it, without eliminating it.

[17]Johan Huizinga, *Homo Ludens* (Boston: Beacon, 1955) 3–4.

Several of the Church Fathers did not hesitate to suggest that the life of God resembles a dance.[18] If the world, by being what it is, exists to give glory to God, the highest form of that glory will appear in music and dance and play. But as Huizinga remarked, following a comment in Aristotle, there is, because of the lack of a higher object, a certain seriousness that appears to be missing in normal play, almost as if to suggest that if the higher object is present, the play will go on with appropriate seriousness (1176b4–12). The serious joy that the inner life of God appears to have in the descriptions of the Creeds seems reflected in the play of the creatures when what is going on is something not "serious" but something delightful yet all-absorbing. The experience of play and the experience of worship seem to belong to the same order.

Several years ago, I was in McDonald's Second-Hand Book Store at the end of Turk Street in San Francisco. A friend and I were exploring this vast emporium of used books and magazines. I believe I was actually looking for Tolkien's *Silmarillion*, but I had not been able to find it. After we had been there for some time, my friend suddenly, to my delight, appeared from a ladder with a British hardback edition of *The Silmarillion*. I had never at the time read it except for some random pages I once skimmed. They had somehow left an impression on me, enough to want to read more. When I had time to look at this marvelous book, I realized that its first few pages may contain the best imaginative description of what God is like ever penned. I read this description to my friend several times, from the section called "Ainulindale: The Music of the Ainur."

This is a mythical account of the creation by God, called Eru, or Iluvatar, of angelic-like creatures called Ainur. In the process there is also a spirit who freely revolts from the original creation, and there are eventually offspring of Iluvatar, an event no one had anticipated. Tolkien described all of this activity in terms of music.

[18]See Hugo Rahner, *Men at Play* (New York: Herder and Herder, 1967); James V. Schall, *Far Too Easily Pleased: A Theology of Play, Contemplation, and Festivity* (Los Angeles: Benziger-Macmillan, 1976).

> There was Eru, the One, who in Arda is called Iluvatar; and he made first the Ainur, the Holy Ones, that were the offspring of his thought, and they were with him before aught else was made. And he spoke to them, propounding to them themes of music; and they sang before him, and he was glad. But for a long while they sang only each alone, or but few together, while the rest harkened; for each comprehended only that part of the mind of Iluvatar from which he came, and in the understanding of their brethren they grew but slowly. Yet ever as they listened they came to deeper understanding and increased in unison and harmony.[19]

What follows is the account of how Iluvatar gave the Ainur a theme to play both in harmony with the rest of the music and with their own innovative contributions. Iluvatar would listen to this music and be glad. However, the evil Ainur, called Melkor, introduced his own themes into the ongoing music that were deliberately not in keeping with the theme that Iluvatar had given to them all. Yet the music went on in spite of the discord and seemed to transcend it by saving it in some higher and more beautiful music.

What puzzled the Ainur, who were beings of great intelligence, was that somehow the music went on and became more beautiful, in spite of the efforts of Melkor.

> As this vision of the World was played before them, the Ainur saw that it contained things which they had not thought. And they saw with amazement the coming of the Children of Iluvatar . . .; and they perceived that they themselves in the labour of their music had been busy with the preparation of this dwelling, and yet knew not that it had any purpose beyond its own beauty.
>
> For the Children of Iluvatar were conceived by him alone; and they came with the third theme, and were not in the theme which Iluvatar propounded at the beginning, and none of the Ainur had part in their making. Therefore when they beheld them, the more did they love them, being things other than themselves, strange and free, wherein they saw the mind of Iluvatar reflected anew. . . .[20]

[19]J. R. R. Tolkien, *The Silmarillion* (London: George Allen & Unwin, 1977) 15.

[20]Ibid., 18.

This astonishing passage is a mythical account of the relation between the Godhead and creation, particularly the creation of the rational beings, angels and human beings. What is to be noted is the freedom both of God and of human beings and angels, yet the mysterious ways in which God's will is done within this very freedom. Again, this astonishment seems to point to what God is like.

God has created us out of no inner necessity. If indeed we are not gods, we must ask, for what are we, each of us, created? In the most basic sense, we are created to be given a life that can receive, if we choose in the course of our earthly lives, the Trinitarian life offered to us. Is this itself an ''abstraction,'' as Huizinga rightly worried about? If God created us for himself and if our hearts will not be at rest until they rest in him, as St. Augustine so beautifully wrote, what is the purpose of all that is not God? We can say that it has no ''purpose'' other than God. The Trinitarian life, complete in itself as all the teachings on this subject affirm, is still fecund, capable of including what is not its own life. This is why, in the Tolkien account, the Great Music was capable of having introduced into its completeness what it did not know before, what was really new, yet what completed the original theme in a way no one but God could have understood.

The great utopian social theories which have replaced the God believed to be dead have been skewed substitutes for the life of the Trinity and our association with it. Their major difficulty, and this is an embarrassing one, is that they can never produce what we actually want. We do not want some perfect society down the ages, or even in our own time. Rather we want some solution to our own personal destiny, which we take to be and want to be social in the sense of having others included in our ultimate joy. Flannery O'Connor again put it well: ''The great difference between Christianity and the Eastern religions is the Christian insistence on the fulfillment of the individual person.''[21] The atheist and radical theorists have not been wrong to envision a highest good for mankind that would be some sort of community. Where they have been erroneous has been in what they offered ultimately to each ex-

[21]O'Connor, *The Habit of Being*, 458.

isting individual. They have not confronted the "awe-ful" desire each person has to remain in existence as himself yet in possession of that which is the highest being in existence. This union with the highest being is what the Trinitarian God does propose as our destiny. The final temptation is that this is too good for us to believe.

"For my part I think that when I know what the laws of the flesh and the physical really are," O'Connor continued "then I will know what God is. We know them as we see them, not as God sees them. For me it is the virgin birth, the Incarnation, the resurrection which are the true laws of the flesh and the physical. Death, decay, destruction are suspensions of these laws. I am always astonished by the emphasis the Church puts on the body. It is not the soul she says will rise but the body, glorified."[22] The central gift that the Son of God received from his Father after his death was the resurrection of his body. Through Christ, the gift is the same for us, the promise of general resurrection of all human flesh, of eternal life before the face of God.

In 1974 Gustave Martelet wrote an essay entitled the "Risen Body and the Beatific Vision." In it he broached the logical but perplexing question of what it is like to be human when we have reached the Beatific Vision, the inner life of the Trinity. He asked about the status and function of those human beings who actually stand within the life of the triune God, of those who have reached the end promised to them. What is done before God is primarily the praise of God. Praise means the response to what is given to us, to what we did not make or even merit—the "Holy, Holy, Holy" of Isaiah and the liturgy. But the creation in which we live remains.[23] We have been given a world to administer, Martelet thought. If death defeats this purpose, it will have defeated God's plan about our relation to the cosmos.

"Our finiteness means we cannot exist without world," Martelet wrote.

[22]Ibid., 100.

[23]See James V. Schall, "On the Condition of Heaven: A Thomistic Reflection on the Completion of Human Numbers," *The Politics of Heaven and Hell: Christian Themes from Classical, Medieval, and Modern Political Philosophy* (Lanham, Md.: University Press of America, 1984) 219–34.

> Without it, we cannot even gropingly discover God (*Acts*, 17:27). Conversely the world cannot fulfill its essential function of "singing out God's glory" (*Psalm*, 18:2) unless there are men around to sing it to. The world makes us conscious of our own identity, both as finite selves and as "otherings" of God. To prevent us from being crushed by his embrace God has planned that we should still be supported by our material world there beyond. Yet it will not be a curtain between us and him, because our vision of him will be immediate. Our sinfulness too in its way is the guarantee that our identity will not be lost in our absorption into God.[24]

We can speculate on what this sort of worldly existence might be like even with the Beatific Vision. St. Thomas at the end of the *Summa Contra Gentiles* devoted a good deal of attention to this very issue. The doctrine of the resurrection of the body may not be the complete Christian answer to the utopianism and radicalism of modernity, of course, though it certainly is the beginning and essence of such an answer.

The Triune life of God, Father, Son, and Spirit, wherein the Father is only the Father, the Son is only the Son, and the Spirit is only the Spirit, is meant for each human person and is the bond of his relationship to others. The doctrine of the Word made flesh is what grounds the Trinitarian life in the particular world and history in which we ourselves exist. The incarnation is a permanent aspect of reality. The friendship within God makes possible the lasting friendship that people have perceived as that which they want above all and which they want to exist as a reality within God himself. It is also the relation they most want to establish with God. This is why the passage from John that reads "I call you friends because I have made known to you everything I have learnt from my Father" (15:15) makes the Trinity itself the source of a communication between God and the human being in the highest things.

Of the Trinity, the German bishops wrote:

[24]Gustave Martelet, "Risen Body and Beatific Vision," *Theology Digest* 23 (Summer, 1975) 125. See also Michael Platt, "Would Human Life Be Better Without Death?" *Soundings* LXIII (Fall, 1980) 321–38.

> The most difficult part and the deepest mystery of the Christian confession of God still stands before us: the confession of the triune or trinitarian God. . . . Unworldly speculations were not the *origin* of this confession. It grew rather out of the experience with Jesus Christ and his Spirit at work in the Church. . . .
>
> This confession of the triune God is a deep *mystery* that no created spirit can discover of itself or ever comprehend. It is the mystery of an unfathomable and overflowing love: God is not a solitary being, but a God who bestows and communicates himself out of the abundance of his being, a God who lives in the communion of Father, Son, and Spirit, and who can therefore also bestow and ground community.[25]

God is not alone. Any possibility that we will be saved in our bodies is grounded in God. This fullness of being, body with soul, is what we actually want. For us then the real drama of the doctrine of the Trinity and of the incarnation and resurrection is that God is like what we indeed want. I do not argue here from wanting to being, that is, from the existence of a desire to the fact of its object. But knowing what we want, if we could have it, we discover in being itself, in revelation, an adequate response: Christ, the Word that was made flesh.

The "awe-ful" subject of the Trinity, in conclusion, is most familiar to us, most often seen by us in the way we address and conclude our prayers: "We ask this [of You Father] through Our Lord Jesus Christ, your son, who lives and reigns with you and the Holy Spirit, one God, forever and ever. Amen." Or, we might again repeat Johnson's prayer: "O Lord, hear my prayer, for Jesus Christ's sake, to whom with thee and the Holy Ghost, three persons and one God, be all honour and glory, world without end. Amen." The Trinity is not merely a theoretical doctrine but a living reality which reaches to our particular destiny, for it is our actual end. If we do not like to recall this truth in "mixed company," it is understandable, for it is, like all Christian doctrines, too good to be true. Because it is too good, it is not easily believable. Yet it is the only dogma worth believing, the only teaching about God for which

[25]German Bishops, *The Church's Confession of Faith* (San Francisco: Ignatius Press, 1987) 72–74.

there really is some evidence. Indeed, it is a doctrine full of ''awe,'' since it tells what God is like.

Chapter X

Intelligence and Holiness: All His Gifts Lead to His Glory

We are made in the image of God. We are no longer called servants but friends, as we read in the Gospel of John. The inner life of God is Trinity, the real communication of Person to Person. What God is like hints at what we are like in our deepest being. God alone is holy. "Holy, Holy, Holy," the traditional praise from Isaiah which is found so often in the liturgy is not a meaningless repetition but a response made in awe to the reality of God in his inner life. If God is holy and we are created in this divine image, we are called to be holy.

But human beings are to be holy as what they are. They do not cease to be human beings in their very holiness. If, as Aristotle said, human beings are rational animals, if this is what defines them, then this is how they are to be holy. In this present life and in the resurrection people are to be not some other sort of being, but themselves. Their speech, their gestures, their very eating and drinking are as natural to them as their reasonings and understandings. That the Body and Blood of Christ should appear to us under the form of bread and wine has its logic for us. Yet we must also think well. The normal result of revelation is accurate thought about the highest things, thought that results from the curious sensation that the highest perplexities of humanity—What is friendship? What is our body? What does loneliness mean even when we have a home?—do indeed have a proper response.

Holiness literally refers to the quality of being godlike. God alone is holy. To be holy means to be like God. The life of God is not our way; yet the very fact that we know God has an inner life inclines us to want to know this life, to belong to it. We cannot anticipate that we will know what God is like. Yet we cannot avoid wondering what he is like. We cannot assume that this knowledge of him is what God wants us to have. We are confronted, nonetheless, with the recurring suspicion that our main problem is not in expecting too much but in too little. The great case for atheism is not that we are offered too little but too much.

Intelligence is a quality or faculty that distinguishes certain beings who can be more than themselves, who can at least partially know what is not themselves. The classic definition of knowledge was simply to "be" all things. To know what is not ourselves changes us, not other things. Yet this knowledge does not make us not to be ourselves. To know seems natural to us, however extraordinary it might be that we can know all that is not ourselves. Human beings are distinguished from other beings with matter in their essence because they possess this faculty of knowing what is not themselves. Only because they know things that are not themselves can human beings know themselves at all. If beings less than God are to be holy, properly speaking, it must be because of something in God, something granted to such creatures by the Being who is holy in Himself. God must want what is not God to know what God as such is like. If we are made in God's image, we must be made to live and exist in the holiness of the inner life of God.

Holiness implies a capacity to receive what God is. God is not generated by the human intelligence but rather encountered through the world or revelation, through God's initiative in creation, redemption, and personal sanctification. Not everything properly speaking can be holy. Holiness will require a certain consciousness. Human beings must both know and choose the holiness offered to them. This double requirement—first, that holiness is not generated from within human beings; second, that it must nonetheless be known and accepted before it can be received—underscores the intimate relation of knowledge and holiness. What does not possess intelligence can be good but not holy. To possess intelligence does not make us for that reason holy. We must also choose to be holy.

By virtue of their respective natures or being as creature and Creator, therefore, a tension exists between a creature's capacity to know and God's inner knowability. What is not God could only know God properly if it were itself God, which it is not. The Divine Being can only be known by a free creature if that creature permits itself to know God, permits itself to be holy. Only in this sense can it be said that God is "dependent" on creation, though this does not imply that God is thereby lacking in anything. What is lacking is in the intelligent creature who can and perhaps does refuse to recognize *what is*. Our intelligence can refuse the intelligence of God, can refuse divine revelation, divine holiness. The consequences of refusing to be holy will manifest themselves in an intelligible counter-order to the being of God. When we refuse God, we concoct for ourselves our own rational account of a world ordered not by God but by us. A perverted mysticism surrounds what is not God.

"I look around: not one word has remained of what was formerly called 'truth,'" Nietzsche wrote in *The Anti-Christ*. "We can no longer stand it if a priest so much as uses the word 'truth.'" All religious representatives from theologian to pope, in Nietzsche's charge, did nothing but tell "lies." Previously they may have been excused by ignorance, but no longer. And why was this radical accusation justified? "The priest knows as well as anybody else that there is no longer any 'God,' any 'sinner,' any 'Redeemer'—that 'free will' and 'moral world order' are *lies*: seriousness, the profound self-overcoming of the spirit, no longer permits anybody *not* to know about this."[1] Nietzsche, the new philosopher, sought to undermine the confidence of the older elite of the priesthood about the proper object of its endeavors.

Nietzsche argued in the name of scientific ethos that "everyone" knew what was said to be "proved," namely that

[1]Friedrich Nietzsche, *The Anti-Christ*, no. 38, *The Portable Nietzsche*, ed. Walter Kaufmann (New York: Viking, 1968) 611.

there was no God. His effort to give the priest in particular a bad conscience is ironically eloquent in its testimony about the centrality of free will and its relation to God, sin, and redemption. The very notion of spirit is identified with "seriousness." "Overcoming," that is, eliminating the truths of faith and reason, is seen to be what the intellectual life is about. Intelligence no longer leads to holiness but replaces it. That is, understanding the arguments against God, sin, redemption, and free will becomes paradoxically the highest manifestation of spirit. Since this understanding is presented as a complete knowledge, it implicitly claims the power to replace God with itself as the highest goal of understanding.

This conclusion is the result of a central strand in modern intellectual life which would place human autonomy at the center of our inner meaning. This is a direct confrontation with all theories, particularly religious ones, that see human life as depending on something other than ourselves. Such an idea entails a vigorous use of human intellect to explain that God, sin, redemption, and free will do not exist as explanations of what human life is about. Thus an intellectual theory or ideology is required that presumably can explain everything by the sheer use of human intellect. So certain was Nietzsche that this effort to remove God had been already accomplished that he could accuse the representatives of the older spirituality of the most base act of moral vice, that of lying about the truth of things.

Nietzsche suspected that the faithful did not hold what they themselves were said to believe. God was not so much disproved but murdered, killed. He needed to be removed not by ignoring him but by a positive act of eliminating him. This act of deicide was spiritual. It took place in the mind after its artistic capacity to imagine another world. A lie was impossible. If nothing but mind was allowed to exist, one could not possibly compare non-existence with the only thing that existed—that is, what the mind formed. No reality existed to check the mind. What was necessary as a consequence of this need to make a new world was, of course, a new person. Here was a claim to construct a world out of human resources. Transcending the existing, historical person was seen to be what human life was about. This was the human vocation, the formation of a new person. The transcending of humanity meant removing the notions of free will, sin, God, and redemption, which had formed the ordered explanation of humanity.

This proposition of creating a new world, of course, was intelligible only in terms of revelation, which had already defined the ultimate human temptation as the human claim to establish by itself the definition of good and evil. To be "beyond good and evil," another favorite expression of Nietzsche's, meant the power to discover and put into effect a view of the world that did not accept the notions of good and evil set forth in reason and revelation. The alternate source of intelligibility in the world to that of the Creator could only be a finite intelligence that sought to define the human being as self-caused. Man announced that he had caused himself. He could act on that assumption. All that existed was caused by the human being.

The Christian tradition holds that simple and uneducated men and women can be holy, but only within a world of free will, redemption, sin, and God. Canonized saints and myriads of good human beings can be identified. Indeed, they may be rather common. That same tradition maintains that people with the most brilliant of intellects can be saints. No conflict between intelligence and faith exists. The priest or the pope properly speaks of "truth." We conclude that saints can be either wise or rather stupid. The foolish and the ignorant, however, need the wise and brilliant. Indeed, faith needs and fosters active intelligence, neglecting it at its own peril. Revelation shocks us out of our intellectual lethargy. It incites us to think about what we otherwise never would have pursued. It is addressed also to the intellectual, such as Nietzsche, who tries to explain the world without the structure of classical belief.

We are accustomed, no doubt, to sympathize with the difficulties intellectuals have with faith. But we cannot separate their difficulties from the equally provocative truth that the greatest sinners, the devils themselves, were depicted, like Plato's tyrant, as of the highest intelligence. The greatest of the sins, pride, is not a vice of the humble or simple, but that of the most learned and wise. Virtue and vice are not functions of comparative I.Q.'s. All walks of life are hazardous because human life as such is a risk. No way of life, however, is more dangerous than that of intellectuals, particularly if they choose as their way of life the pursuit of their own knowledge. But we should be sure in what this risk of the intelligent consists. It is not in misunderstanding mere life or existence itself. Rather it involves the risk of not achieving that for which each individual exists. The problem lies in the order of doing, not merely existing. But doing follows understanding. If we understand the nature of ourselves and the world incorrectly, we will not act properly or in the easiest way to achieve our personal ends.

The pursuit by intelligence to understand the why of reality often results in a "theory" to explain why no human life is at ultimate risk, why, as Nietzsche claimed, there are no sins, no freedoms, no choices. The outcome of intelligence is the erection of a duller world than the world in which risk exists, ultimate risk, even for the most humble. The elimination of sin and choice implies the removal of any real drama or story in human life. Holiness, like sinfulness, since it requires choice, is an aspect of human freedom. The alienated intellectual replaces the accurate description of the world which contains the choice of God or ourselves by his or her own understanding of the world which leaves out the transcendent meaning of God's creation.

In his book on St. Thomas, Chesterton remarked, perhaps cryptically, that "the work of hell is entirely spiritual."[2] This position requires an explanation of the whole metaphysics of the goodness of things, about evil as a lack of a good, about the nature of the will which is determined by no particular object, so that even in acting wrongly, it chooses some real good. We could be paradoxical and state that the closer one is to pure spirit the more danger one is in. St. Paul wrote, "In my speeches and the sermons that I gave, there were none of the arguments that belong to philosophy; only a demonstration of the power of the spirit. And I did this so that your faith should depend not on human philosophy but on the

[2]G. K. Chesterton, *St. Thomas Aquinas*, in *The Collected Works of G. K. Chesterton*, vol. 2 (San Francisco: Ignatius Press, 1986) 485.

power of God'' (1 Cor 2:4-5). Philosophy is seen here as opposed to holiness and the things of God.

We should not and do not conclude that philosophy is intrinsically hostile to God. But we do suspect that it can be, and is very likely to be, so used. The capacity for self-deception in the highest things is very great, and self-deception is of the most serious sort because it is the self which is primarily the alternative to God in all of our actions. Yet, as I said, revelation was given to us in order that we might exercise our intelligence more acutely. If God is all-knowing, God's existence, insofar as the human mind confronts God's presence or action in the world, cannot but cause knowing in what is not God.

Harry Blamires, in *The Christian Mind,* wrote that intelligence is capable of substituting itself for its own proper object, which it only meets but does not create: ''Your beliefs, as a Christian, are not yours in the sense that you have rights over them, either to tamper with them or to throw them away. Of course, the very fact that nowadays we look upon convictions as personal possessions is a symptom of the disappearance of the Christian mind.''[3] What is this? ''A Christian mind?'' Is not mind just mind? Surely there are not two sorts of minds.

Yet it is true. Thinking is a strange enterprise because it is so influenced by what we want, by what we allow ourselves to think. The example of Socrates is never far from this question. He was the philosopher who, if he would philosophize, if he would seek the truth, had to remain a private citizen. This privacy of the philosopher is the other side of the question of the saint who is not a philosopher. The non-philosopher saint, the simple holy person who is not recognized to have any intellectual pretensions, teaches both that human life is more than philosophy and that, normally, few are going to disturb the simple soul in his or her belief. The fool and the philosopher can look pretty much alike in most cities. Likewise, true goodness or holiness in many cities or

[3]Harry Blamires, *The Christian Mind* (Ann Arbor: Servant Publications, 1978) 40.

in many times can survive only because neither goodness or holiness is recognized for what it is.

In a letter she wrote on July 5, 1958, Flannery O'Connor explained the reasons why she wrote her stories and novels in such a striking, often grotesque manner.

> The setting in which most modern fiction takes place is exactly a setting in which nothing is so little felt to be true as the reality of a faith in Christ. . . . Fiction may deal with faith implicitly but explicitly it deals only with faith-in-a-person or persons. What must be unquestionable is what is implicitly implied as the author's attitude, and to do this the writer has to succeed in making the divinity of Christ seem consistent with the structure of all reality. This has to be got across implicitly in spite of a world that doesn't feel it, in spite of characters who don't live it. Writers like myself who don't use Catholic settings or characters, good or bad, are trying to make it plain that personal loyalty to the person of Christ is imperative, is the structure of man's nature, his necessary direction. The Church as institution doesn't come into it one way or another.[4]

This analysis is an attempt to save those outside of the Church, those who believe in some way but not fully, wholly, coherently.

A personal loyalty to Christ remains "the structure of man's nature." This is a bold, forceful statement. O'Connor was not content to depict her characters in action. She showed them in a world in which doctrine was missing or confused but in which the reality of Christ was the central purpose of each particular life, even though the characters seldom realized it. What O'Connor did not do, however, was to say that it made no difference what was believed. She looked for an explanation of the world in which a given individual could be saved even though he could not understand in any orthodox manner the formal intelligibility of the world. She did not invent a new inner order of the world but addressed herself to the question of how individuals, wherever they find them-

[4]Flannery O'Connor, *The Habit of Being*, ed. Sally Fitzgerald (New York: Vintage, 1979) 290.

selves, live in the one world *that is,* the one that includes free will, redemption, sin, and God.

Spiritual, not material, things are the most dangerous ones. A good deal is written about "transcendence," but it often takes a inner-worldly form such as a more perfect world order, eternal truth, justice, perfect benevolence, all of which become politicized. These notions of perfect order are "spiritual" or abstract. They do not defend the existing reality but propose something that might be. They are not necessarily for that reason, however, either Christian or realist. They can and often do represent a refusal to be incarnational at all, to grant any sort of imperfect existence to finite creatures. They represent a rebellion against any idea of an imperfect world in which the actual incarnation could have happened. The chief alternatives to God will be spiritual, even when they appear as materialist and are embodied in history. Although classical spirituality has sought to accept, as signs of a higher human aspiration, efforts to put into reality ideals of beauty, truth, or goodness, these ideals are not, as they stand, God. "Spirituality" or "holiness" can appear to be opposed to God who is, in the orthodox view, incarnate and powerful enough to save mankind in any existing, sinful order.

In a culture veering away from Christianity, the initial deviations from order will appear as an abstraction, as "ideal." The holy person formed by virtue and grace will be replaced by the philosophical person of ideas, who will finally be replaced by the political person. This political person will have been freed by philosophy from any grounding in an order that is not purely a structure of the mind of the philosopher-politician. Politicized "holiness" will be identified with justice, and justice will be the conformity of a political order with what the philosopher proposes. Upholding the "truth" of the order, even an order based on a theoretical position of skepticism, will be the only nobility or piety allowed.

True holiness is not merely the understanding that there are spiritual things in the universe. Holiness includes the understanding of what is meant by spiritual things, of the operation of our intellects by which we understand and of that through which we understand. Gerard Manley Hopkins wrote:

I say more: the just man justices;
    Keeps grace: that keeps all his goings graces;
Acts in God's eye what in God's eye he is—
    Christ. For Christ plays in ten thousand places,
Lovely in limbs, and lovely in eyes not his
    To the Father through the features of men's faces.[5]

The abstractions, justice or beauty, must be seen to live in grace, in a divine Being who grounds such ideas in something more than themselves. What we are to our neighbor, to ourselves, is revealed in the faces, in the concrete lives we have and are given, in the lovely eyes not ours.

Eric Mascall wrote of the exercise of analyzing just what the alternatives to Christianity would look like by comparison: ''Compared with the historic faith of Christendom, the world which is offered to us by modern secularism is restricted, impoverished and quite incapable of satisfying our real needs and aspirations. . . . Most mysterious of all is the fact that many Christians themselves give the impression that their religion is dull and cramping.''[6] (To give him credit, this is what Nietzsche also observed of Christians). Mascall realized how this faith was the only theory that could give a cogent reason why each life might be exciting and significant, because it contained with its every choice a possibility of ultimate good or evil.

Flannery O'Connor again put the theoretical position well, tying it to the dogmas that ground the issues involved in sin and will:

> My reading of the priest's article on hell was that hell is what God's love becomes to those who reject it. Now no one has to reject it. God made us to love Him. It takes two to love. It takes liberty. It takes the right to reject. If there were no hell, we would be like the animals. No hell, no dignity. And remember the mercy of God. It is easy to put this down as a formula and hard to believe it, but try believing the oppo-

[5] *The Poems of Gerard Manley Hopkins*, ed. W. H. Gardner and N. H. MacKenzie (4th edition; London: Oxford, 1967) 90.

[6] E. L. Mascall, *The Christian Universe* (London: Darton, Longman & Todd, 1966) 22–23.

site, and you will find it too easy. Life has no meaning that way.[7]

Nietzsche's rejected principles—free will, God, sin, redemption—reappear. O'Connor made the doctrine of hell intelligible and required us to think out the alternative to it. She did not come to any conclusion different from Nietzsche. Both writers understood that we choose our ultimate status. The nature of our spirituality will depend on our will and intelligence, on what we choose. To "try to believe the opposite," as Nietzsche in fact did try to do, deprives individual life of transcendent meaning. But this very thinking through of such consequences is a necessary intellectual aspect of holiness, for it demonstrates what is at stake, that understanding the truth is essential to genuine holiness.

Samuel Johnson once wrote to Boswell about the real alternative to a world that is self-constructed by the human intellect, a world that presupposed only itself: "To what degree fancy is to be admitted into religious offices, it would require much deliberation to determine. I am far from intending totally to exclude it. Fancy is a faculty bestowed by our Creator, and it is reasonable that all His gifts should be used to his glory, that all our faculties should co-operate in His worship; but they are to co-operate according to the will of Him that gave them, according to the order which his wisdom has established."[8] Fancy, freedom, and order are seen by Johnson to belong together. The risk of freedom is not contrary to the existence of freedom. The use of freedom, however, is to be governed not by the intellect creating its own order but by the discovery of an order already given to it. All God's gifts should freely lead to his glory. Spirituality and holiness are also obedient.

In the German *Confession of Faith*, we find this comment on holiness: "When Holy Scripture speaks of 'holiness,' it does not primarily mean ethical perfection, but rather *being singled out from the domain of the worldly and belonging to God.*"[9] We can

[7]O'Connor, Letter to Louise Abbot, 1959, *The Habit of Being*, 354.

[8]*Boswell's Life of Johnson* I (London: Oxford, 1931) 532.

[9]German Bishops' Conference, *The Church's Confession of Faith* (San Francisco: Ignatius Press, 1987) 234.

reject this singling out. The belonging to God that is implied in holiness is not something that is done apart from that which is specifically the character of a person, the capacity and necessity to choose how to see the world and the worldly. There is no involuntary holiness. The intelligence of the person is the instrument of holiness insofar as it must judge what is the source of this singling out. For the classical definition of pride, the primary vice, is the singling out of ourselves, the explanation of the world in terms of our own mental picture of what it ought to be, checked by no outside source of truth.

In a famous passage Thomas à Kempis remarked that he would rather feel compunction than know how to define it (*Imitation of Christ* I, 1, 3). Contained within this brief passage is both an awareness of the dangers of intelligence and an appreciation of the fact that people can be holy without being able to give a philosophical definition of holiness. For Nietzsche the priest and the Christian had bad consciences because they "knew" the falsity of the central dogmas of the faith. The one flaw of Nietzsche concerned this "knowing." Was it true? Christianity cannot and ought not ever neglect its philosophical component which addresses the validity of its truth.

For Flannery O'Connor, on the other hand, the task of intelligence was to spell out carefully what a world without freedom, grace, God, sin, and redemption looked like. Nietzsche's challenge ought not to be left as something unable to be analyzed. It is a part of holiness to know why alternative mysticisms are attractive and why they deviate from the given good to which the intellect is ordered. Holiness cannot neglect intellect. But intellect can seek to put its own world into being since it can imagine something other than *what is*. We must be "singled" out from the imprisonment of our own independent intellectual systems by what is not formed by our own intelligence itself. God it is who frees us from our own self-constructed theoretical systems.

The character of human holiness is initially receptive. The virtue of humility, Nietzsche was quite right, is the typical Christian virtue. Humility admits that we do not create our own purpose in the world. We do not constitute by ourselves the highest things. We discover what we are and what we are for from outside ourselves. For this reason Nietzsche had to call humility a vice. Yet once having received and prayed on what we are drawn into by the active presence of God, we can act. For there are indeed virtues and graces in the world that also make our lives different, even though the primary end of holiness is not to make the world different but to live the life of God. Aquinas at this point argued that because of our intellects this possibility of actually receiving the vision of God is open to us. We are given to anticipate more than we can imagine or create by ourselves. This is the root of the real astonishment of the faith, and of its incredibility. The real temptation remains our suspicion that we are given not too little but too much. No other holiness is so exalted or so welcome or so intellectually satisfying as that described by the doctrines of the Creed.

Intelligence and holiness are aspects of a spiritual life that needs to grasp the truth that spirit is close both to evil and to good. The risk of the life we are offered is rooted not only in our inner being but in the being of God. Holiness, in conclusion, is the drama of our understanding and action in the world in which we live. If that world is our own exclusive world, as it can be, we risk never being drawn into the holiness of God. But if we use our intelligence to discover what exactly a world might be like in which sin, God, freedom, and redemption do not exist, we can see that we must reject that which leaves us only with ourselves, with the exalted loneliness of a Nietzschean superman.

The classical description of God as God is that he is holy. This is the praise most proper to him, the "Holy, Holy, Holy." It is the recognition that his world is that for which we exist. Any world we choose exclusively for ourselves is its own punishment. We are given, in a kind of divine irony, what we ask for, both when we ask for ourselves and when we ask for the God that singles us out. Mascall was right; no other doctrine about our lot and condition is less dull than this relationship of intelligence and holiness. "For Christ plays in ten thousand places, / Lovely in limbs, and lovely in eyes not his / To the Father through the features of men's faces."

In his *Spiritual Exercises,* St. Ignatius always asks us, when we pray, to visualize with our senses and imagination any scriptural scene we may be considering in our prayer. But he also characteristically directs our attention to understanding the subject matter of our prayer and our faith. Holiness is not separate from our understanding. He will thus, in his "Principle and Foundation," explain what our purpose in life is and how we are to attain it. "Man is created to praise, reverence, and serve God Our Lord and by this means to save his soul." In this context, he explains that the purpose of the other things on the face of the earth, life and death, fame and humiliations, wealth and poverty, is to assist us in reaching our purpose. God had us in mind when he created out of nothing everything *that is*. Everything that is and comes to us, he holds, is to be used to gain our purpose, which is eternal life with God himself.

When St. Ignatius came to his "Contemplation for Obtaining Love" at the end of the *Exercises*, he insisted that we "ask for what we wish." And the first thing we are to request is "an *intimate understanding* of so many goods we have received from God." Only in the light of this proper, intimate understanding, which we are again and again requested to seek, can we properly recognize God's majesty so that we can love and serve him in all things. All other things on the face of the earth, through our understanding their truth and using them for our good, are saved through our relation to God—such is our dignity. Intelligence is not the fullness of holiness, to be sure. But it is an essential element, the neglect of which can easily lead us to a kind of anti-godly mysticism which pits us against God's redemptive purpose for us.

In his "Contemplation on the Incarnation," moreover, St. Ignatius asked us to understand the context in which holiness was possible for mankind. We are to reflect on "how the three Divine Persons looked over the whole range and circumference of the world full of men and women. This Trinity saw how so many were descending into Hell. Realizing this, the most Blessed Trinity in its eternity decided that the Second Person should become Man to save the human race. Thus in the plenitude of time, they sent the Angel Gabriel to our Blessed Lady." This reflection is a summary of why and how holiness exists in the world and how it both is intended for us and can reach us. We are to understand not only what holiness is, but how it is we are to live in the holiness that the Lord has sent into the world.

Origen, in his notes on prayer, wrote that "he who prays for the coming of God's kingdom prays rightly to have it within himself. . . . For God reigns in each of his holy ones." Holiness is intended for each of us individually. It is the least abstract reality there is. We do not first define holiness and then discover that it is a property of God. Rather as we are graced by God's redemptive purpose, we can understand what the life of God is, what it means that our highest praise is simply the praise of *What Is*, the "Holy, Holy, Holy." We rejoice that we do not have to be gods because God already *Is*. What is God like? The angel Gabriel was sent to Our Lady. The Word was made flesh and dwelt amongst us. All God's gifts lead to the divine glory.

Chapter XI

Augustine: On Teaching and Being Taught

Flannery O'Connor recalled that "somewhere St. Augustine says that the things of the world poured forth from God in a double way: intellectually into the minds of the angels and physically into the world of things."[1] For this reason the search for what God is like can take many turns and twists. I have suggested in the account of Raissa Maritain (see above, chapter 3) that often we must simply look carefully at what happens in the lives of people we do not know in order to see how God has related himself to these people. In this endeavor no one is more provocative, more insightful than St. Augustine. Augustine's account in his *Confessions* of what he did, of what happened to him, his memory, his record of his life, is one of our most precious instructions in what God is like.

The *New Yorker* once had an end-filler that was listed under the rubric: "Letters We Never Finished Reading." This particular letter was post marked "Salem House Publications, 462 Boston Street, Topsfield, MA 01983" and began: "Dear Sinner: Perhaps you're wondering what I, God, am doing writing an autobiography. . . ." No doubt the *New Yorker* editors were rightly amused by such a beginning. We must say that Augustine's *Confessions* were not written by God but by an admitted sinner. They were autobiographical and addressed to God. We can say that *The Confessions* too are something we

[1]Flannery O'Connor, *The Habit of Being*, ed. Sally Fitzgerald (New York: Vintage, 1979) 128.

never finish reading, even when we have read them many, many times.

I want to bring together through Augustine all that I have been thinking about the topic of what God is like. Let me begin by recalling two passages from Augustine that seem to me to catch something of his spirit, something of O'Connor's sense of how things pour forth from God and how such a mercurial Augustine was able to catch some of this superabundant outpouring.

> 1) And what did it profit me that, when scarce twenty years old, a book of Aristotle's, entitled *The Ten Categories*, fell into my hands—on whose very name I hung as on something great and divine, when my rhetoric master of Carthage, and others who were esteemed learned, referred to it with cheeks swelling with pride—I read it alone and understood it? (St. Augustine, *Confessions*, IV, 16).
>
> 2) Mary heard God's word and kept it, and so she is blessed. She kept God's truth in her mind, a nobler thing than carrying his body in her womb. The truth and the body were both Christ: he was kept in Mary's mind insofar as he is the truth; he was carried in her womb insofar as he is a man; but what is kept in the mind is of a higher order than what is carried in the womb (St. Augustine, *Sermo*, 25, *PL* 46, 937-8).

Augustine boasted both about how easily he understood Aristotle and how he appreciated the role of the Blessed Mother in her own relation to God. Augustine began his road to God by rather too confidently starting with the philosophers, with Aristotle and Cicero. "And what did it profit me," he asked himself at twenty-five, "that I, base slave of vile affections, read unaided, and understood, all the books that I could get of the so-called liberal arts?"[2]

Wise philosopher-politicians like Cicero himself had sent their sons off to Athens to learn philosophy. "To everyone who proposes to have a good career, moral philosophy is indispensable. And I am inclined to think that this applies particularly

[2]St. Augustine, *Confessions*, IV, 16, in *The Basic Works of St. Augustine*, vol. 1, ed. Whitney J. Oates (New York: Random House, 1948) 56.

to [you] yourself,'' Cicero wrote solemnly to his son, Marcus, in Athens, about his obligations toward learning.

> For upon your shoulders rests a special responsibility. People have high expectations that you will work hard, as I have. . . . It would be discreditable, then, if you came back empty. . . . So make every effort you can. Work as hard as possible (if study comes under the heading of work and not of pleasure!) and do your very best. I have supplied you with all you need, so do not let people say that the failure is on your side. But enough of this! I have sent you similar exhortations times without number.[3]

Such sons, we know, often find these sober fatherly instructions to be merely burdensome. The sons are busy about other things. Nor do all philosophers produce worthy sons, and other philosophers, as Socrates himself, are accused of neglecting their sons by engaging in philosophy and its somber consequences.

Other more precocious young men, like Augustine in Thagaste in Africa, were sent by their poorer fathers first to near-by Carthage, mainly to learn not philosophy but how to speak and how to make a living—to the law schools and the business schools, in other words. The first thing that Augustine did on arriving in Carthage was read this same Cicero, which changed his life forever. How sad it is that we no longer have this dialogue, the *Hortensius*, which so intellectually inspired the young Augustine. One is tempted to think that Cicero's true spiritual son, though born some five hundred years after him, was not young Marcus, who never amounted to much, carousing in Athens, but rather the turbulent Augustine, who, apparently, did a fair amount of carousing himself, both in Carthage and in Rome.

Augustine, though reluctantly, pursued philosophy to its very limits. He learned that truth is not merely something we are given, but something we must choose. We may, in fact, not choose it, even if we know it is true. This is our risk. The record of Augustine's *Confessions* is so dramatic because it ac-

[3]Cicero, *On Duties, III*, in *Cicero: Selected Works*, vol. 1, ed. Michael Grant (Harmondsworth: Penguin, 1977) 161.

knowledges the number of times a potential young philosopher can choose wrongly, can choose willfully against *what is*. Hence the tragedy of our lot is more disturbing than that of the universe itself. For it is only in the drama of our wills that the true end of the universe can ultimately be understood or achieved. This explains why classical philosophy began with pre-Socratic cosmology and, with its exhaustion, proceeded in Socrates to ethics, and finally in Augustine to the Word made flesh.

Augustine's dialogue *De Magistro* was written at the end of his thirty-second year. In it, Augustine's own son, Adeodatus, then about fifteen, was discussing the problem of learning and teaching. He told his father that he had indeed learned something from this particular conversation about words and what was behind them. "Man is only prompted by words in order that he may learn, and it is apparent that only a very small measure of what a speaker thinks is expressed," the young man explained to Augustine.[4] He added that we learn "whether things are true" from him who dwells within us by grace.

What had his human father, Augustine, done for his son in this lesson and exchange between them? In fact, Augustine did not break the "thread of his thought" for he "anticipated and dissolved all the objections" which had occurred to Adeodatus. That is to say, error, confusion, and controversy can indeed prevent us from knowing the truth within us. The function of the teacher is first to address himself to what is not true so that the pupil can see with his own powers the truth of things. Whatever "unquiet" Adeodatus had carried into his soul had been dissolved; thus in the end there seemed to the young man to be a perfect conformity between what Augustine had stated and that inner truth to which all words or argument led. This inner truth was something that was independent of the teacher and, in a sense, of the learner.

If we wonder how this independence of truth might be understood, we must look a little earlier in the same dialogue at what Augustine had been teaching his son. We observe that he was most concerned to keep the integrity of the teacher by

[4]St. Augustine, "On the Teacher," 14, in *Basic Works*, vol. 1, 395.

disassociating the teacher's own words as such from the truth itself. Words led to truth; they were not themselves truth. The dialogue had carefully distinguished between sounds, words, and meanings or that to which words led. This inability of words to be themselves simply "truth," though they could lead us to it, was why Augustine insisted upon an inner truth, which was not, however, merely subjective.[5] Augustine, as a follower of the Platonic tradition, was disturbed by the difference between the stability of truth and the changeableness of things. As a Christian, however, he could not find in the created cosmos itself sufficient cause for the order and truth which the mind clearly saw. He found this cause of stability and truth not in himself, in his own powers, but in his own inner illumination, which came from God, not from himself or from the cosmos.

An Aristotelian thinker would find this same metaphysical certainty rather in the world and its causes, but both Augustine and Aristotle must finally reach some reason why things are as they are. The central doctrine of Christianity is the incarnation—expressed by the most philosophical of the evangelists as "the Word made flesh and [dwelling] amongst us." Aristotle had defined the human mind, the highest of the soul's own powers, as that faculty which was *capax omnium* (capable of all things), that power by which what was not ourselves came to exist in us to be ours.

What was beyond us, however, came to be ours without changing what was outside of us. Knowledge as knowledge did not change the world. But knowledge did discover a truth in things, a truth that was not fashioned by the human mind but one to which the mind was open as its natural object. Augustine saw this same truth in the ultimate origins of why something was this way not that, of why it was at all, so that for him each thing needed to be "illuminated" in his inner soul. As his son understood, we could say truly of ourselves that we see the truth of the thing in itself.

[5]See Matthias J. Smalbrugge, "Les Notions de"Enseignement' et 'Parole' dans le *de Magistro* et l'*in Joannis Evang*. Tr. 29," *Augustinianum* 27 (December, 1987) 523–38.

For Augustine, we "applaud" not the teachers or learners in themselves but only the truth. Indeed, teachers really are learners if they know what they are doing. Usually, Augustine admitted, very little time elapses between our speaking of something and our comprehending it. Students are bright and quickly grasp what the teacher intends his words to mean. But the fact is, both teacher and pupil see the same truth. For this reason Augustine asked pointedly, "Who is so stupidly curious to send his son to school in order that he may learn what the teacher thinks?"[6] For Augustine, an intellectual institution is not a place for the private opinions of the faculty. Thus no truth is the possession of the teacher; it is not his private property or original invention.

The sciences, virtue, and wisdom which the teacher professes to teach, are, to be sure, explained through words. Through these words the pupils must "consider within themselves whether what has been explained is said truly." The pupil makes such consideration not by attending to what the teacher thinks, but by attending "to that inner truth according to the measure of which each is able."[7] We should not attribute to words "more than is proper." For Augustine, both the teacher and the disciple arrive at something neither owns or makes for himself.

The Confessions follows how Augustine himself looked on his having been taught and on his own teaching. We will consider *The Confessions* up to the point of his full conversion and return to Africa. This account of his early life is the classic text of the young potential philosopher in all his turmoil. We know more of the inner life of Augustine than of any other ancient or perhaps even modern person.[8] His only classical rival is, perhaps, Cicero or Marcus Aurelius. Of the interior life of Plato or Aristotle we know practically nothing. This extraordinary self-reflection which Augustine exposed to us is his legacy of teaching. Here is the "great teacher" of whom

[6]Augustine, "On the Teacher,"14, in *Basic Works*, vol. 1, 394.
[7]Ibid., 395.
[8]Cicero is the only ancient writer we know about as well as Augustine.

Leo Strauss spoke, the one whom we can only encounter in his books.[9]

In the first chapter of *The Confessions* Augustine announced that he had been "preached to" by Ambrose. Augustine knew his own heart to be "restless." He also acknowledged that he was meant to "praise." We are "moved to delight in praising" the Lord. In this book he wanted to know and understand the order of which should be considered first, the knowing or the calling on God. He understood that he could not call on anything without knowing about it, but if our knowledge is not good, just who are we calling on? So he wondered instead if, in order "to know Thee," we first must call on God.[10] The endeavor to know requires both a belief and a call.

By the time Augustine reached Ambrose in Milan, in 386 A.D., he had already recapitulated in himself almost all the major errors about God open to a most intelligent young man. Monica, his mother, earlier had been badgering him to visit a certain learned bishop to discuss his intellectual problems. But the good bishop, after listening to Monica, decided that as yet Augustine was simply "unteachable." He was, in his own words, "inflated with the novelty of that heresy [Manicheanism], and that [he] had already perplexed divers inexperienced persons with vexatious questions."[11] Interestingly, the bishop told Monica that Augustine himself would figure his way out of Manicheanism if first she would pray to God for him; in the end he would "by reading, discover what the error is." Evidently, the unnamed bishop had had much the same problem as a young man as Augustine. He did not see why Augustine would not be able to puzzle it out in due time. Everyone, in Augustine's view, was at some time or other in his life unteachable, so that until some change of will took place, he would remain in this voluntarily obtuse condition.

Augustine was aware of his own transgressions, even those beginning in infancy and boyhood. "The iniquities of

[9]Leo Strauss, "What Is Liberal Education?" *Liberalism: Ancient and Modern* (New York: Basic Books, 1968) 3.

[10]Augustine, *Confessions*, in *Basic Works*, vol. 1, 3.

[11]Ibid., 41.

his heart'' explained in part why he did not sooner come to truth. He did not, however, ''contend in judgment'' with God who is the Truth. He did not seek to set himself up as a maker of truth. He did not want to ''deceive himself'' any longer. He was acutely aware that truth is given, that one does not make it; he could not stand it if his own iniquity ''lied against itself.''[12]

Augustine frankly admitted that as a young man he would rather have been playing ball than studying. He even cheated a bit at the games he played. He certainly felt this deception was a fault. However, he had ''no love of learning, and hated to be forced to it.''[13] Though he loved Latin, he hated the study of Greek, and later wondered why. He consoled himself that he had at least learned to read and write, but he felt, reminiscent of the classic Platonic question of poetry and philosophy, that he had worried too much about Dido and the love stories he found in the Latin classics.

Like Plato, Augustine was concerned about the charm or fascination one often feels towards the classical literary and philosophical texts. But he understood that ''a free curiosity has more influence in our learning these things [Latin] than a necessity full of fear.''[14] Clearly a bright young man, he was constantly being praised and applauded for his own learning and accomplishments. In his more sober moments, he finally, like Agamemnon or Oedipus, had to learn by suffering—from God ''who teachest by sorrow.''[15] Nor was he unmindful ''of that small part of the human race who may chance to light upon these my writings.''[16] He was most conscious of the fact that his own experience, his own book, was intended, through his own path recounted in *The Confessions,* to lead its readers to the truth.

As a young man hardly twenty years old, Augustine became the head of a School Rhetoric in Carthage. The students, who were none too disciplined, showed a ''vagrant liberty.''

[12]Ibid., 6.
[13]Ibid., 10.
[14]Ibid., 14.
[15]Ibid., 21.
[16]Ibid., 22.

They mostly wanted to become lawyers, a profession in which, as Augustine quipped, one excelled in proportion to his craftiness. It was as schoolmaster that Augustine encountered Cicero's *Hortensius*. We "admire Cicero's language but not his heart," he said, rather unkindly, of the great Roman.[17] None the less, the book simply "inflamed" him. He yearned for an "immortality of wisdom," but he was also aware that Scripture had warned that philosophy could seduce us (1 Cor 1:17-25; Rom 1:19-20). He quickly cast aside all the religious sects with which he had dallied in order, like the young men of *The Republic*, to embrace philosophic wisdom itself.

First, he tried to relate Scripture to philosophy, but Scripture "appeared to be unworthy to be compared with the dignity of Tully."[18] In his "inflated pride," he could not get at Scripture's "inner meaning." This dilemma led him into the hands of the Manichees, which only made things worse. In retrospect, he thought, even "the poets and the grammarians" seemed to make more sense than the Manicheans.[19] He himself was too ignorant of "that which really is."[20] Yet he suddenly began to realize that evil was not in things, as the Manicheans would have had it, but "was naught but a privation of good, until in the end it altogether ceases to be." When he was to encounter the Platonists later on, he would perfect this line of thought.

From his nineteenth to his twenty-eighth year, Augustine went on his merry way deceiving himself and others, in public "by sciences which they style 'liberal'—secretly with a falsity called religion."[21] He discovered, that is, astrologers, mathematicians, and determinists. At this point he encountered an old doctor who told him to toss out all these books of horoscopes which he had been considering.[22] As he learned more about the nature of chance, he began to doubt the wisdom of these "star-gazers." In the midst of these controver-

[17]Ibid., 32.
[18]Ibid., 33.
[19]Ibid., 34.
[20]Ibid., 35.
[21]Ibid., 42.
[22]Ibid., 44.

sies a young believing friend of his died. Augustine had jested with him about his beliefs, only later to discover that the young man was serious about his faith.

During these years Augustine reminds us of the democratic youths whom Plato discussed in *The Republic*, who go around from day to day changing what they want to know or do (557a–564a). But he was learning. He had tried and rejected a number of basic and recurring philosophical or religious positions. As he got over his grief at his friend's death,

> What revived and refreshed me especially was the consolations of other friends, with whom I did love what instead of Thee I loved. . . . There were other things in them which did more lay hold of my mind—to discourse and jest with them; to indulge in an interchange of kindnesses; to read together pleasant books, together to trifle, and together to be earnest; to differ at times without ill-humor, as a man would do with his own self; and even by the infrequency of these differences to give zest to our more frequent consentings; sometimes teaching, sometimes being taught; longing for the absent with impatience, and welcoming the coming with joy.[23]

Here is the mind of the potential young philosopher and his friends, clearly reminiscent of Glaucon, Adeimantus, and Polemarchus in *The Republic*, who wanted to hear philosophy praised for its own sake (367c-d). It is a picture of the need such young men have for both knowledge and companionship, aware even in their supreme self-assurance that there are truths which they do not yet possess.

In Carthage, when about twenty-six or twenty-seven, Augustine wrote several books "On the Fair and the Fit." Exactly how many even he could not recall. He dedicated these books to one Hierius, a Roman orator, whom he did not know.[24] Augustine himself wanted to be an orator. He pondered his vocation. He already knew that "man himself is a great deep." That Roman orator was of the kind that Augustine loved, "as I wished myself to be such a one." "I erred through

[23]Ibid., 48.
[24]Ibid., 52.

an inflated pride, and was carried about with every wind, but yet was piloted by Thee, though very secretly.'' He did not suspect that he could himself go ''astray of free will, and end as a punishment.''[25]

A couple of years later, when Augustine was twenty-nine, the most learned of the Manichean bishops, Faustus, came to Carthage. Faustus enjoyed a high reputation. In preparation for this meeting Augustine spent his time checking up on the Manichean system. For nine years he had been wanting to discuss things with this Faustus, especially as other members of the sect ''were unable to answer the questions I raised.''[26] Augustine was nothing if not brash. However, even Faustus turned out to be a major disappointment, though he was ''of pleasant speech.'' Faustus was not well read; he knew only ''some of Tully's orations, a very few books of Seneca, and some of the poets,'' together with a few Manichean books. This realization of Faustus' lack of knowledge was the final blow for Augustine. Poor Faustus ''was ignorant of those arts in which I believed him to excel.''[27] Augustine began to despair that his problems would ever be solved. Faustus did not want to check the calculations of the Manichean books, ''for he was aware that he had no knowledge of such things.'' Instead of being eloquent, he said exactly ''nothing.'' But grudgingly Augustine admired his honesty. Augustine finally went back to teaching rhetoric, but released by Faustus from the ''snare'' in which he had been caught.

Disgusted with the greed and lack of discipline of the students in Carthage and naively believing that students were different in Rome, Augustine sailed to Rome to begin teaching. Immediately he fell in with a Gnostic ''elect'' group, which seemed to prove that we ourselves did not sin, but that some other nature in us did.[28] This view, of course, was quite welcome to Augustine as it confirmed him in his ways. He began, however, with the help of one Helpidius, to realize that the Scriptures did not say exactly what the Manicheans taught,

[25]Ibid., 55.
[26]Ibid., 63.
[27]Ibid., 64.
[28]Ibid., 68.

or even what he had thought about them.[29] He also learned that students in Rome cheated their teachers out of their pay, just as they did in Carthage.[30] Meantime, the prefect of Milan was looking for a teacher of rhetoric. He interviewed Augustine and hired him, apparently "with the aid of those identical persons, drunk with Manichean vanities," from whom Augustine was trying to escape. And as he put it, "to Milan I came, to Ambrose the bishop, known to the whole world as the best of men."[31]

It was in Milan that Augustine encountered the Platonists. In the meantime his own life underwent profound changes under the influence not only of Monica and Ambrose but also of the sophisticated intellectual culture of Milan. He eventually rejected his mistress, a profitable marriage proposal, a second mistress, and even his job as a professor in order to pursue his quest for truth wherever it might lead him. Later he would return to Africa, via Ostia, where Monica was to die. What was remarkable about his stay in Milan and Cassiciacum was, however, his persistent effort to see in his faith a direct relation both to the philosophical problems with which he had struggled throughout his life and the new ones he discovered as he learned more about Greek philosophy.

The young Augustine, the brilliant young potential philosopher, from his nineteenth to his thirty-third year, who looked continually for books and teachers, who taught and who was taught, is of interest to us. For perhaps better than in any other instance in the history of philosophy do we have a singleminded young man who in his own soul, yet in a soul he revealed openly to us, had to go through all the passions, all the heresies, and all the philosophies in order to arrive at truth. As he worked his way through the great moral and intellectual problems that confront any intelligent young man or woman, we can sense how he can touch the soul of anyone who "chances" to read him. He wrote his *Confessions* for the ages. He wrote it consciously for posterity, it seems, because he realized that this life, which he "confessed" to us, accurately

[29]Ibid., 70.
[30]Ibid., 70.
[31]Ibid., 71.

described him; and in describing himself, he revealed our own souls to us.

The intellectual heritage of Augustine is still alive in *The Confessions*. His heritage is for those who realize that in the end we must finally understand what possible answers have been given to the questions posed by any intelligent, young, potential philosopher. But Augustine forces us to realize that we not only must understand truth but also choose it. We must allow ourselves to be attracted by it, and we must finally transcend any fault that prevents us from following it. Augustine, perhaps more than any other single person in the history of philosophy, stands for this fact: *we must also choose the truth*.

At the beginning of book six of *The Confessions,* Augustine recounted how Monica had managed to follow him to Milan. The good lady hit stormy seas on the way but spent most of her time comforting her frightened fellow passengers. When she finally arrived at Milan where her son had launched his teaching career, Augustine said, "She found me in grievous danger, through despair of ever finding the truth."[32] This extraordinary admission of Augustine to his mother defines perhaps better than any other passage in philosophic literature the sort of open soul the seeker of wisdom must have. By the time Augustine reached Milan and had heard Ambrose preach, however, he had begun to suspect there was more to what Monica believed than he had been willing to admit in his younger years. Even of Ambrose Augustine confessed that he was mainly interested in "how skillfully" he spoke, but he could not help suspecting "how truly he spoke."[33]

Augustine began to wonder whether he had been wrong all along about Scripture. He found that "the greater part of the philosophers held much the more probable opinions" than the Manicheans to whom he had been attached.[34] Imitating the academic skeptics who "doubted everything and fluctuated between all," he abandoned the Manicheans. But the philosophers did not much satisfy him either. He decided to be a catechumen, which did not imply that he believed every-

[32]Ibid., 73.
[33]Ibid., 71.
[34]Ibid., 72.

thing, but only that he no longer believed what he had held up to this time.

From the very busy Ambrose, Augustine determined to learn what he could. What he was discovering was that the revelational side of his family background had some sense in it. He remained wary, of course. Ambrose taught "nothing that offended me, though he taught such things as I knew not as yet whether they were true."[35] Faced with this bewilderment, Augustine admitted, rather humbly, that "for all this time, I restrained my heart from assenting to anything, fearing to fall headlong; but by hanging in suspense I was the worse killed." Again, one sees the attention to will, to the fact that truth does not force itself on us but must be sought (something Augustine claimed he did) and chosen. His very reticence testified to his awareness that something more was at work in him than just understanding.

Augustine ironically was attracted by the traditional doctrine because "it was with more moderation and honesty that it commanded things to be believed that were not demonstrated."[36] In his reflections on "so many self-contradicting philosophies" he came to believe both that "Thou wert, and hast care of us." The more metaphysical questions of "what was to be thought of Thy substance, and what way led, or led back to Thee" remained perplexing to him. Such questions hint at his own Platonic background. These first two questions, whether God exists and whether he cares for us, are two of the three positions—(the third is that God can be bought off by prayers and sacrifices) which Plato in *The Laws* maintained are those that cannot be doubted in a true polity (885b).

With two young men, Alypius and Nebridius, then in Milan, Augustine formed a philosophical circle to pursue excitedly what they were discovering. Alypius had been Augustine's pupil in Africa. Though mostly a virtuous young man, in a memorable scene he did succumb, with subsequent sorrow, to the base attractions of the Circesian games both in Carthage and in Rome. Nebridius, also from near Carthage, followed Augustine to Milan "for no other reason than that

[35]Ibid., 77.
[36]Ibid., 77.

he might live with me in a most ordered search after truth and wisdom."[37] These young potential philosophers considered together the most "abstruse questions" but could not quite figure out why they could not quickly find the whole truth. Their earnestness is both disingenuous and charming. So they were frustrated "for as yet we had discovered nothing certain to which, when relinquished, we might betake ourselves."[38] Clearly, they were not merely searching for the truth, after the manner of classical philosophy, but they expected that, when they found it, they would have something "to do" about it.

Augustine was now about thirty and decided to take stock of where he was going. He informs us that ever since he was nineteen he had been "inflamed with the desire of wisdom." When he had found her, he intended to "forsake all the empty hopes and lying insanities of vain desires."[39] But where was he? Faustus did not help, nor the academics. He decided rather to follow the "ecclesiastical books" which once had seemed "absurd." But who would teach him? "Ambrose has no leisure—we have no leisure to read. Where are we to find the books?" What the three young men decided to do was to give up all teaching and to "betake themselves solely to the search after truth."

Finally, Augustine resolved that maybe this philosophical search for truth had moral consequences; so he valiantly, in his view, gave up his beloved mistress. He then set up a sort of philosophical household in the home of his friend Romanianus. In this more peaceful environment he began to consider more carefully the questions of God's substance, of good and evil, of change. At first he suspected that Epicurus would have been right "had not I believed that after death there remained a life for the soul."[40] He realized that he could not be happy without his friends.

In his continuing philosophical discussions during this period Augustine instructs us that these philosophical questions are to be taken seriously. The great issues needed to be

[37]Ibid., 84.
[38]Ibid., 85.
[39]Ibid., 85.
[40]Ibid., 89.

confronted, not just as a youthful philosophic pastime, as Callicles had argued in the *Gorgias* (485), but with that inner agony which Monica had perceived in Augustine when she found him in Milan. He eventually met the Platonists, but on the way he teaches his readers in any age that they must elaborate the philosophical questions for themselves so as to be able to consider questions that, as he put it, "cannot be demonstrated." What did these Platonic doctrines mean for him?

> But having then read these books of the Platonists, and being admonished by them to search for incorporeal truth, I saw Thy invisible things, understood by those things that are made, and though repulsed, I perceived what that was, which through the darkness of my mind I was not allowed to contemplate—assured that Thou wert, and wert infinite, and yet not diffused in space finite or infinite; and that Thou truly art, who art the same ever, varying neither in part nor motion; and that all other things are from Thee, on this most sure ground alone, that they are.[41]

All of this was heady stuff. He confesses that he "chattered as one well skilled," but would have perished had he not sought a higher way than philosophy. He desired "to seem wise; yet mourned I not, but rather was puffed up with knowledge."

At this point he wondered whether it would have been better for him to have encountered Scripture before the books of the philosophers. He concluded that it was best not to have met the Scriptures first. He needed to know just how the books of the philosophers impressed his memory. Thus, after he was "subdued by Thy books," he could know the difference between "presumption and confession."[42] William Stevenson's comment on this expression is worth citing here:

> Augustine identified the essence of this attack in book 7 of the *Confessions* when he posed the rhetorical question, "When would these books (of the Neoplatonists) teach me . . . the difference between presumption and confession!"

[41]Ibid., 107.
[42]Ibid., 107.

> The basis of the distinction, summarized so elegantly by the two contrasting words *praesumptio* and *confessio*, lies in the mediation of grace. God's love for individual human beings, as symbolized by the Incarnation and Crucifixion, is the source of all right human love. Without the gift of grace all human love falls short of true love because it rests on a "presumption" by individual human beings that they are its source. Only in the humility of "confession," of the simultaneous "accusation of oneself" and "praise of God," can true love find a home.[43]

The roots of modernity, the gnostic claim for complete human autonomy and its response, are already seen in Augustine's analysis of presumption and confession.[44]

Had he studied Scripture first and then read the philosophers, Augustine felt on reflection that he might have withdrawn "from the solid ground of piety," or even have thought that his "wholesome disposition" of piety could have been "attained by the study of those (philosophical) books alone."[45] He was not a Pelagian, although he understood its humanistic appeal. He was beginning more clearly to understand that truth is tenuous and that it might arise from his very piety leading him to genuine philosophical insights.

In his thirty-second year Augustine was finally converted. In the process he decided to consult Simplicianus, Ambrose's successor in Milan, who, Augustine observed, had "lived most devoted to Thee."[46] He wanted Simplicianus to tell him "which would be the most fitting way for one afflicted as I to walk in Thy way?" At this time he saw himself as someone who had figured out the essential things, yet he was not ready fully to glorify God in his deeds. "To Simplicianus

[43]William R. Stevenson, Jr., *Christian Love and Just War: Moral Paradox and Political Life in St. Augustine and His Modern Interpreters* (Macon, Ga.: Mercer University Press, 1987) 91.

[44]For Leo Strauss' statement of this modern project (what Voegelin called "gnosticism"), see his *City and Man* (Chicago: University of Chicago Press, 1964) 3–4. See Eric Voegelin, *Science, Politics, and Gnosticism* (Chicago: Gateway, 1968).

[45]Augustine, *The Confessions*, in *Basic Works*, vol. 1, 107.

[46]Ibid., 110.

then I went."[47] When he told Simplicianus that he had read some Platonic books, which Victorinus, a Roman professor of Rhetoric, had translated into Latin, the old man was delighted that it was precisely these books he had encountered and not books of "other philosophers which were full of fallacies and deceit."[48]

The Platonists in Simplicianus' view led "to belief in God and His word."[49] Augustine knew that Victorinus even had a statue in the Roman Forum. Simplicianus had known him and been told by him that he was a covert Christian. But Simplicianus would not believe it unless Victorinus were seen in church. To which, in a famous phrase, Victorinus retorted, "Is it then the walls that make the Christian?"[50] But he decided that Simplicianus, who was telling this story to the wavering Augustine for a purpose, was right; he consequently asked for baptism. The local clergy were, because of his fame, going to let him be baptized in private, but he preferred to have the baptism before the local congregation, who shouted in approval when he approached the font, "Victorinus! Victorinus!" What is of significance here is that when Augustine recalled his own inner state as he listened to this story of Victorinus, he "burned to imitate him."[51] For when Julian the emperor forbade any Christian to teach grammar or oratory, Victorinus chose rather to "abandon the wordy school than Thy word."

While Augustine was continuing his teaching in Milan, Alypius and Nebridius were getting their lives and affairs in order. A certain Pontitianus, evidently a public official, also paid a visit to Augustine and Alypius while Nebridius was in Rome. Pontitianus, rather to his surprise, spotted on a gaming table a book by St. Paul. It was not one of those books of which Augustine says quaintly, "I was wearing myself out in teaching."[52] This Pontitianus turned out to be a Christian and proceeded to tell Augustine of his encounter, by way of a book,

[47]Ibid., 111.
[48]Ibid., 112. See 99–101.
[49]Ibid., 112.
[50]Ibid.
[51]Ibid., 116.
[52]Ibid., 118.

with Anthony the Egyptian hermit. Pontitianus was with some other Roman officials, also "Agents for Public Affairs," in Triers on a walk when he came across a cottage inhabited by some simple Christians, who evidently had a copy of Anthony's *Life*. One of these officials read it. Suddenly the young man began to "read, marvel at, and be inflamed by it; and in the reading, to meditate on embracing such a life, and giving up his worldly employments to serve Thee."[53] Listening to this vivid account of how others had changed their lives, Augustine wondered why he could not do the same.

Chapter seven of book eight of *The Confessions* bears this delightful title: "He Deplores His Wretchedness, That Having Been Born Thirty-two Years, He Had Not Yet Found Out the Truth." Augustine was profoundly moved by these stories of Simplicianus about Victorinus and of Pontitianus about Anthony. These narratives caused Augustine again to recall his initial reading of Cicero. "For many of my years (perhaps twelve) had passed away since my nineteenth, when, on reading Cicero's *Hortensius*, I was roused to a desire for wisdom; and still I was delaying to reject mere worldly happiness, and to devote myself to search out that of which not the finding alone, but the bare search, ought to have been preferred before the treasures and kingdoms of this world. . . .[54] Augustine, never one to hide behind a modest self-opinion, confessed himself to be at this time simply "a miserable young man."

Exasperated, Augustine threw up his hands to Alypius. "What is wrong with us?" he pleaded with his friend. "Where is this? What heardest thou? The unlearned start up and 'take' heaven and we, with our learning, but wanting heart, see where we wallow in flesh and blood!"[55] Almost unconsciously Augustine was most aware of the particular difficulty any potential young philosopher would have because he was "learned." After this outburst, he and Alypius went into the quiet garden away from the house. Here in a classic passage Augustine reflected on his own will and how difficult it is to

[53]Ibid., 118.
[54]Ibid., 120.
[55]Ibid., 121.

choose properly. "The mind commands the body, and it obeys forthwith; the mind commands itself, and it is resisted."[56] With his experience with the Manicheans, he knew that there are not two minds within us. Meanwhile, as he fought over his own will, Alypius sat beside him in the garden "awaiting in silence the results."[57] Just what was going on? Clearly, for Augustine "this controversy in my heart was fought out self against self." Again it is clear that with Augustine we are aware that the ultimate struggles are not over the kingdoms of this world, or even over philosophical truths, but over ourselves and how we ultimately orient ourselves. No teaching of political philosophy is more fundamental than this struggle of Augustine in the garden about himself against himself. This struggle takes place no matter in what polity a person may live. Augustine would have little difficulty in agreeing with Plato that the external forms of polities reflect this basic struggle, which is deeper than any civil order and in the end transcends any of them.

Still unsatisfied with his life, Augustine decided that he needed solitude, so he slipped away from Alypius. Not without drama he told us, "Solitude was fitter for the business of weeping," as if what he was about was no longer philosophical argumentation alone.[58] Like Socrates in his agony of deciding what to do, Augustine heard a voice which told him to "take and read." He recalled a similar incident that happened to Anthony in the desert. So Augustine took his copy of the Apostle's text and read, apparently at random, the famous passage from Romans: "Not in rioting and drunkenness, not in chambering and wantonness, not in strife and envying; but put ye on the Lord Jesus Christ, and make not provision for the flesh, to fulfill the lusts thereof" (13:13-14). Naturally, Augustine figured that this passage had him in mind. When he told Alypius, the latter applied to himself the passage and what followed: "Him that is weak in the faith, receive ye." They both told what had happened to Monica, who was, of course, quite delighted.

[56]Ibid., 122.
[57]Ibid., 125.
[58]Ibid., 125.

Needing more time to reflect on such things, Augustine's pagan friend Verecundus lent him his villa at Cassiciacum. There Nebridius and Alypius went too. Soon, however, Verecundus died, and later, just after he returned to Africa, so did Nebridius. Alypius too had been converted. Augustine retired to this villa, where he finally decided to give up his own professorship. "The vintage vacation being ended, I gave the citizens of Milan notice that they might provide their scholars with another seller of words. . . ."[59] What did he do at Cassiciacum during the holidays, which lasted "for long and many [days] they seemed, on account of my love of easeful liberty. . .?"[60] He returned to the theme of his writing, what he had to say to the ages. "What I accomplished here in writing, which was now wholly devoted to Thy service, though still, in this pause as it were, panting from the school of pride, my books testify—those in which I disputed with my friends, and those with myself alone before Thee; and what with the absent Nebridius, my letters testify."[61] Augustine, mindful of vanity, nevertheless wanted his own account as a young man to be there for others to follow. He remained in the end a teacher who had been taught, taught not merely philosophy. From beyond philosophy, he heard answers to the questions that arose within philosophy and within the city.

Of all the classical young men, potential philosophers, who sought the truth, Augustine perhaps was the first to stress that this same truth must also be chosen. But he also realized that the answers to his quest were given, though his capacity to know them depended on the penetration of his most acute philosophic mind into the questions themselves. On this basis he could listen to grace as an element of his philosophical quest.

"Take and read": these are the Christian words that most correspond with the message of Socrates from Delphi (19e–21e). For when Socrates, whose voice followed him everywhere but to his trial, learned that the oracle had called him the wisest man in Greece, he wanted to know why. This curi-

[59]Ibid., 134.
[60]Ibid., 131.
[61]Ibid., 131.

osity began his philosophic career, which ended when he learned that only in the city in speech can the philosopher be safe. Augustine, on the other hand, struggled not with the poet, statesman, and craftsman, as Socrates did, to find out what was the truth. Rather, Augustine turned finally to himself, to his life. But he did this, be it noted, while he struggled all through his early years of manhood with the most profound of philosophic questions, those of evil and good, of the supreme being, of friendship, of beauty, of truth. He not only conversed with Adeodatus, Alypius, his friends, his mother, and Faustus, but also with himself in his *Soliloquies*. In knowing himself, however, Augustine remained a true follower of Socrates.

When Augustine was scarcely twenty, as we recounted at the beginning, he read Aristotle's *The Ten Categories*. He read about substance and accident and, as he proudly told us, "understood" them. Later he said of the Virgin that she was more blessed in her discipleship than in her motherhood because her whole life testified to the truth of her Son. This truth Augustine went out of Carthage to find, and he realized at last, when he was thirty-two, as he told his son, that the truth we must look for is a truth we do not make. His teachings began with his recognition that the highest things must be first taught to him, initially in ordinary words. And he is both satisfying and unsatisfying because in the end the truth which he despaired of finding in his twenties depends in part on our own lives, as he reluctantly admitted to himself.

Our beatitude, to recall, is "contingent" because we are free. Augustine, more than any other single person, I think, realized that without this same freedom, truth would not be worth having. He meditated long on evil because of this same freedom. At first he accepted the erroneous proposition that evil is a material, necessary thing. This position was initially presented to him by the Manicheans but he willingly accepted it out of his need to justify his own life. He came to realize with some clarity that evil exists not in things, nor in some dual god, nor in our political institutions. Neither is it caused by our property divisions, our family structures, or by our states, the great theses of the modern political ideologies. Rather evil arises in our wills under any sort of regime, from the best to the worst. Augustine can lay claim to being the political philosopher who is the true son of Cicero and the writer of "the true apology of Socrates."[62] Augustine located the true drama of our existence in our wills. Our final destiny he found in the "city of righteousness," the "faithful city" not of this world, but in "the City of God."[63] He knew no states but those limited by our sins and by our final destinies.

In so arguing Augustine addressed himself directly to the young philosopher and to the old philosopher, to the dying Socrates, to tell them that their quest was not in vain. Death was indeed that preparation for wisdom as Socrates defined it. Socrates held that, in the end, he was wise because he did not know and knew that he did not know. Augustine taught rather differently. "I would therefore confess what I know concerning myself; I will confess also what I know not concerning myself. And because of what I do know of myself, I know by Thee enlightening me; and what I know not of myself, so long I know not until the time when my darkness be as the 'noonday' in Thy sight."[64] The "noonday" in this passage comes from Isaiah 58:10. But note also that in the Myth of the Cave in the seventh book of *The Republic* some unspecified potential philosopher turned around from the shadows and chains to ascend out of the cave into the open sun, where he was blinded until he could finally witness the Good in all its brightness.

The "theme" of political philosophy is "the city of righteousness, the faithful city." This theme, we are told by Leo Strauss, is taken more seriously in Jerusalem than anywhere else on earth.[65] The other name given by Augustine to the subject of his great work, *The City of God*, was indeed Jerusalem, the heavenly Jerusalem. No one, perhaps, has taken this same theme in all its ramifications more seriously than this young philosopher from Carthage, who went to Rome grieving because at thirty-two he had not yet found the truth.

[62]Ernest Fortin, *Political Idealism and Christianity in the Thought of St. Augustine* (Villanova: Villanova University Press, 1972) 16.

[63]See Leo Strauss, *The City and Man*, 1.

[64]Augustine, *Confessions*, in *Basic Works*, vol. 1, 150.

[65]See Strauss, *City and Man*, introduction; *What Is Political Philosophy* (Glencoe, Ill.: The Free Press, 1959) 9.

Speaking of Aquinas, who was Augustine's most diligent reader, Josef Pieper observed: "The teacher looks not only at the truth of things; at the same time he looks at the faces of living men who desire to know the truth."[66] Preaching on the Blessed Mother, Augustine explained: "For her it was a greater thing to have been Christ's disciple than to have been his mother." And expounding to his son about the nobility of the teacher Augustine affirmed: "Those who are called pupils consider within themselves whether what has been explained has been said truly; looking of course to that interior truth, according to the measure of which each is able. Thus they learn, and when the interior truth makes known to them that true things have been said, they applaud. . . ."[67] For Augustine being taught preceded teaching, and teaching meant teaching that truth which we despair at not finding but, when discovered, is worthy of noonday light, of applause, because it is found, given, and not made by us. We can only rejoice in it.

Augustine passed philosophically from Carthage to Jerusalem to Rome to Athens to the heavenly Jerusalem, the *City of God*, the faithful city. That is, Augustine, in the history of philosophy, and particularly of political philosophy, stands for one fact—*we must also choose the truth*, even when it is given to us. "The mind commands the body, and it obeys forthwith; the mind commands itself, and it is resisted." To choose the truth is what Augustine was taught by his own life in his search for what God is like. This lesson is what he intended to teach to us, his chance readers, if we too are not, as he saw himself for a time, "unteachable." This realization of the difficulty to know and to choose the highest things, ultimately, was the poignant drama of the young man in *The Confessions*. *Tolle, Lege*.

[66]Josef Pieper, *The Silence of St. Thomas* (Chicago: Gateway, 1965) 23.
[67]Augustine, "On the Teacher," in *Basic Works*, vol. 1, 394.

Conclusion

"Man's Fleshbound Spirit, Unencumbered"

Philosophers and "hereticks" have, if we read them well, written and spoken much about the Triune God. Psalm 37 reads, "Do not fret because of the wicked; do not envy those who do evil." The mystery of evil and the mystery of God exist in the same universe, the one in which we find ourselves. The same Psalm tells us that "the Lord laughs at the wicked," almost as if he knows that out of their wickedness will come a lovely good of which they know not, a good even for themselves if they choose. The Lord also laughs in the delight of his creation. We read in the Book of Wisdom: "When he laid the foundations of the earth, I was by his side, a master craftsman, delighting him day after day, ever at play in his presence, at play everywhere in his world, delighting to be with the sons of men" (8:29-31). What exists was created out of the abundance of God.

We are given intelligence to understand rightly this relationship of God, world, evil, and ourselves. "It was not by way of cleverly concocted myths that we taught you about the coming in power of Our Lord Jesus Christ," we read in the Second Epistle of Peter, "for we were eyewitnesses of his saving majesty" (1:16). Not mere myths, but eye witnesses—this is the dogged insistence of those who saw. "The Word was made flesh and dwelt amongst us" (John 1:13). We pray to God that we might know what God is like. God is like someone who answers even our sins with the gentlest of gifts, with the harmonies we least might have expected. This is why I have recalled Tolkien in reflecting on the Trinity: "In every age there comes forth things that are new and have no foretelling, for they do not proceed from the past." We are not the only actors in our lives.

After former President Reagan and Mr. Gorbachev met in Moscow in 1988, Professor Richard Pipes of Harvard, a well-known foreign-relations specialist, made a trip to Moscow to see if everything had changed as drastically as the public was led to expect. Pipes was a highly respected critic of the Soviet Union and skeptical of all the announced progress. After some days in Moscow he was quite astonished to hear a young woman on a Soviet television documentary on religion tell the TV audience, *"You have to believe in God. Otherwise, you are dead.* Religious faith keeps you alive."[1] Such almost prophetic words, as we subsequently realize, are a far cry from the affirmation that "God is dead."

Pipes was fascinated with the Soviet scene. He found, not entirely without irony, that the conversation was considerably better there than in America because intellectuals did not have any outlets besides talk. At a dinner one evening Pipes discovered, for example, that many of the guests had spent time in prison camps. They talked until the wee hours of the morning. Pipes reflected: "You'd never see that at Harvard, I can tell you that for sure. You get this nowhere else but here. People don't care about ideas in America that much. They get such fulfillment from action and getting what they want. Intellectuals here (in Moscow) have never been part of the system. There have been no outlets for them but sitting and talking." Pipes seemed to reflect Solzhenitsyn's idea that there is great spiritual strength in Russia because of the need in one's soul to resist the system. "Still, it's fascinating to be here," Pipes concluded. "Everywhere you go you see something. You can't walk out of the hotel without an adventure. *Every morning I go off to Harvard, and absolutely nothing happens.*"[2]

[1]David Remnick, "The Moscow Spring of Richard Pipes," *The Washington Post,* June 18, 1988. Italics added.

[2]Ibid. Italics added.

What are we to make of this remark? That it is possible to be quite bored even at Harvard because there is no real issue of truth at stake? And what is it, ultimately, that would not bore us? The thesis of this book is that, because of our very human condition, there will always be something in the order of the world that leaves us with a sense of emptiness. We should not, perhaps, be ''bored'' with *what is*. Chesterton was right to remind us of the ''inexpressible value of existence,'' the existence of ordinary things like doors and eggs and windows. But St. Augustine was right too. We should not fully rest in anything less than God, even in the ''all these lovely things'' Augustine encountered in his life.

In a review of Jean-Luc Godard's disorganized film, ''King Lear,'' we read, in a mood similar to what we saw in Nietzsche, Camus, and even sometimes Raissa Maritain or St. Augustine: ''A subcurrent in the film—in fact, in many of Godard's later films—is the filmmaker's despair over the impossibility of ever making sense. Behind this is Godard's inability to resolve an essential contradiction in his work—his reverence for ideas and theories and all sorts of philosophical speculation, and his utter disregard for a sustained, coherent presentation of them. *It's as if he believes that a jumble is the best anyone could ever hope to make of things*.''[3] We have here both an acute awareness of the unimportance we give to ideas or truths and a sense of exhilaration when we are in an atmosphere wherein it counts what we hold.

What is God like? It seems clear that both of these views—the seeming littleness of things and the exhilaration of choice—are rooted in the notion that, without a kind of absolute risk pressing on us, we have no strength or energy to seek the truth. In these reflections on God and how we relate to him, on what he is like, however, I have suspected otherwise. I have argued that we do seek the truth, particularly the truth about God, about what God is like. We are frail creatures but we are not helpless. The ''jumble'' is not something that is necessary, but is the result of our own choosings. ''It is not every spirit, my dear people, that you can trust,'' we are

[3]Hal Hinson, '' 'King Lear' as Conundrum,'' *The Washington Post*, June 18, 1988. Italics added.

reminded in the First Epistle of John; "test them, to see if they come from God. . . . You can tell the spirits that come from God by this: every spirit which acknowledges that Jesus the Christ has come in the flesh, is from God . . ." (4:1-2). Clearly, we need to have the intellectual understanding of the evil that exists in the universe and in ourselves: not every spirit can we trust.

The world is there for us to figure out. This we must do as best we can, not forgetting that we most likely will die still not knowing all we might about the ultimate things. I have written these pages to suggest that politics or human inner-worldly history is not enough, however important each might be as the actual context of our ways to God. Our attention needs for once in our lives to be directed to the perplexing question of what then *is* enough. Again we are confronted with the enigmatic, if not actually troubling suspicion that what causes us the most difficulty is our failure to be liberal enough, free enough to receive a salvation, a gift of God that is far greater than anything we could bring forth by ourselves.

Joseph Sobran wrote an essay on why C. S. Lewis did not pay too much attention to politics. Sobran wrote, citing Lewis:

> The doctrine of the immortality of the soul had a very practical and urgent bearing on "the difference between totalitarianism and democracy. If individuals live only seventy years, then a state, or a nation, or a civilization, which may last for a thousand years, is more important than the individual. But if Christianity is true, then the individual is not only made important but incomparably more important, for he is everlasting and the life of a state or a civilization, compared with his, is only a moment."[4]

We are more lasting than our polities. The abiding substance that is ourselves is what gives politics its importance, and not the other way around. This is why I have cited, and cite again here, Flannery O'Connor's observation that she is "always

[4]Joseph Sobran, "Happy at Home," *Single Issues: Essays on the Crucial Social Questions* (New York: Human Life Press, 1983) 157.

astonished by the emphasis the Church puts on the body. It is not the soul she will rise but the body, glorified.''

I continue to think that the providence of God reaches us not so much in the grand movements of history, though culture can make a difference, but in the more concrete events of our lives within whatever civil or family history is actually given to us or chosen by us during our lifetimes. George William Rutler wrote: ''Particularity is the ground of devotion, at least from the Christian point of view, because Christianity is the account of how God became particular. There was a period—one period of thirty-three years, to be precise, and a moment—or three hours of a Friday, to be quite precise, when God was as specific with us as he ever was. That is called salvation history, and not simply salvation, because it happened.''[5] This particularity, this fragility is our context for discovering what God is like. The divine really happened in our world.

A friend, pondering such things, once wrote to me: ''What am I living for? What is the bedrock and foundation of my life? I thought love was the bedrock, and I still thought so, but, I thought, how is love shown? What does love mean? How does it act? And as I saw my whole life lying open before me, I concluded that what is there at bottom—the form of love—is fidelity and loyalty.'' God, in both Testaments, is presented as someone faithful to us. God is loyal to the divine promises made to us. These are promises, of forgiveness, joy, and trust, that deal with us, in our particularity, as they dealt with Christ in his once only life. We are not abstractions, nor is God. In our very choices and deeds, God acts when we act. But he acts to lead us, within the fabric of our lives, to his end and to invite us to make our end his. ''One of the most convenient Hieroglyphicks of God, is a Circle,'' John Donne wrote one Christmas Day, ''and a Circle is endlesse; whom God loves, hee loves to the end: and not onely to their own end, to their death, but to his end, and his end, that he might love them still.'' Few passages are more beautiful than this. I love to cite and hear it.

[5]George William Rutler, *The Cure D'Ars Today* (San Francisco: Ignatius Press, 1988) 13.

I began these reflections with those who insist that in practice, our God is dead, or that we act as if this were so. I ended with Augustine, the whole of whose life is accounted for before God in his own very words, words we can read and follow. Indeed, Augustine showed us how his own life—with Monica, Alypius, Nebridius, Adeodatus, and Ambrose—was in fact a response to God's search for him. He recounted how his restless heart sought the truth and, once he found it, sought to live the new life within this truth. The story of Augustine is, perhaps, not everyone's story, but it is there for everyone to know about. Few will find it totally alien to their own lives. Augustine would not necessarily want us to follow him just to prove we could do it. Most of us probably could not so follow him, so weak and frail are we. Rather he told us about his life in order that we might see that even there, even in a life he thought so sinful, there is God not merely redeeming the sinner, but through this redeeming teaching him, teaching us. Salvation is also an intelligence, meant for us to understand.

The ultimate "heretick," I think, to recall Samuel Johnson's word, but with Chesterton's suspicion that the only real "heretic" today is the one who holds what is called intellectual and doctrinal orthodoxy, is the one who believes in the Trinity, the inner life of God. This inner life is also meant for and given to us. It is the very purpose of our lives and the reason the world exists. No matter how we have lived our lives, God intends "to save everything that can be saved," to state again Raissa Maritain's powerful phrase.

The existence of God also reminds us that not everything whatsoever can be saved. This very fact makes the universe full not of boredom, of places where nothing is happening, but of risk and adventure, even in Moscow, even indeed at Harvard, especially in our own daily lives wherever we might be at home. We can to be sure obscure what is very plain; we can doubt, though we need not, that there is mirth in God, that prayer is testimony to the fact that we are not alone, even when we are alone or wherever we "walkest," that friendship is not lacking in the Divinity, nor in our relationship to God. We are to be loyal, to be faithful.

In Washington, I once took a walk over across Key Bridge, into the Iwo Jima Memorial area, across the lawn by the Netherlands Carillon, into Arlington Cemetery, by President Taft's Tomb, back across Memorial Bridge, to the Lincoln Memorial, by the Vietnam Memorial, over through the Octagon House with a friend, whom I chanced to meet on entering, on through George Washington University, and back into Georgetown. (God is like someone who answers our sins and our joys with the gentlest of gifts.) On Pennsylvania Avenue, just across Rock Creek, I passed a book store with some sale items displayed. I am a rather easy target for such things, so I bought, as I only had a couple of dollars in my pocket, a Penguin edition of Plato's *Phaedrus*, with the Seventh and Eighth Letters, the latter of which alone I did not already have.

The Seventh Letter was Plato's effort to justify himself, or at least to explain himself. Plato had admired the Syracusan politician Dion, but together they could not succeed in establishing a better rule in his city. Dion was finally exiled from his city. Dion, like Socrates, believed that ''it was better to be the victim of wickedness than to be its author.'' Dion did not succeed in ruling well. Plato did not think Dion was wholly ignorant of what went on in the world, so he should not have been too surprised by it all. However, Plato explained: ''This was what undid Dion. He knew that those who brought about his destruction were thoroughly bad men; what he did not realize was the depth of their ignorance and wickedness and greed. To this he fell a victim, and brought upon Sicily infinite grief'' (351).

P. G. Wodehouse, though more mildly, made the same essential point about our human condition, about what I have called our ''frailty,'' when he had his hero Bertie Wooster describe his nephew Sacheverell's ''extraordinary mildness and timidity'' in this way: ''He belonged definitely to the class of humanity which never gets a seat on an undergound train and is ill at ease in the presence of butlers, traffic policemen, and female assistants in post offices. He was the sort of young fellow at whom people laugh when the waiter speaks to them in French.''[6] It is in such a world that we are called to redemption.

[6]P. G. Wodehouse, *The World of Wodehouse Clergy* (London: Hutchinson, 1984) 57-58.

Might we therefore say, for it is the other side of our freedom, that God recognizes this depth of ignorance, wickedness, and greed in our kind? And might we also acknowledge that good people, in not realizing thoroughly what goes on in the world, are responsible for making things worse? Many wicked things actually occur, to be sure. Yet our belief in God ought not to be based on the notion that such dire things do not happen among us. Nietzsche wanted to make, as grounds for rejecting God, Christian ethics which calls for turning the other cheek. This approval of weakness, as he called it, was fatal. He thought Christian morality at its best was the cause of increased evil. Nothing about our belief in God, however, requires us to ignore the depths of our evils, and if not ours, as in the case of Dion, those of others. Nevertheless, I have been arguing here a proposition about God. It holds that ultimately, God—Father, Son, and Holy Spirit—is full of joy, friendship, and humor, that in him there is no evil nor sadness. Something is indeed amusing when the waiter speaks to us in French, in a language we do not know a word of.

On April 17, 1778, a Good Friday, Boswell told of a walk with Samuel Johnson. After a collation at which Johnson forgot to fast, they entered St. Clement's Church which had quite a "numerous congregation . . . which Dr. Johnson observed with pleasure." When they left the church, they passed along Butcher-row and ran into an old school mate of Johnson's, Mr. Oliver Edwards, whom Johnson had not seen since 1729. Here Boswell noted that he wished "to give a pretty full account of one of the most curious incidents in Johnson's life."[7] The two school companions were delighted to see each other. Immediately they recalled oft-told tales, discussed how old they did or did not look. Edwards had become a solicitor. He possessed a house in the country, so they talked about country versus city living. Edwards praised the grass, corn, and trees in their growing. Johnson reminded him, "You find, Sir, you have fears as well as hopes," as if the gentleman forgot to mention the difficulties of farming, which he did. Boswell marvelled at Johnson's attentiveness.

[7]*Boswell's Life of Johnson* II (London: Oxford, 1931) 228–30.

Johnson, Boswell, and Edwards, after their walk, returned to Johnson's house, to enter the library. Edwards recalled that Johnson would not let him use the word "prodigious" at college. The question came up whether Edwards had earned a lot of money at the law. "But I shall not die rich," he concluded, after suggesting he had made a little. Edwards, evidently a kind of eighteenth century college drop-out, confessed that he wished he had stayed in college, maybe to have become a parson, and "live comfortably." To this Johnson replied: "Sir, the life of a parson, of a conscientious clergyman, is not easy. I have always considered a clergyman as the father of a larger family than he is able to maintain. I would rather have Chancery suits upon my hands than the cure of souls. No, Sir, I do not envy a clergyman's life as an easy life, nor do I envy the clergyman who makes it an easy life."

At this point, Johnson suddenly was distracted with a recollection about their college days, and to prove he remembered Edwards, asked him: "Do you remember our drinking together at an alehouse near Pembroke Gate?" Johnson then recalled a pun in Latin which Edwards had formed over the incident of Our Saviour's turning water into wine. Edwards, somewhat taken with this vivid recollection, answered Johnson: *"You are a philosopher, Dr. Johnson. I have tried too in my time to be a philosopher, but I don't know how, cheerfulness was always breaking in."*[8]

This sentiment of cheerfulness, of the alehouse at Pembroke Gate, is where I will terminate these thoughts on what God is like. "God is dead," Nietzsche told us of ourselves. "You have to believe in God. Otherwise you are dead," a young woman was heard to say on Soviet television. Whether we deal with the philosopher Plato warning us about how bad people can be, with my friend's son preferring perhaps a little "messiness," with the French film-maker seeing it all as merely a philosophic "jumble," with another friend who knows that loyalty and fidelity are the basis of our loves, or with the conscientious clergyman whose life is not so easy and would be uneasy if it were, we can end with the realization that the real

[8]Ibid. Italics added.

"trouble" with our world and our philosophy is that, as Oliver Edwards told Samuel Johnson, we don't know how, but "cheerfulness is always breaking in."

Such too was Chesterton's instinct about mirth in the Deity, the real mystery about the origin of comedy, humor, and joy in our lives. From whence does it all break in? Why does it come, to put it quaintly, into our very particularity? "Do you remember our drinking together at an alehouse near Pembroke Gate?" Let us recall again, to the same point, the phrase of Hopkins which sums up both what we are and what we will be: "*Man's spirit will be flesh-bound when found at best, / But unencumbered. . . .*" The ultimate heresy, the mystery full of awe, the awe-ful mystery of the Trinity, of the inner life of God, remains to teach us what God is like. And God usually teaches us, as my friend explained about our condition, "with a smile and a Head shake." We exist, but we are not perfect. Yet it is we who seek, as St. Ignatius told us about why we should be holy, "to save our souls."

Let me end, finally, by recalling one last time the Prayer which James Boswell cited from the great lexicographer's notes, which Boswell used to demonstrate, on the matter of the Trinity, that Samuel Johnson, unlike Samuel Clarke, was no "condemned heretick": "O Lord, hear my prayer, for Jesus Christ's sake, to whom with thee and the Holy Ghost, three persons and one God, be all honour and glory, world without end. Amen." We can all hope that some James Boswell will one day find such a prayer somewhere in our remaining papers, even perhaps in a loquacious Moscow, or at Harvard, where, it is said, every morning, absolutely nothing happens. It begins with our mothers, who "give a totally dependent being his first definition of 'is,' and they identify that which is good and that which is evil in an ordered environment, the structure of which ultimtely allows the child freedom of choice." The great dramas of our existence begin here, with what we do with the choices we make, in our wills, as St. Augustine taught us.

We are not, however, "deprived of grace." The Christ we deserve was not the Christ who was sent to dwell amongst us. This is why "Allelujah" and "Amen" are our best prayers.

The inexpressible value of existence incites us to be grateful, to act in a world of lovely things that we can use wrongly. But if we do so use them, we have an Advocate with the Father, Jesus Christ, as St. John said in his First Epistle. "All that can be saved will be saved." But what will be saved will be saved through the incarnation of the Son of God into our world, into an ordinary place, Nazareth, in a time when Caesar Augustus was Emperor in Rome. Particularity is the ground of devotion. "Do you remember our drinking together at an alehouse near Pembroke Gate?" God was quite specific with us.

The fact that our existence is at risk reveals better than anything else what God is like. "You have to believe in God. Otherwise you're dead." The Blessed Trinity observes us, some of us even "descending into Hell," as St. Ignatius put it, in order to lead us through the incarnation and Passion of Christ to the purpose for which we are called out of nothing, that is, to be given as the goal of our existence the inner life of God in eternal life. "Man's spirit will be fleshbound when found at best, / But unencumbered. . . ."

The risk God takes is that we can refuse God's grace. The world was not created because something was lacking in the Godhead but because of God's fullness. Man learns by suffering, as the Greeks taught us. We are, however, in the words of St. Paul, to make up what is lacking in the suffering of Christ—we, not someone else. Human glory and holiness consists in this, that the risk of God was worth taking. "*All His gifts lead to His glory*." For God can do no more for a free, finite creature than to give him the power to understand him and the grace to choose him. We are not saved in some other world, but in this one, with all its poignancy. The Word was indeed made flesh and dwelt amongst us. "The Lamb who was sacrificed is worthy to be given power, riches, wisdom, strength, honor, glory, and blessing" (Rev 5:12). *This is what God is like.*

Index